Japanese Military 'Comfort Women'

Sharing and Remembering
the Historical Pain

NAHF
History & Culture
Series

Japanese Military 'Comfort Women'

Sharing and Remembering the Historical Pain

Yoon-soo Cho

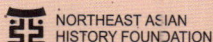
NORTHEAST ASIAN
HISTORY FOUNDATION

Publisher's Note

The countries of the East Asian region have historically shared close ties. Since ancient times, various ethnic groups have emerged on the Asian continent and formed nations. Conversely, wars of conquest have sometimes caused ethnic groups and nations to disappear. Countries such as Korea, China, and Japan have evolved from ancient times to the present day, developing through conflict and war on the one hand, and through exchange and cooperation on the other. As civilizations developed on the continent from the earliest times, they formed unique cultures through the exchange of materials and cultures. Modernity has been marked by conflicts between continental and maritime powers, as well as invasive imperialist wars. A particularly unfortunate period in history unfolded when Japan forcibly annexed Korea and invaded China.

Establishing a system of peace in East Asia requires overcoming the unfortunate history of the past and establishing a new paradigm of international relations. Unfortunately, however, unproductive nationalistic historical perspectives have tended to predominate in the early 21st century. When countries strongly emphasize a nationalistic viewpoint, distrust increases among neighboring nations, resulting in the regrettable situation of escalating conflicts and tensions.

The Northeast Asian History Foundation was established in 2006 with the aim of resolving conflicts arising from differences in historical perceptions in the East Asian region in order to promote cooperation and prosperity within a framework of peace. Over the years, the Foundation has conducted research on East Asian history and held international academic exchanges to bridge differences in historical perceptions. The results have been published in various series of historical publications and have received acclaim from many readers. However, most of these publications are in Korean, which has limited their ability to reach a global audience and facilitate cross-border communication with global citizens. Therefore, in order to share research results with the international community and create a platform for communication aiming to resolve differences in historical perceptions, the Foundation plans to publish the <History & Culture Series>.

The series will cover topics that can help people around the world understand issues that have caused disputes in East Asian history, encompassing territorial and maritime issues, among others. We hope that this series, published by the Northeast Asian History Foundation, can make a significant contribution to the accurate understanding of historical conflicts in the East Asian region and to bridging differences in historical perceptions.

Young-ho Lee
President of Northeast Asian History Foundation

Preface

In order to write this book, I re-read the historical documents and testimonies of the former Japanese military 'comfort women.' The more I read and pondered, the more I empathized with the pain of the victims embedded between the lines. I had to stop many times to take a deep breath and calm myself.

Memories of youth can be beautiful and glorious for many, but the youth of the 'comfort women' was completely destroyed by the Japanese military. Thinking of those days made me angry and unable to suppress my resentment, so I tried to erase those feelings from my memory and heart. But just as a torn piece of paper cannot be glued back together, the scars of the 'comfort women' did not disappear completely. These women had to live in constant fear that their career of 'comfort women' might be revealed. Those survivors who happened to be known to others were forced to live with the label of "tainted women" and faced social prejudice and discrimination. Their dream of living a normal life like everyone else did not come true. Half a century later, however, their courage transformed that suffering into hope for the future. They have moved us forward by sharing a bit of that pain in their hearts. I hope that this book can be a small support for those steps forward.

The cover of this book is based on the artwork of a former 'comfort woman,' Shim Dal-yeon. She was dragged into the war and suffered violence at the hands of Japanese soldiers. Her body and mind were damaged in ways that are hard to imagine, and she was repeatedly hospitalized in mental institutions throughout her life. In an effort to heal from the trauma, she underwent horticultural therapy, which encourages creative work with flowers, and it worked for her.

People called Shim Dal-yeon the "Flower Grandmother" because she painted many flowers during her lifetime. She preferred dried flowers to fresh flowers because "fresh flowers wither and twist when the water inside them dries up, but dried flowers last longer and do not convey the feeling of death." Whenever I think of her youth, which never blossomed, my heart aches. Among her artworks, the one that caught my eye was "Wearing Flower Socks." She uses the shapes of flowers, leaves, and stems to decorate the elegant lines of traditional Korean socks. Departing from the image of 'comfort women,' often symbolized by the "Statue of Peace," I wanted to express my desire to lay down a path of flowers and blossoms for them. I also pray that the flowers will bloom in the heart of Shim, who passed away in 2010, and the hearts of other 'comfort women.'

The publication of this book was made possible with the help of many people. The manuscript was revised several times, and the work was like a "battle" because of its complicated texture. I would like to thank Nikebooks and Young-ho Lee, president of the Northeast Asian History Foundation, for their encouragement and support.

November 2023

Yoon-soo Cho

Contents

Publisher's Note ▪ 4

Preface ▪ 6

Introduction ▪ 11

Chapter 1 The Hidden Truth Unveiled by the Victims' Courage

1-1. Breaking the Silence: "I was a Japanese Military 'Comfort Woman.'" ▪ 20

1-2. Testifying to the Truth ▪ 30

**Chapter 2 Japan's Invasion War and
the Japanese Military 'Comfort Women' System**

2-1. Fraudulent Recruitment and Forced Mobilization: The Involvement of
the Japanese Government and Military in Illegal Activities ▪ 46

2-2. Comfort Stations Established and Managed by
the Japanese Military ▪ 90

2-3. Unimaginable Abuses and Inhumane Treatment of
Women in Comfort Stations ▪ 109

2-4. The Japanese Military Sexual Slavery System:
Why Comfort Stations? ▪ 118

Chapter 3 How Did the Korean and Japanese Governments Respond?

3-1. Both Countries Stuck in the 1990s:
 Fact-Finding and Reconciliation Incomplete ▪ 134

3-2. Two Crucial Incidents in 2011 and 2015: A Constitutional Court Decision and a Korea-Japan Agreement ▪ 150

Chapter 4 How Did the Global Community Respond?

4-1. Universal Values: The Issues of Sexual Slavery and Forced Mobilization ▪ 196

4-2. Japan's Denial and the Global Reaction ▪ 207

Epilogue: Sharing and Remembering the Courage and Pain of the Victims ▪ 219

Chronology of the Japanese Military 'Comfort Women' Issue ▪ 227
Bibliography ▪ 300
Index ▪ 304

Notes

1. This book is a translation of 『일본군'위안부'-역사의 아픔을 함께 나누고 기억하다』 (Northeast Asian History Foundation, 2019).

2. Chinese and Japanese names of people and places are spelled as they are pronounced in the respective local languages.

3. Historical materials with the original text in English are included directly, and the other materials are translated from Chinese, Japanese, and Korean.

Introduction

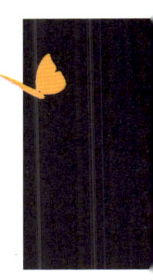

> "So when we got to the statue there I brought the paper bag with me holding it up because it will be appropriate saying that this ugly hunk of junk deserves a paper bag on her head, on its head."
>
> "They were not sex slaves. They were prostitutes."

These are the arguments presented by American mouthpieces for Japanese ultra-nationalism in the documentary film *Shusenjo* (主戰場): *The Main Battleground of the 'Comfort Women' Issue*, which addresses the issue of the Japanese military 'comfort women.' The film, made by Japanese-American director Miki Dezaki, shows the Japanese far right's distortion of history and their blind nationalism and racism. They seem not to care what is true and what is false. What they want to believe became a false truth.

Movie Poster for *Shusenjo: The Main Battleground of the Comfort Women Issue*
(Image Provided by Cinema Dal Co., Ltd.)

The documentary contains the passionate voices of the people who fought to resolve the issue of the Japanese military 'comfort women' and ordinary U.S. citizens. The movie shows that the 'comfort women' as we understand them and the 'comfort women' vilified by the Japanese right wing are completely different concepts, even though they share the same words. The Japanese right-wingers claim that the women were not victims of sexual violence by the Japanese military, but were prostitutes who sold their bodies for money. Could it be possible to bridge this gap in perception?

Musical Poster for *Eyes of Dawn* (Image Provided by Suki Company)

It seems impossible to fill the gap. This is because, as the title of the documentary suggests, it is a war of historical memory. So, what weapons are needed to win the ongoing war of memory? The only weapon I can think of is historical facts.

The 1991 Korean drama *Eyes of Dawn* was the first drama that brought the existence of the Japanese military 'comfort women' to public attention. Until then, it had only been whispered about. The drama's main characters, Dae-chi Choi, a Korean student soldier mobilized for the Japanese military, and Yeo-ok Yoon, a 'comfort woman' recruited for the Japanese front, were in love, and their tragic love story became very popular in Korea, with an average viewing rating of 44%. Yeo-ok, the daughter of an independence activist, lived a hellish life at the comfort station of the 15th Division of the Japanese military in Nanjing, China. Dae-chi and Yeo-ok fell in love with each other. The secene of the lovers parting over a barbed wire fence deeply touched the hearts of many viewers. *Eyes of Dawn* was rebroadcast on a Korean cable television network in 2019 to commemorate the 100th anniversary of the March 1st Movement. The heartbreaking love story between the two colonial subjects was also made into a musical.

The reason why so many people accepted the story of the 'comfort women' in this drama was that it was based on historical facts. On August 14, 1991, two months before the drama aired, a very surprising press conference was held. A 70-year-old woman came forward and said that the Japanese government lied about its wartime atrocities, including the military comfort stations. The old woman said that she was a 'comfort woman' for the Japanese military. Her name was Hak-soon Kim. Her testimony had a huge impact on people, and it was natural for people to empathize with the female character of *Eyes of Dawn*, Yeo-ok Yoon.

As soon as the 1990s entered, Korean society began to take an interest in the issue of the Japanese military 'comfort women.' In January 1990, Professor Jung-ok Yoon of Ewha Womans University started the series "Tracing the Footprints of the 'Labor Corps Victims': An Investigative Report" in the *Hankyoreh newspaper*. While the Japanese government continued to deny the existence of the 'comfort women,' no one could deny the reality when Hak-soon Kim, a survivor of the 'comfort women' system, accused the Japanese government of lying. She said, "Even though someone like me, who has actually experienced such things, is still alive, they are lying."

In December 1991, the South Korean government requested intergovernmental discussions with the Japanese government to resolve the issue of Japanese military 'comfort women,' and Japan accepted the request. In response to Hak-soon Kim's testimony, the Japanese government began collecting information at the government level. In January 1992, Chief Cabinet Secretary Koichi Kato (加藤紘一) issued a statement acknowledging the Japanese military involvement in the recruitment of 'comfort women' and the operation of comfort stations, expressing apologies and remorse. In August 1993, Chief Cabinet Secretary Yohei Kono (河野洋平) acknowledged in his statement that the mobilization was carried out against the will of the victims. He also pledged to transmit this fact to future generations through historical education.

Victims and support groups believed that it was only a matter of time before the issue of Japanese military 'comfort women' would be resolved. This was because many victims were coming forward not only in Korea, but also in other countries. Furthermore, with the

Japanese Military 'Comfort Women' After the War

international community, including the United Nations, showing interest, it seemed impossible for Japan to evade responsibility.

However, even in 2019, the issue of the Japanese military 'comfort women' remains heated. The Japanese government criticizes the South Korean government for not abiding by the 2015 Agreement between the two countries. Why is Japan, the perpetrator, criticizing Korea when Koreans are the victims?

The victims are not making any extraordinary demands. They are seeking recognition of historical facts, an apology, and compensation as an acknowledgment. Why should the hearts of the victims be heavy when they ask for something so reasonable?

Above is a powerful photograph showing the suffering of the Japanese military 'comfort women.' What do you feel when you look at this photo?

The pregnant woman on the far right is Young-sim Park, a 'comfort woman' survivor from North Korea. She passed away in 2006. Who are the other three women? What happened to them? Who is the smiling man with the rifle? Why is he in this photo?

This book aims to answer these questions. Knowing the historical facts is the first step in restoring the honor of the victims. Documenting and remembering this issue will make it possible to resolve it one day. For that day, this book begins the story of the Japanese military 'comfort women.'

Chapter 1

The Hidden Truth Unveiled by the Victims' Courage

1-1
Breaking the Silence: "I was a Japanese Military 'Comfort Women.'"

On August 14, 1991, a gray-haired old woman appeared at the office of the Korean Council for the Women Drafted for Military Sexual Slavery by Japan (hereinafter referred to as the "Korean Council").[1] She seemed to be an ordinary elderly person that we meet in our daily lives. After a pause, she began to talk about her experience in front of the media reporters. It was the first time a victim of the Japanese military 'comfort women,' which the Japanese government denies its involvement in, appeared in public.

"I was taken to a remote area in China at the age of sixteen and suffered as a Japanese military 'comfort woman.' How

---

[1] 韓國挺身隊問題對策協議會. It is commonly known as the Jeongdaehyeop or "Korean Council."

could you deny the existence of the 'comfort women' when I myself am a witness to it, having experienced it as a victim?"

She said she would testify to what she had gone through in the name of history. She had buried the painful past in the deep and dark corner of her heart for more than 50 years. She calmly testified to the reality of being a Japanese military 'comfort woman' as she experienced it.

"In the spring of 1940, I was sold to a remote place in central China, and I did not know why this was happening to me. The Sino-Japanese war was raging at that time. They turned the private houses abandoned by the Chinese villagers into comfort stations. They gave me a new name, Aiko, and I had to serve three or four soldiers a day at the front. There were about 300 soldiers."

Hak-soon Kim was furious. Her audience was confronted with an unpleasant truth of history.

Let us turn back the clock by one year. On May 18, 1990, the Korean Women's Associations United[2] and other relevant NGOs held a press conference in advance of President Tae-woo Roh's visit to

---

2   韓國女生團體聯合

Newspaper Article on *Chosun Ilbo* on August 16, 1991

The first Korean witness to the Japanese military 'comfort women,' whom the Japanese government denies, has come forward. "When I was 16 years old, I was taken to a remote area in China and suffered as a 'comfort woman' of the Japanese military. I am still alive and the denial of my existence makes no sense."

Hak-soon Kim (66, female, Chungshin-dong, Jongno-gu, Seoul) spoke out on August 14 from the office of the Korean Council for the Women Drafted for Military Sexual Slavery by Japan (Korean Council), and declared that she would testify to what she had buried in her heart for 50 years in the name of history. She spoke of her experience as a member of the Joseon Women's Volunteer Corps.

"In the spring of 1940, I was sold to a place called Cheolbyeokjin in central China, where the Sino-Japanese war was raging. They were building comfort stations out of the houses that the Chinese had abandoned because of the war."

When Kim arrived, there were already three Korean women between the ages of 17 and 21 who had served as 'comfort women' for the Japanese troops. They were named Miyako and Sadako. Kim was given a new name, Aiko, and had to serve three or four soldiers a day at the front. There were about 300 soldiers stationed in the area at that time. Terrified, Kim tried to escape several times, but was caught and punished.

After spending three months in the comfort station, she managed to escape with the help of a Korean merchant. She lived with the merchant in Shanghai, China, and returned to Korea one year after liberation [in 1946]. She lost her entire family during the Korean War and currently lives on welfare.

Kim demands that "the Korean government immediately reveal the facts about the Japanese military 'comfort women' and seek an official apology and compensation from the Japanese government." She also stated that "I am angry at the stark reality that Japanese songs are being played on the streets without restriction."

- Reported by Seon-ju Lee

Japan scheduled for May 24 [1990]. They asserted, "The Japanese authorities should thoroughly investigate and reveal the truth, apologize and compensate for their past criminal acts, especially for the long-buried 'comfort women' issue among others."

On June 6 of the same year, during a meeting of the Budget Committee of the Japanese House of Councilors, a lawmaker of the Japan Socialist Party, Shoji Motooka (本岡昭次), asked whether "there were women who were taken as 'comfort women' among the forced laborers. In response, Tsudao Shimizu (清水傳雄), director of the Labor Ministry's Occupational Safety Bureau said, "Regarding the issue of 'comfort women' considering various long-standing stories, it seems that private business owners accompanied such individuals with the military, or that such situations existed. Frankly, it's impossible for us to investigate these matters and produce results."

Amidst these circumstances, the testimony of Hak-soon Kim, who said, "I was a 'comfort woman' victim" created an opportunity to bring to life our nation's hidden painful past. Her testimony gave strength to the voices calling for Japan to reveal its past wrongdoings on behalf of the victims who were abducted and suffered harsh experiences at a young age and demanding a formal apology and compensation from the Japanese government.

The testimony of Hak-soon Kim, who courageously revealed the suffering she endured under her name, spread beyond Korean border. It reached the Philippines, Indonesia, Taiwan, and even as far as the

Netherlands, where testimonies of victims of the Japanese military 'comfort women' exploded. Jan Ruff O'Herne, a Dutch woman who served as a 'comfort woman' in Indonesia, remembered Hak-soon Kim in the following way.

> For the past 50 years, we, the so-called 'comfort women' of the Japanese military, all kept silent. We were ashamed of what had happened to us. We felt that we were dirty and it was terrible. I sat in my room and watched television. I saw Hak-soon Kim. Then I thought, "I was a Japanese military 'comfort woman' myself. I should help her." I had to support her. She had already spoken the truth, but the world did not recognize her voice and the Japanese military system of 'comfort women.' That was when I decided to speak out.
> (Provided by Jan Ruff O'Herne, July 2014, Part of a Video Message to Pope Francis)

Hak-soon Kim's testimony gave other victims the courage to talk about their own painful experiences. Her testimony reached out to the victims, telling them that the problem they had suffered alone was not their fault, but the fault of the perpetrator, Japan, and that they should work together to solve it. Encouraged by her initiative, victims began to tell their stories. Heartbreaking stories that had been kept hidden became a source of mutual comfort, and they no longer felt alone.

Soon-ak Kim, another former 'comfort woman,' recalls that her body trembled when she saw her fellow survivor in Cambodia, Hoon (Korean name: Nam-yi Lee) appeared on television. Hoon had already forgotten both her native language and her Korean name. She was taken to Cambodia at the age of 19 and became a 'comfort woman' for the Japanese soldiers. She rode in a truck with other local girls, not understanding what was happening, and was transported on a large ship via Singapore to Phnom Penh. Soon-ak Kim remembers the moment she saw Hoon on television:

"I was alone. I had nothing to rely on. One day I saw Hoon on TV and started beating my chest with my hands. Oh, someone like her lives on. A former 'comfort woman' for the Japanese soldiers... torn apart, stabbed... It was a story I kept to myself for so long. I was so alone, with no one to talk to... Then I realized that it was not my fault and I could say that I was a 'comfort woman' for the Japanese military."

The testimonies of the victims of the Japanese military 'comfort women' attracted the attention of the international community. The excavation of related historical documents soon followed. Professor Yoshiaki Yoshimi (吉見義明) of Chuo University (中央大) in Japan, who first discovered and published documents on the Japanese military involvement in the recruitment of 'comfort women' and the establishment of the comfort stations, said that he began searching for the historical materials after hearing Hak-soon Kim's testimony.

The victims not only testified to their pain and suffering, but also stepped forward to resolve the lingering issues of the past. They realized that by revealing the truth and receiving an apology and compensation from the Japanese government, they could help prevent the unfortunate history from repeating itself. Here is Ok-sun Lee's testimony:

> "My story must be told. I don't really want to talk about what I went through. It's too painful to even think about. But we need to keep talking about it. To protect other women from similar exploitation and to prevent these heartbreaking experiences from happening again. The truth must be known."

So why was the suffering of the 'comfort women' forgotten for so long? As many victims like Hak-soon Kim testified, they regarded their personal pain as something they had to bear alone. Maybe even the victims themselves did not want to accept what had happened and tried to forget their unbelievable circumstances. Summoning and sharing those painful memories was a cruel task that took a lot of courage.

Society as a whole should also be held partly responsible for the long silence. Until one woman finally came forward with the truth after 46 years of silence, no one bothered to ask what happened to them. Our society chose not to know and not to remember. Was it because we did not know what had happened to them?

More than 300,000 Korean men were conscripted into the Japanese army as soldiers and military personnel, so it is unreasonable to say that people were unaware of the fate of the women. It would be fair to say that society did not see the issue as a problem for the state to solve, but rather as a personal problem of the individual victimized women. As a former 'comfort woman,' Yong-soo Lee said, "Although the world has changed a lot, we [Korean society and its people] have not changed.' Even after Japan's surrender, no one took the plight of the 'comfort women' seriously. Not only the victorious nations, but also the South Korean government failed to address the issue during the 14 years of bilateral negotiations that preceded the signing of the Treaty on Basic Relations Between Japan and the Republic of Korea[3] in 1965. We as a society refused to listen to the women's silent cries.

The pervasive patriarchal culture of Korean society played an important role. It was not easy for the former 'comfort women' to say that their bodies had been forcibly violated by the Japanese soldiers because of the gendered social atmosphere. The victims could not return to their hometowns for fear of being blamed for what had happened and criticized for tarnishing the nation's honor. They had no choice but to remain silent. Therefore, it took great courage to relive the past and share their experiences. Even with the passage of time,

---

3　韓日基本條約

their wounds did not heal. Many more of the former 'comfort women' than those who revealed their suffering continue to live with their stories hidden from the world.

In the summer of 2017, I met Yong-soo Lee, a former 'comfort woman,' in Tokyo, Japan. She said the following:

> "I can forgive Japan, but I can't erase what I experienced from my mind. Maybe if I die, my memories will be erased. So, the answer is to die to erase my memories. It has been a long time, but I have never forgotten the pain of those moments, not even for a second."

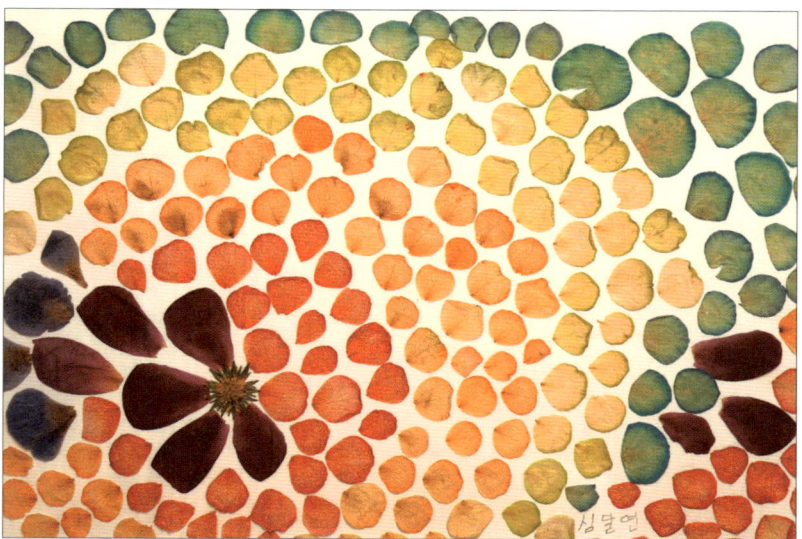

All Wars Must Stop II by Dal-yeon Shim
(Provided by Daegu Citizen's Forum for Halmuni)

The words of the victim, who said that she had to grit her teeth and endure even in happy moments because the dark memories resurfaced, still echo in my mind. It was heartbreaking to hear that many victims could not sleep at night after testifying. People want to hear their stories. Courts demand highly precise details in their testimony. Victims testified for the sake of the historical truth, but they had to endure fear and loneliness while doing so. Some even trembled with shame every time they repeated their horrible memories. We should bear the responsibility of passing on to the next generations the memories that the victims shared with difficulty and that still shake their bodies to the core.

1-2
Testifying to the Truth

On July 30, 2007, Congressman Mike Honda introduced Resolution 121 in the U.S. House of Representatives, calling for the resolution of the Japanese military 'comfort women' issue. The Congress listened to the testimony of victims before passing the resolution. But Japan's right-wing groups argue that the survivors' testimonies are unreliable because they keep changing. For example, they point to instances where survivors initially stated that they followed willingly because of persuasion, but later claimed that they were forcibly taken by people dressed in "police-like uniforms."

In the absence of relevant records, the conditions to which women were subjected in the comfort stations and the extent of the harm they suffered can only be revealed through the testimony of survivors. Memories may become incomplete with the passage of time, but the brutal wounds of such suffering are not easily forgotten. The cruelty of the 'comfort women' system comes to light through the victims' own words.

The discrepancy in memory is a peripheral matter, not the crux of the issue. If someone was forcibly taken and transported to a place they had never been before, they might not remember exactly where that place was, or whether they were transported by boat or truck. The victims of the Japanese military 'comfort women' would have seen people of an unfamiliar ethnicity in unfamiliar places. The grass and trees they saw in the streets would have been very different from those in their hometowns. They would have been very frightened. It is a stretch, then, to discredit all the testimony of 'comfort women' who were taken to such unfamiliar places, simply just because their memories have a few discrepancies.

The same goes for the memories of the soldiers who lived through the same war. Their memories may differ from the facts, but that does not make them liars. Even if their memories blend with what they heard from other soldiers, those memories are not considered false. However, right-wing groups in Japan insist on applying exceptionally strict standards to the words of the 'comfort women' victims.

Memories can be a crucial means of uncovering historical facts that are missing from official documents, or point the way to find new documents. In some cases, testimonies have been the basis for finding related documents and even for locating suspected sites of

Japanese military comfort stations.

Victims' testimony can also be supported by physical evidence. For example, the basis for the Japanese right-wing claim that the 'comfort women' had high incomes comes from the savings records of Ok-joo Moon, a former 'comfort woman.' Moon left the port of Busan in 1942, passing through Taiwan and Singapore, and was victimized as a 'comfort woman' in Mandalay, which located near Rangoon (the former capital of Myanmar). She had been told that she would work at a Japanese military canteen, but when she arrived, she found that it was a comfort station. Some of the women who had been mobilized together protested against Matsumoto, a business owner, for misleading them about the work, but eventually they had no choice but to give up. Ok-joo Moon was called Fumihara Yoshiko during her time there.

In the comfort stations, the managers controlled the money. The women were given military coupons by the soldiers as payment, but the managers took away all the coupons. The women could not afford to buy food, clothes, or cosmetics. In Ok-joo Moon's case, the soldiers gave her military coupons as tips and she saved them. Due to the severe inflation in the area, the military coupons did not mean much to the soldiers. According to the Japanese Prisoner of War Interrogation Report No. 49, written by the U.S. forces, life was very difficult for the 'comfort women' because the owners charged them extravagant amounts for food and other necessities.

Chapter 1 Unveiling the Hidden Truth Through the Victims' Courage   33

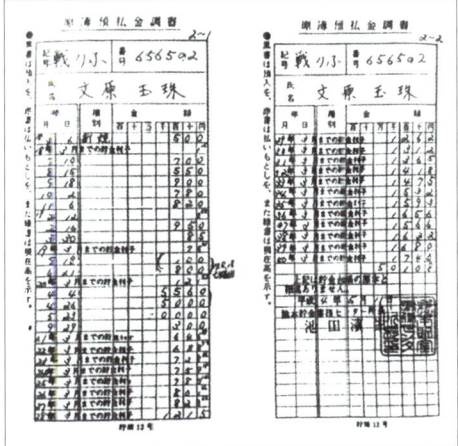

Military currency issued by the Japanese Military

Military Postal Savings Account of Ok-joo Moon

The revelation of victim Ok-joo Moon's savings records was sparked by the "Gathering for Returning Ok-joo Moon's Military Postal Savings," which produced a report covering its activities from March 1992 to April 1993. The photo above is a document stored in the Kumamoto (熊本) Savings Office.

Contrary to the claims made by Japanese right-wingers and the book *Anti-Japanese Tribalism* by Young-hoon Rhee that 'comfort women' earned more than generals, the region in question suffered from severe inflation, which greatly distorted the value of Moon's income. If we look at the actual value of the deposits printed in Ok-joo Moon's bank book, the value of the 2,150 yen (in local currency) saved from April to September 1943 was actually 264 to 405 yen (in Japanese currency), and the value of the 2,641 yen saved from October

1943 to March 1944 was actually 148 to 266 yen. In other words, if an apple cost 1 yen in Japan at that time, the same apple could have cost more than 1,000 yen in Mandalay. And if withdrawals were made in Joseon, they would have been based on the actual value of the deposit, not the inflated value. Moreover, Ok-joo Moon never received a penny of her savings. In March 1992, she went to Japan and asked the Shimonoseki Post Office for her military postal savings. However, the Japanese government responded that it could not make the payment because her rights to the savings had been extinguished by the 1965 Agreement on Claims and Economic Cooperation between the Republic of Korea and Japan.

The testimonies of the victims should not be discredited. Rather, they reveal historical facts that are not conveyed through documents. Therefore, close attention should be paid to the historical facts recounted by the victims.

Understanding the Terminology: Comfort Corps, War Comfort Women, Japanese Military Comfort Women, and Japanese Military Sexual Slaves[4]

In the newspaper article about Hak-soon Kim's press conference in 1991, the main text reads, "I suffered as a Japanese military 'comfort woman.'" However, in the title of the article, "I am a proof of the existence of the comfort corps," the term "comfort corps" was used instead of 'comfort woman.' The Korean Council for the Women Drafted for Military Sexual Slavery by Japan, which was established on November 16, 1990, to address the issue of Japanese military 'comfort women,' also includes the term "comfort corps" in Korean. When this issue became a social concern, the term "comfort corps" was commonly used.

From the end of 1989, Korean women's organizations took the

---

4   挺身隊, 從軍慰安婦, 日本軍慰安婦, 性奴隷

lead in raising the issue of the "comfort corps," and the Korean government also officially raised the "comfort corps" issue with Japan through the media. Here, the term "comfort corps" refers to the Japanese military 'comfort women.' What exactly is the "comfort corps"? How are these terms different? Or were they the same? It can be quite confusing.

The term "comfort corps" or "Volunteer Corps" originally referred to units formed voluntarily to serve the emperor, an embodiment of the Japanese state, by offering their bodies. Japan used this term to emphasize voluntarism when mobilizing troops and workers to support Japan's war effort. It was also used as a term to describe labor mobilization, such as the "Women's Labor Corps."[5] The reason why the term "comfort corps" was used to refer to the Japanese military 'comfort women' was derived from the historical fact that Japan extensively mobilized the women of Joseon under that name.

The term "war comfort women" has been used mainly in Japan. Some criticize that the word "war" should not be used in the term because it contains a sense of voluntariness, as seen in terms such as "war correspondent" or "war nurse." This is a valid criticism. Currently, this term is hardly used even in Japan. However, the term "war comfort women" is sometimes used not to emphasize the spirit of volunteerism, but to demonstrate the involvement of the Japanese mil-

---

5   女子勤勞挺身隊

itary in the operation of the comfort stations. In other words, the term provides a very important clue to refute the Japanese government's denial of military involvement. The Japanese right-wingers who claim that there is no connection between the military and the Japanese military 'comfort women' launched a movement to remove the term "war comfort women" from textbooks, asserting that while 'comfort women' may have existed, "war comfort women" did not.

The term 'comfort women' was coined by the Japanese military. In 1932, a battle took place between the Japanese Navy's land squadron stationed in Shanghai, China, and the Chinese 19th Army. This battle is known as the 1st Shanghai Incident. After the Shanghai Incident, as the Japanese troops began a large-scale deployment in the area, Japanese military comfort stations were established.

The women mobilized to the comfort stations were called 'comfort women' under the pretext of providing "comfort" to the soldiers. The literal translation of the term is "women who comfort and soothe the mind," which could lead one to mistakenly think that they performed roles similar to modern psychological counselors. We often find comfort in good books, movies, beautiful flowers, or a green forest. As such, the word "comfort" connotes positive and warm emotional experiences. However, the term 'comfort women,' created by the Japanese military, completely reflects the perspective of the Japanese military men. The Japanese government and military wanted 'comfort women' who could provide comfort to the soldiers. However, from the viewpoint of the women who suffered, they were not 'comfort women,' but rather "sexual slaves."

At the International Public Hearing on Post War Compensation of Japan, held in Tokyo in 1992, a former 'comfort woman' Jan Ruff O'Herne argued as follows:

> "I totally reject the term 'comfort women.' It means something warm and soft and cuddly. We weren't 'comfort women,' we were Japanese war rape victims."

Recently, the term Japanese military 'comfort women,' with quotation marks has been used. These quotation marks indicate that the meaning of the 'comfort women,' as used by the Japanese military, is not agreed upon, but that it is employed as a term to describe historical facts. In addition, specifying the "Japanese military" in the term is intended to clearly point out the perpetrator of the crime.

In the international community, the term "Japanese military sexual slavery" is increasingly being used instead of the term 'comfort women.' The report by Radhika Coomaraswamy, the UN Special Rapporteur on Violence against Women, submitted to the UN Commission on Human Rights in 1996, argued that the term 'comfort women' should be replaced by the term "wartime military sexual slavery." She explained that the term 'comfort women' does not reflect the pain and suffering the victims endured during

Chapter 1 Unveiling the Hidden Truth Through the Victims' Courage   39

A Portion of Report No. 49, "Report on Interrogation of Japanese Prisoners of War," Produced by the Psychological Warfare Team, Office of War Information (OWI), Based on the Interrogation of 20 Korean 'Comfort Women'

A "comfort girl" is nothing more than a prostitute or "professional camp follower" attached to the Japanese Army for the benefit of the soldiers. The word "comfort girl" is peculiar to the Japanese. Other reports show the "comfort girls" have been found wherever it was necessary for the Japanese Army to fight. This report, however, deals only with the Korean "comfort girls" recruited by the Japanese and attached to their Army in Burma (now Myanmar). The Japanese are reported to have shipped 703 of these girls to Burma in 1942.

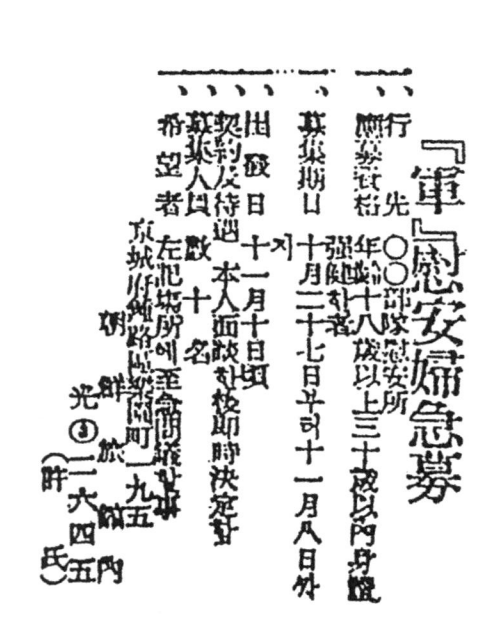

Maeilsinbo, October 27, 1944

"Military" Comfort Women Urgently Wanted

- Destination: ○○ Unit Comfort Station
- Eligibility: Applicants between the ages of 18 and 30 in good health
- Recruitment period: October 27 through November 8
- Departure date: Approximately November 10
- Contract and work conditions: To be determined immediately after interview
- Number to be recruited: Dozens of women
- Applicants: Please contact us as soon as possible at the following address

Joseon Inn, 195 Rakwonjeong, Jongno-gu, Gyeongseong City
(Phone) Gwanghwamun 3-2645 Mr. Heo

forced prostitution and sexual violence. Coomaraswamy argued that because the women were subjected to daily rape and severe physical abuse, the term "military sexual slavery" is much more accurate and appropriate.

In 2012, U.S. Secretary of State Hillary Clinton also advocated for the use of the term "forced sex slaves" instead of 'comfort women.' The UN Human Rights Commission and resolutions of various countries' legislatures have also described the Japanese military 'comfort women' system as the worst human rights violation committed by Japan during World War II, constituting a de facto system of "sex slavery." It can even be said that the comfort stations were "rape centers" operated by the military. In the international community, the term "comfort station" is also considered inadequate to convey the brutal reality, and terms such as "rape centers" are sometimes used instead.

Recently, the term "Japanese military sexual slavery" has become more popular. The Korean Council[6] changed its name from the "Korean Council for the Women Drafted for Military Sexual Slavery by Japan[7]" to the "Korean Council for Justice and Remembrance for the Issues of Military Sexual Slavery by Japan[8]" in July 2018, when it merged with the "Foundation for Justice and Remembrance.[9]"

---

6 挺對協
7 韓國挺身隊問題對策協議會
8 正義記憶連帶
9 正義記憶財團

In the Boat being Dragged Away by Soon-deok Kim
(Provided by House of Sharing)

Regardless of what the victims are called, the fact remains that they were subjected to forced sexual acts during their captivity under the Japanese military, making them "sexual slaves." However, there are people who feel uncomfortable with the term "sexual slaves." The victims themselves often find the term quite disturbing. At a meeting organized by a citizens' group in Tokyo in 2016, Yong-soo Lee asked not to be called a "sexual slave."

"My name is Yong-soo Lee. Please call me by my name, Yong-soo Lee, a human rights activist."

Chapter 2

Japan's Invasion War and the Japanese Military 'Comfort Women' System

2-1
Fraudulent Recruitment and Forced Mobilization: The Involvement of the Japanese Government and Military in Illegal Activities

When the issue of the Japanese military 'comfort women' was first raised, the Japanese government responded that civilian women voluntarily followed the troops. Those who deny the Japanese government's responsibility for the Japanese military 'comfort women' argue that it was merely an extension of the legally sanctioned prostitution system to war zones. In other words, they claim that 'comfort women' were people who engaged in prostitution of their own free will. The circumstances of women who became 'comfort women' through human trafficking are indeed unfortunate and deplorable, but legally, there was no problem at all, they claim.

The methods used to mobilize the victims of the Japanese military 'comfort women' were diverse. Even if it is acknowledged that some mobilization took place through the licensed prostitution system, as argued by the Japanese right-wing or former Prime Minister Shinzo Abe, is it fair to absolve the Japanese military and government of their responsibility?

The following is a process of recruitment and transfer in the 'comfort women' system based on the Japanese governmental documents.

1) Japan's invasion of China and the expansion of the Japanese army

Beginning with the invasion of the Korean Peninsula, Japan continued its territorial expansion into Manchuria, China, and the Pacific. The Korean Peninsula and Manchuria served as stepping stones for Japan's aggressive expansion into the continent. The Mukden Incident,[10] which broke out in 1931, provided an opportunity for the large-scale deployment of Japanese troops in China.

At 4:50 a.m. on July 7, 1937, the Japanese army launched a surprise attack on the Chinese troops at the Lugou Bridge[11] on the Yongding River in the southern outskirts of Beijing. Japan's Japanese Army Dispatched to China[12] was already stationed in the area, and around 20,000 troops, including two divisions of the Kwantung Army and the 20th Division of the Joseon Army, had joined to support the

---

10 滿洲事變
11 蘆溝橋, also known as the Marco Polo Bridge
12 支那派遣軍

Shina Garrison Army in northern China.[13]

The war that began in Lugou spread to Shanghai as the Chinese troops retreated from northern China. In Shanghai, a naval and ground force was deployed along with the 10,000-ton armored cruiser "Izumo." Additionally, the 3rd and 4th fleets were reinforced to form the Shina Fleet. On August 15, 1937, the cabinet of Fumimaro Konoe (近衛文麿) dispatched the 3rd Division and the 11th Division to Shanghai, forming the Japanese Army in Shanghai with General Iwane Matsui (松岩岩根) as its commander.

In August 1937, General Matsui's Army in Shanghai fought a fierce battle with the Chinese military. In the early stages of the battle, General Matsui, recognizing that the Japanese forces were being pushed back due to insufficient manpower, requested the deployment of three additional divisions. With the reinforcement of troops, the Japanese Army in Shanghai grew to approximately 100,000. From then on, the Shanghai area became the stronghold of the Japanese army with about 300,000 soldiers, including nine divisions, two independent infantry regiments, and two field artillery regiments, led by General Matsui, commander of the Japanese Army in Central China (the higher command of the Japanese Army in Shanghai).

With the sudden deployment of 300,000 Japanese soldiers in the Shanghai area, the demand for comfort stations increased sharply.

---

13   支那駐屯軍

Previously, the soldiers used the brothel designated by the command. As the number of troops increased, however, it became impossible to accommodate all the soldiers.

The Japanese army issued regulations to establish comfort stations as military support facilities. The problem was how to mobilize the 'comfort women.' It was not possible to recruit women to work in the comfort stations without the cooperation of the Home Ministry and the Ministry of Foreign Affairs. Moreover, it was not easy to recruit Chinese women because of the simmering resentment against the Japanese military in China.

Daiichi Saloon, The First Japanese Military Comfort Station in Shanghai.
[Provided by *Encyclopedia of Japan's Invasion of China,* by Su Zhiliang et al. (2014)]

From the beginning of the Sino-Japanese War until 1938, comfort stations were set up on a large scale. This is the reason why many documents related to the Japanese military 'comfort women' at that time were produced in the Shanghai area, and most of the correspondence was sent to Japan by the Shanghai Consulate General. It is also possible to determine the status of the recruitment and transfer of the 'comfort women' for the Japanese military by examining these official records.

2) Transportation of 3,000 'comfort women' to the Japanese Army in Shanghai in utmost secrecy

The Japanese army committed all kinds of plunder and atrocities in every area it passed through. In particular, Japanese soldiers brutally raped Chinese women regardless of their age, occupation, or social status. In response, the Chinese people resisted fiercely, even prepared to face death. The Shanghai police, under the jurisdiction of the Japanese consulate, strongly protested to the Japanese military command, stating that the security in the region had become more unstable due to the actions of the Japanese army.

The Japanese military command faced serious difficulties in occupying and ruling Shanghai and Nanjing because of the assaults, murders, and sexual violence committed by the Japanese soldiers against the civilians. It was considered urgent to set up more comfort stations in order to quickly stabilize the occupied area and concentrate the military forces in other areas.

The battle of Nanjing began on December 6, 1937, and the city fell on December 13. In mid-December 1937, as the Nanjing Massacre was beginning, a secret meeting was held in Shanghai to devise measures to prevent sexual assaults on civilian women and to maintain public order. Why was such a meeting necessary?

First, the looting and sexual assault of civilians by the military were war crimes under international law. Moreover, such unruly behavior needed to be controlled as a matter of discipline, which should not be compromised. In addition, the international community strongly condemned Japan when the foreigners in the Shanghai International Settlement directly witnessed the atrocities committed by the Japanese military, and exposed them to the world. The Japanese military command had no choice but to focus on countermeasures to deal with these problems.

The participants of the meeting included government officials from the Ministry of Foreign Affairs who were in charge of consular affairs at the Consulate General in Shanghai, Tokuhisa Major (徳久), General Araki (荒木), and Toyama Mitsuru (頭山満), among others. Major Tokuhisa and General Araki were members of the military police and the Defense Attaché Office. Military medical officials were concerned that due to the rapid increase of sexually transmitted diseases (STDs) among the soldiers in Shanghai and Nanjing, the soldiers would likely be rendered unfit for combat by these diseases before ever fighting against the Chinese forces.

Among the participants of the secret meeting, there were unknown people. They were people involved in the sex industry in Japan. Ouchi (大内) from Kobe City, Fujimura (藤村) and Konishi (小西) from Osaka City, and merchants hired by the military were also present. There is no record of the names of these merchants.

The military police said that they would need at least 3,000 'comfort women,' given the number of troops currently stationed. The problem was how to recruit and transport them to Shanghai.

However, the brothel owners who attended the secret meeting expressed confidence that they could recruit women in Japan and its colonies, but were concerned that transporting them to Shanghai would be more difficult. At that time, when Japan started the war with China, the movement of civilians to the Shanghai area was restricted, and the issuance of passports and visas was limited to essential cases only. The business owners explained that moving women for the purpose of prostitution could be a violation of Japanese domestic law, and that it was difficult for the women to obtain visas and passports to work in brothels because the public brothel system had been abolished in China. Nevertheless, the military police insisted that the comfort stations under construction must be filled with women as soon as possible.

After listening to the business owners, the consulate officials decided to take measures to allow the women to travel to Shanghai with only identification documents, without visas or passports. This decision was made with an awareness of domestic criticism that visas were issued for the purpose of prostitution. They also simplified the administrative procedures for transporting the women to avoid violating domestic law. This was aimed to prevent possible future accusations of traveling abroad without visas or passports.

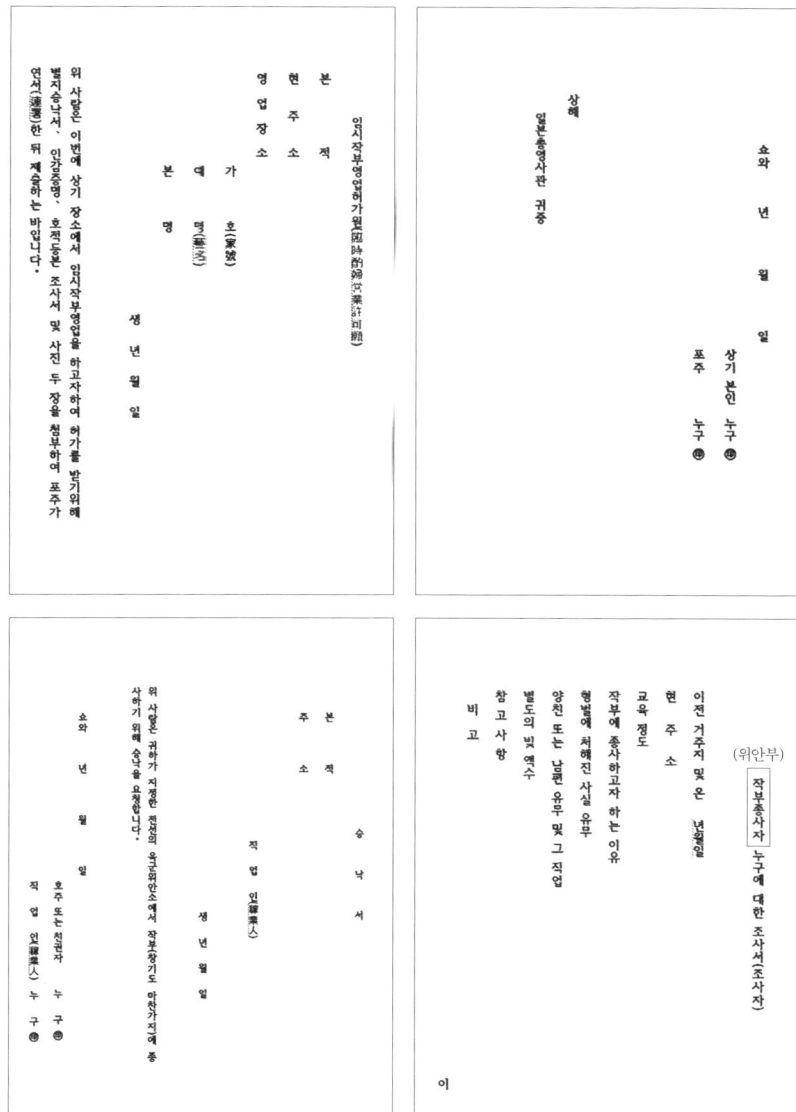

Travel Documents Prepared by the Shanghai Consulate

The documents on page __ were prepared by the Shanghai Consulate. As the phrase "the above person hopes to obtain permission to engage in temporary work as a hostess in the above-mentioned place" suggests, these documents formally indicate that the women themselves wanted to become 'comfort women' and move to China. As the war began and civilian control tightened, the Shanghai Consulate required the women to attach two photographs of themselves to the temporary work permit in order to identify people posing as 'comfort women.' In addition, the women were required to undergo security checks, as no formal procedures were in place. This allowed the local police to request background checks on the women at the Shanghai consulate. In any case, the consulate promised to respond quickly to 'comfort women' recruiters who wanted to bring women from Japan or Korea to Shanghai.

The military police were responsible for the safe transportation of the recruiters and 'comfort women' once they were handed over by the consulate. The cost of transportation to the military police was borne by the recruiters. The recruiters, in turn, deducted the cost from the wages of the recruited women. When transporting women from the places like Nagasaki (長崎) or Taiwan (臺灣) to Shanghai, the military police sometimes took charge and used military ships for transportation. These were called "government ships." While there were cases of transportation by rail or military trucks, military ships were used when sending large numbers of 'comfort women.' In particular, the army was directly involved in the transportation process.

The Defense Attaché Office (DAO) set up comfort stations. They also took measures to ensure that the 'comfort women' received immediate medical check-ups and STD tests upon their arrival. In the presence of police officers at the consulate, a specialist doctor examined the 'comfort women' for STDs once a week. This was not for the well-being of the women, but to prevent infection among the soldiers.

3) Collusion between the Japanese military and government to mobilize 'comfort women'

The document outlining the division of tasks after the secret meeting at the Shanghai Consulate was titled "Request for Provision of Convenience Regarding the Arrival of Imperial Army Soldiers' 'Comfort Women.'"[14] On December 21, the Japanese police stationed at the Shanghai Consulate drew up a memorandum of cooperation, with the aim of secretly recruiting around 3,000 women, and notified the kens in Japan through the Home Ministry. Three brothel owners from the Kansai area returned to Japan after the meeting at the Shanghai Consulate. Based on the decisions made at the meeting, the brothel owners began recruiting 'comfort women' from each ken. The phrase in the blow document reads, "Activities to recruit prostitutes are already underway in Japan and Joseon." This proves

---

14　軍将兵慰安婦女渡来ニツキ便宜供与方依頼ノ件

Request for Provision of Convenience Regarding the Arrival of Imperial Army Soldiers' 'Comfort Women'

December 21, 1937

This matter is under consideration by various related agencies as a comfort measure in response to the advance of the Imperial Army on the frontlines. Based on the previous agreement between this office [the Consulate], the Army DAO, and the Military Police, it has been decided to establish military comfort stations at various locations along the frontlines, according to the following guidelines.

Details

Consulate
(A) Determine whether to grant permission to business support personnel
(B) Verification of the identity of 'comfort women' and general contractual procedures for the business
(C) Post-arrival convenience measures after transit
(D) Inquiries and correspondence between relevant government agencies regarding identity verification of the business owner and women
(E) In principle, the women should stay in Shanghai upon arrival. After the approval is determined, they should be transferred directly to the military police.

The Military Police
(A) Procedures for transporting businessmen and women received from the consulate.
(B) Protection and supervision of the businessmen and women.

The Defense Attaché Office (DAO)
(A) Preparation of workplaces and accommodations
(B) Supervision of general health and venereal disease testing

According to the above guidelines, we are expediting the establishment of the facilities. Activities to recruit prostitutes are already underway in Japan and Joseon, and they will travel for important missions in the future. Please ensure that they carry the identification document issued by this office [Shanghai Consulate General] with the reason for travel, and provide them with conveniences for boarding and other matters. In addition, please instruct the recruiters or their representatives to carefully fill in the form below on the way to the job site after arriving in Shanghai, so as not to repeat the complicated process. After reviewing the documents, we kindly ask for your assistance.

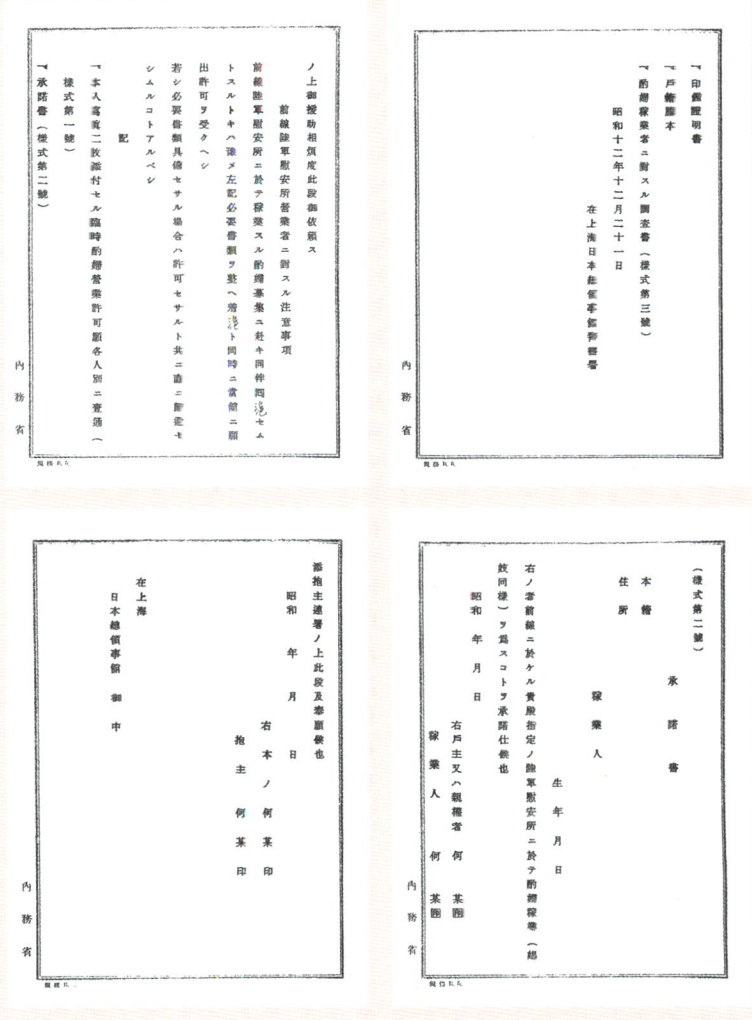

that recruitment was carried out in Joseon as well. However, no documents have been found that detail how recruitment took place in Joseon or how the Japanese Government General of Joseon cooperated. We can only speculate based on the circumstances in Japan.

The three brothel owners recruited 3,000 women from all over Japan and Joseon, including Nagasaki-ken (長崎県), Ibaraki-ken (茨城県), Gunma-ken (群馬県), Wakayama-ken (和歌山県), and Miyagi-ken (宮城県). During this process, the local police in each region cooperated in recruiting and transporting the women.

The document entitled "Request for Women Traveling to Shina"[15] is a request for cooperation Japanese Army in Southern China sent to the Japanese Home Ministry, especially to the police department, in recruiting 400 women for the comfort stations. The number of 'comfort women' to be recruited from each ken was as follows: 100 from Osaka, 50 from Kyoto, 100 from Hyogo, 100 from Fukuoka, and 50 from Yamaguchi. Based on the specific numbers determined by the military for each region, the request asked for the government's assistance in selecting business owners, recruiting and transporting the women, and ensuring the convenience of these processes. Notably, the document emphasized the discreet selection of trustworthy head contractors. This was because the head contractors had to operate the military comfort stations in cooperation with the military. Communication regarding

---

15   支那 渡航婦女ニ関スル件伺

the transit of the 'comfort women' was managed by the General Staff Headquarters and local Military Commands. The military was responsible for overseeing "contract details and the protection of the local women." This indicates that the transportation of the 'comfort women' was conducted similarly to military operations. The military's responsibility for contract details implies that if there were any illegal activities including labor fraud, the military would take responsibility, punish the wrongdoers, and repatriate the victims. However, there is no record of the military repatriating any victims.

The response of the Home Ministry to the "Request for Women Traveling to China" was shown in the document entitled "Concerning the Handling of Women Traveling to Southern China."[16] The Home Ministry found it difficult to comply with the police's request for cooperation, even under the special circumstances of the war, for the contractors in various regions to recruit 'comfort women' for the Japanese military. It stated that the Home Ministry would accept the military's request, but would do so discreetly. The Home Ministry recognized the possibility that recruiting 'comfort women' in Japan and transporting them overseas might violate international treaties and domestic laws, but it turned a blind eye to this. The operational structure was that the police in each ken responded to the military's specific requests for women and selected local recruiters. The police were

---

16　南支方面渡航婦女ノ取扱ニ関スル件

Request for Women Traveling to China

November 4, 1938

Today there was a request from Arifumi Kumon (久門有文), a major of the Army Air Corps in the Army Dispatched to Southern China, to support the travel of about 400 prostitutes needed to set up comfort stations in southern China. How about handling this request in accordance with the Home Ministry's Notice No. 5 (内務省発警第五号) of February 23 this year, and notifying each local office to secretly select qualified leaders to recruit the women to be sent to the site?

P.S.: There was news from the Japanese Governor General of Taiwan that about 300 local women have already completed their preparations for embarkation.

Details

1. The number of prostitutes to be recruited from Japan is about 400; 100 from Osaka, 50 from Kyoto, 100 from Hyogo, 100 from Fukuoka, and 50 from Yamaguchi. To accomplish this, select leaders, recruit women, and send them to the locations.
2. The above-mentioned leaders will be people who manage military comfort stations at the locations and should have trustworthy identities.
3. The aforementioned women will be transported discreetly from Japan to Kaohsiung, Taiwan at the leaders' expense. From Kaohsiung to the destination, they will board government ships. If the above method of transportation is not feasible, they will take regular scheduled ships between Kaohsiung (高雄) and Pingtung (屏東), under the control of the leaders.
4. Major Imaoka (今岡) and Captain Yoshida (吉田) of the 2nd Division of the General Staff Headquarters will manage the communication regarding this matter, and Major Mineki (峯木) of the Military Command will be in charge of the local matters.
5. If and when these women are needed elsewhere, the Furusho (古荘) Unit Headquarters will coordinate all the requests regarding the Southern Shina Expeditionary Force and the issuance of the leaders' permits. [General Staff Kumon (久門) will give this instruction to each unit after returning to his own unit.]
6. Regarding this matter, the Home Ministry and the local government offices will only provide assistance in recruiting and transporting the women. The details of the contracts and the protection of the women at the local places

will be the responsibility of the military.

7. In view of the above and in accordance with the government's Notice of February 23 this year, this matter will be referred to each of the above kens for implementation. (Please make initial contact by telephone and follow up with written communication.).

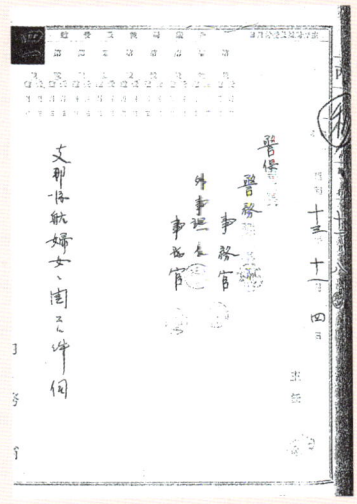

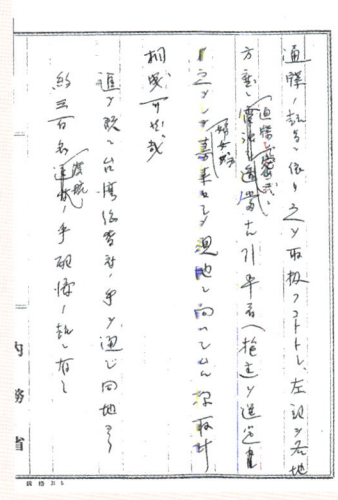

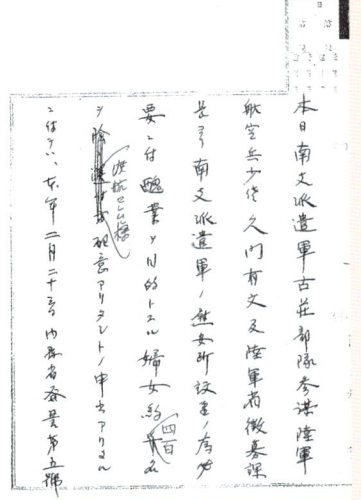

Notice

Public Safety Bureau, Issue No.136 [effective November 8, 1938]
From: Director of the Public Safety Bureau
Attention: Governors of Osaka, Kyoto, Hyogo, Fukuoka, Yamaguchi

Concerning the Handling of Women Traveling to Southern China

On February 23 this year, the Home Ministry issued Notice No. 5 regarding the women traveling to China. It seems that the southern China region also needs specialized women for the comfort stations, but there is no report that such a trip has taken place yet. According to the local request, resolving the current situation is considered inevitable, but we intend to keep this matter strictly confidential. We ask for your understanding and consideration.

Details

1. Selection and Handling of Women Recruitment Leaders
(A) The leaders will be selected from among those who have passed the identity check and are suitable to manage the military comfort stations in the southern China region. In addition, considering the approval for the establishment of military comfort stations in the southern China area, meetings should be held with those who wish to manage such operations to discuss the provision of convenience. The procedures will be carried out based on the voluntary wishes of the operators.
(B) The number of women who went to the southern China area for the purpose of "comfort business" was about 400. Among them, about 100 were assigned to be obtained from Osaka-ken, 50 from Kyoto-ken, 100 from Hyogo-ken, 100 from Fukuoka-ken, and 50 from Yamaguchi-ken. Appropriate persons will be selected as guide leaders in accordance with the preceding clause, and only these leaders will be allowed to secretly hire the above woman. The women's travel will be managed as stipulated in the following clauses. However, the women recruited from the area outside the above-mentioned kens will have no obstacle to travel.
(C) The number of women led by each leader should be between 10 and 30.
(D) If there are people who want to run comfort stations according to the previous three points, the information of the leaders, such as their address, name,

experience, and the expected number of women under their leadership, should be reported confidentially to the Home Ministry.
(E) Based on the report in the previous clause, official documents from the military will be provided to enable the discreet recruitment of women to work in comfort stations.
(F) The name of the leader, the number of women traveling, the port of disembarkation, the expected date of departure, and the expected date of arrival in Kaohsiung, Taiwan will be reported to the Home Ministry as mentioned in the previous clause. (Ships to Taiwan will be arranged in accordance with this notification.)

(Text omitted)

6. Location and Management of the Comfort Station
(A) The location and buildings for the comfort stations will be initially decided by the military based on the local situation. When changes are made, the same rule will be applied.
(B) The rest will be directed and supervised by the military.

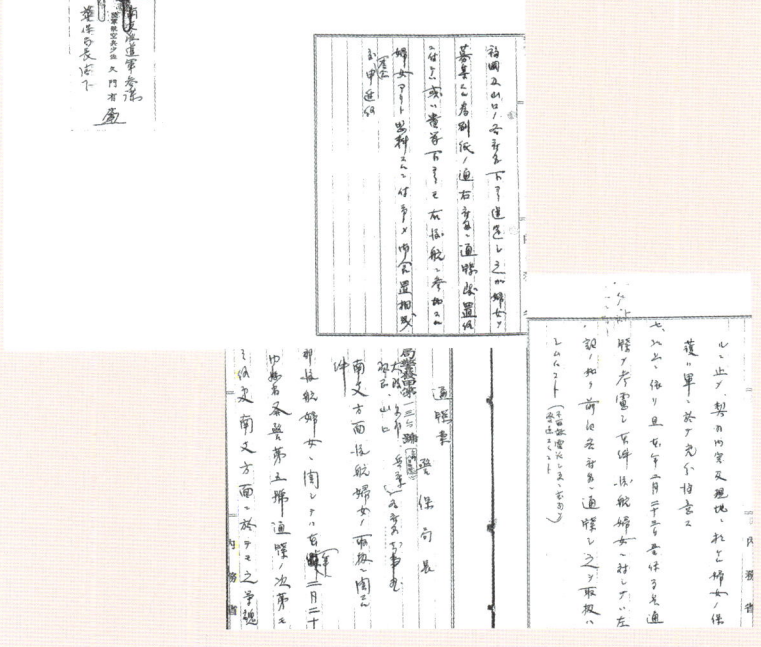

involved in the selection of recruiters at the request of the military, but the intention was to place all recruitment-related responsibilities on the recruiters. Thus, the military and the government cooperated extensively in the recruitment of women.

4) Condoning employment fraud and human trafficking

In the 1930s, deceiving women into prostitution and transporting them overseas was illegal in Japan under both domestic and international law. According to Article 60 of the Japanese Criminal Code and Article 61 of international treaties, it is evident that the recruitment of 'comfort women' for the Japanese military itself was unlawful at that time.

In 1932, there was a court case in which the pimps and brothel owners in Nagasaki-ken were convicted for sending 15 women to comfort stations in Shanghai. They had recruited the women while concealing information that they would be involved in the sex trade. On March 5, 1937, the Supreme Court of Japan issued a verdict in this case. Ten people who recruited women were sentenced to prison terms ranging from 1 year and 6 months to 2 years and 6 months. Both the Nagasaki District Court and the Supreme Court ruled that the recruitment and transportation of 'Comfort Women' violated Article 226 of the Criminal Code. The ruling classified the act of deceiving women and sending them overseas as illegal.

The Criminal Code (April 23, 1907)

Chapter 33. Kidnapping and abduction

Article 224. Anyone who kidnaps or abducts a minor shall be subject to imprisonment for a term of not less than 3 months and not more than 5 years.

Article 225. Anyone who abducts or kidnaps a person for the purpose of profit, obscenity, or marriage shall be subjected to imprisonment for a term of not less than 1 year and not more than 10 years.

Article 226. Anyone who kidnaps or abducts a person for the purpose of transporting them outside the Empire shall be subjected to imprisonment for not less than 2 years. Anyone who trades a person for the purpose of transporting them outside the Empire, and anyone who transports a kidnapped or traded person outside the Empire, shall also be subject to the same punishment.

Article 227. Anyone who accepts, hides, or assists in the escape of a person who has been kidnapped or traded, for the purpose of aiding individuals who have committed the above three offenses, shall be subject to imprisonment for a term of not less than 3 months and not more than 5 years. Anyone who accepts a person who has been kidnapped or traded for profit or obscenity shall be subject to imprisonment for a term of not less than 6 months and not more than 7 years.

Article 228. Attempts to commit the crimes mentioned in this chapter shall be punished.

Article 229. Except for the crimes under Article 226, the crimes under Article 227 (1) for the purpose of assisting the crimes of Articles 226, and their attempted crimes, all crimes mentioned in this chapter shall be prosecuted if they are not committed for the purpose of profit but complained of. However, if the abducted or sold person marries the perpetrator, there will be no prosecution unless the marriage annulment or dissolution case is completed.

(Omitted below)

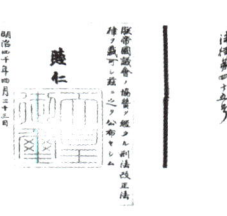

International Treaty Prohibiting the Trafficking of Women for Prostitution[17]

December 21, 1925

Treaty No. 28

After consultation with the Privy Council Adviser, I declare that our country is a party to the Final Protocol of the International Treaty Prohibiting the Trafficking of Women for Prostitution, signed by 21 countries, including Germany, in Paris, France, on May 4, 1910. However, our country has reservations that Paragraph B of the Final Protocol be applied only to those under the age of 18. This is promulgated in conjunction with the International Agreement for the Suppression of the Prostitution, adopted by 12 countries, including France, in Paris, France, on May 18, 1904.

Hirohito Mutsuhito (嘉仁 裕仁)

December 21, 1925 (14th year of the Taisho era)
Prime Minister, Viscount Takaki Kato (加藤高明)
Minister of Foreign Affairs, Baron Kijuro Sidehara (幣原喜重郎)
Minister of Internal Affairs, Reijiro Wakatsuki (若槻禮次郎)
Minister of Justice, Tasuku Egi (江木翼)

Treaty No. 18
INTERNATIONAL CONVENTION FOR THE SUPPRESSION OF THE WHITE SLAVE TRAFFIC

The Sovereigns, Heads of States, and Governments of the Powers hereinafter designated,

Being equally desirous of taking the most effective steps for the suppression of the traffic known as the "White Slave Traffic," have resolved to conclude a Convention with this object, and a draft thereof having been drawn up at a first Conference which met at Paris from 15 to 25 July 1902, they have appointed their plenipotentiaries, who met at a second Conference at Paris from 18 April to 4 May 1910 and agreed upon the following provisions:

17　醜業ヲ行ハシムル為ノ婦女賣買 禁止ニ関スル國際條約

Article 1 Whoever, in order to gratify the passions of another person, has procured, enticed, or led away, even with her consent, a woman or girl under age, for immoral purposes, shall be punished, notwithstanding that the various acts constituting the offence may have been committed in different countries.

Article 2 Whoever, in order to gratify the passions of another person, has, by fraud, or by means of violence, threats, abuse of authority, or any other method of compulsion, procured, enticed, or led away a woman or girl over age, for immoral purposes, shall also be punished, notwithstanding that the various acts constituting the offence may have been committed in different countries.

Article 3 The Contracting Parties whose legislation may not at present be sufficient to deal with the offences contemplated by the two preceding Articles engage to take or to propose to their respective legislatures the necessary steps to punish these offences according to their gravity.

Article 4 The Contracting Parties shall communicate to each other, through the intermediary of the Government of the French Republic, the laws which have already been or may in future be passed in their States relating to the object of the present Convention.

Article 5 The offences contemplated in Articles 1 and 2 shall, from the day on which the present Convention comes into force, be deemed to be lawfully included in the list of offences for which extradition may be granted in accordance with Conventions already existing between the Contracting Parties.

In cases in which the above provision cannot be made effective without amending existing legislation, the Contracting Parties engage to take or to propose to their respective legislatures the necessary measures.

(Omitted)

FINAL PROTOCOL

At the moment of proceeding to the signature of the Convention of this day, the undersigned plenipotentiaries deem it expedient to indicate the sense in which Articles 1, 2, and 3 of that Convention are to be understood, and in accordance with which it is desirable that the Contracting States, in the exercise of their legislative sovereignty, should provide for the execution of the stipulations agreed upon or for their extension.

A. The stipulations of Articles 1 and 2 are to be considered as a minimum, seeing that it is self-evident that the Contracting Governments remain entirely free to punish other analogous offences, such, for example, as the procuring of women over age, even where neither fraud nor compulsion may have been exercised.

B. As regards the suppression of the offences provided for in Articles 1 and 2, it is fully understood that the words "woman or girl under age, woman or girl over age" refer to women or girls under or over twenty completed years of age. A law may, nevertheless, fix a more advanced age for protection, on condition that it is the same for women or girls of every nationality.

(Omitted below)

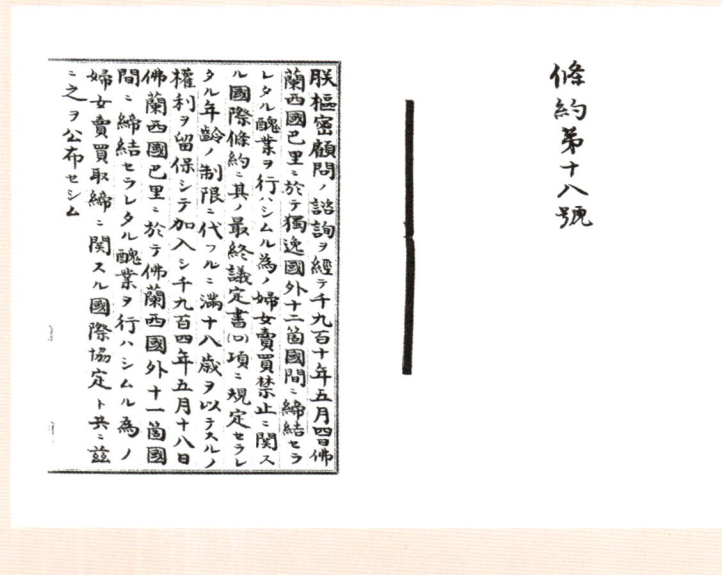

After the Sino-Japanese War, such illegal activities were increasingly tolerated. Particularly concerning minors, the Home Ministry turned a blind eye despite the need for strict supervision. Many of the recruited 'comfort women' were under the age of 20. This can be confirmed by the testimony of victims and the records of STD tests conducted by military doctors.

Recruiters, actively supported by the Japanese military and government, lured women through various schemes. On January 6, 1938, the Mori (文里) Police Office in Wakayama-ken arrested three contractors who were recruiting women to be sent to the Imperial Army comfort stations in Shanghai. The contractors said they were on a business trip to Wakayama-ken to recruit 3,000 women for the Japanese troops stationed in Shanghai. But Wakayama-ken intelligence detectives determined that they were trying to kidnap the women and smuggle them overseas. They issued arrest warrants for the three contractors. They worked in the sex industry in Osaka-shi and recruited women from Wakayama-ken at the request of an unknown brothel owner who attended the secret meeting in Shanghai. They were Kintaro Saga (佐賀今太郎) and Jinemon Kanazawa (金沢甚右衛門), and the third person, Shigenobu Hiraoka (平岡茂信), introduced the women to Saga and Kanazawa.

Under the direction of the Japanese Army in Shanghai, Saga and Kanazawa conspired with Hiraoka, who knew the local situation in Wakayama-ken. In order to recruit women for the sex industry, it was necessary to have someone familiar with the local situation. Hiraoka had been in the entertainment business in Wakayama-ken for a long time, and he first approached three women he knew well, enticing them with the promise of making a lot of money by helping the Japanese military. He then took the women to the recruiters.

The Wakayama-ken Police determined that the actions of the three men were highly reprehensible for several reasons. First, they never told the women that they were going to work as prostitutes. They deceived the women with false claims that the work would be easy and that it was for the Imperial Army. They also enticed the women with the promise that they would be fed, clothed, and housed, which would make them earn a lot of money. The plan to send the women abroad was considered particularly heinous. The main reason for the arrest of the contractors by the Wakayama-ken Police was their statement that they were recruiting at the request of the Imperial Army. The Wakayama-ken Police could not believe that the esteemed Imperial Army would engage in such degrading activities.

The Wakayama-ken Police, while compiling statements against them, found that all their testimonies were consistent. The information they provided about transporting women to Shanghai with the help of the police and military police in Nagasaki-ken and Osaka City, was confirmed after verification. Nagasaki-ken confirmed to Wakayama-ken that the perpetrators recruited the women in accordance with the "Request for Provision of Convenience Regarding the

Arrival of Imperial Army Soldiers' Comfort Women" issued by the Shanghai Consulate Police Department. Their identities were also verified by the Shanghai Consulate.

The mobilization of 'comfort women' occurred when the expeditionary force made a request, after which the Shanghai Consulate notified the director of the Police Bureau at the Home Ministry and each ken governor through the Ministry of Foreign Affairs. Then, the governor of each ken notified the local police stations. In the case of Wakayama-ken, the failure to receive this notification led to the incident.

The recruitment of 3,000 'comfort women' requested by the Japanese Army in Shanghai caused social problems not only in Wakayama-ken, but also in other kens (県, prefecture) in Japan. The governor of Gunma-ken expressed his concern to the police chiefs of other kens, the Minister of Internal Affairs, the Minister of the Army, and the Japanese Army Dispatched to Shanghai. In January 1938, Kobe-shi issued an order for a strict crackdown on the recruitment of 'comfort women,' which lured women under the false pretense of recruiting them for the Imperial Army. This was because such actions were considered to be not only detrimental to the good reputation of the Imperial Army, but also against public order and traditional propriety. Since Gunma-ken had abolished the public brothel system in 1893, the governor's reaction was natural.

As such illegal activities became rampant, the Japanese government

Regarding the Treatment of Women Traveling to China

February 23, 1938

Notice No. 5 of the Director of the Public Safety, Home Ministry

From: Director of the Public Safety Bureau, Home Ministry
Attention: Ministers of each cho (庁), fu (府), and ken (県)

Regarding the Treatment of Women Traveling to China

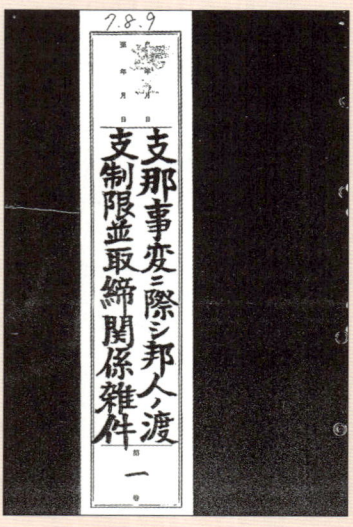

With the recent restoration of order in various parts of China, there has been a significant increase in the number of people traveling to China. Many of these women are seeking to work in restaurants, cafes, brothels, or similar businesses. In addition, there have been a number of cases of people in Japan arranging for the recruitment of these women, and making statements as if they have the support of the military authorities. The women's travel abroad may be necessary in view of the special situation. The authorities also recognize this necessity and should take appropriate measures. But they are trying to recruit women beyond the acceptable limits, undermining the reputation of the Empire and tarnishing the image of the Imperial Army. This has a negative impact on the people on the home front, especially the families of the soldiers who have been deployed. In the current situation, it is difficult to comply with the international treaties on trafficking of women. Considering the local and other relevant circumstances, this office issues the following Notice for your compliance.

(Omitted below)

tried to strictly control the transportation of women to China. On February 23, 1938, the Home Ministry issued a notice entitled "Regarding the Treatment of Women Traveling to China."[18]

According to the notice, only women over the age of 21 who were engaged in prostitution were allowed to travel. The women were required to appear at the police station and apply in person for an identification document. In order to issue the document, the police had to investigate the possibility of human trafficking, fraud, and kidnapping. The police were to take action against false or exaggerated work-related information. The directive reflected the reality that during recruitment, it was "difficult to comply with the international treaties on trafficking of women."

At first glance, this directive might appear to be an effort by the Japanese government to crack down on the recruitment of women through abduction or deception. However, it was a rhetorical gesture articulated in the form of an official document. In reality, the military controlled the recruitment of women, and the police cooperated with pimps. The document as such was a calculated attempt to evade any responsibility for these operations in case of future problems.

How did the military and police respond to the order? The response of the military and police to the government order was minimal. According to the document "Regarding the Treatment of Women

---

18 支那渡航婦女ノ取扱ニ関スル件

Traveling to China" sent to the Minister of the Hokkaido Government by Seijiro Yoshizawa (吉澤清次郎), Director of the American Bureau of the Japanese Ministry of Foreign Affairs, the police chiefs overseeing the recruitment process issued identification documents to women under the age of 21.

"Notice No. 5, Regarding the Treatment of Women Traveling to China, issued by the Director of the Public Safety of Home Ministry on February 23, 1938, was sent to every minister of the provincial, municipal, and prefectural governments. According to the document, only women over the age of 21 were allowed to travel to China to engage in prostitution. However, during the crackdown by the bureau under my supervision on the 10th of this month [May 1938], three out of four prostitutes who went to Beijing through the Shanhai Pass (山海關) were under 21 years of age. One was born in 1922 and two were born in 1921. Based on the nature of the business, it was very clear that they all came here for the purpose of prostitution. Despite the circumstances, they all had identification documents issued by the Asahikawa City [Hokkaido-ken] Police Chief. Although we were fully aware of the violation, we had to let them pass. There are two or three similar cases."

In other words, among the women recruited as 'comfort women' were underage girls between the ages of 17 and 18. Since the recruitment of 'comfort women' was carried out on a large scale, we can assume that the Japanese police tolerated illegal activities in order to meet the quota.

Even the Japanese Ministry of the Army was aware of the social problems caused by the recruitment of 3,000 'comfort women.' This fact is evident in the document entitled "Regarding the Recruitment of Military Comfort Station Workers"[19] prepared by the Ministry of the Army on March 4, 1938.

This document shows that the women were essentially "abducted" and the intention was to ensure that the relationship between the brothel owners and the military remained undisclosed. Although on the surface there appears to be a strict determination to enforce the law, the reality is that the expeditionary forces selected recruiters under their control, and ensured close cooperation between the police and the military police during the recruitment process to prevent possible investigations of the recruiters.

While such illegal activities were common in Japan, the government turned a blind eye to these illegal transactions. The situation must have been even worse in colonial Joseon. Although we have not found any materials that reveal the direct involvement of the Japanese

---

19　軍慰安所従業婦等募集ニ関スル

Regarding the Recruitment of Military Comfort Station Workers

Letter from the Adjutant (Ministry of the Army) to the Chief of Staff of the Northern Area Army and the Central Expeditionary Force

In the recruitment of 'comfort women' to be sent to the areas of the Sino-Japanese War in the past 4 years, there is concern that deliberately using the military's name may defame the reputation of the military and mislead the general public. Recruiting 'comfort women' in situations where war correspondents and morale-boosting visitors come and go without control could potentially cause social problems. In addition, the recruitment methods resemble kidnapping, which in many cases leads to police arrest and interrogation. This requires careful attention. Therefore, in future recruitment, it is recommended that the expeditionary forces take control and lead in selecting the recruiters, while maintaining close coordination with local military police and police authorities to uphold the reputation of the military. We hope that there will be no further social problems related to this situation.

Army Confidential Information No. 745
March 4, 1938

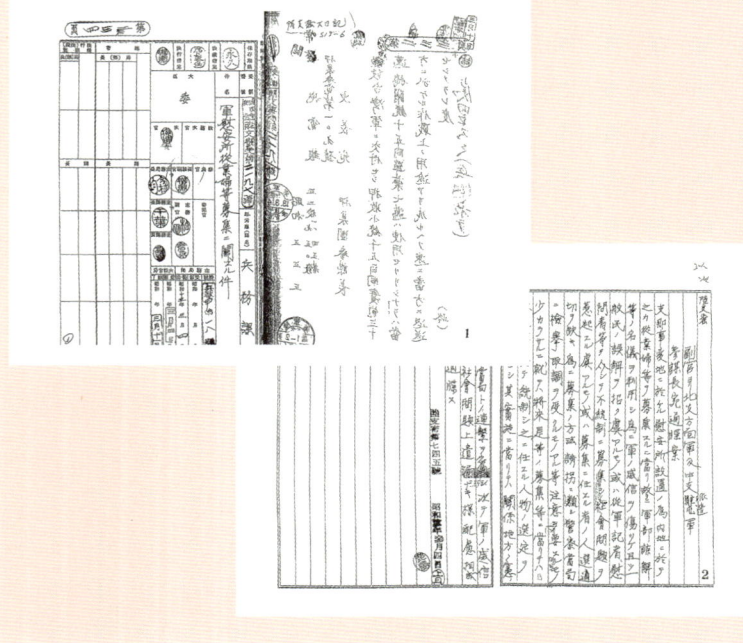

Government General of Joseon[20] in the mobilization of 'comfort women,' judging from the recruitment advertisement for 'comfort women' in the aforementioned Maeil Shinbo, it can be inferred that a similar approach was likely taken as in Japan. In other words, it is speculated that the military command in Joseon would have requested the recruitment of 'comfort women' and the Japanese Government General of Joseon would have been directly or indirectly involved in selecting recruiters to mobilize the 'comfort women.'

The number of 'comfort women' transported at one time during the war ranged from 700 to 3,000. It was a large number. After trial and error in the recruitment process, the recruitment became more methodical. After the document "Regarding the Recruitment of Military Comfort Station Workers" was written, cooperation between the military and the recruiters and between the Home Ministry and the Ministry of Foreign Affairs became closer. In particular, the military and the government were extremely reluctant to say that the recruitment of 'comfort women' was "directed by the military" or "involved the military." They didn't want to admit that the military had given the order.

However, the military was directly involved from the allocation of the number of 'comfort women' to be recruited to the transportation of the women. The Home Ministry assessed how many 'Comfort Women' needed to be recruited in each area and allocated the

---

20　朝鮮總督府

recruitment quotas. The military then sent relevant documents to each ken to encourage mobilization. The military also intervened, directly or indirectly, in the selection of the leaders who would lead the women during the transportation process. When it was difficult to obtain identification documents, the recruiters contacted the military, skipped all procedures, and handed the women over to the military police to transport them to their destinations.

Comfort Women of the Empire by Yu-ha Park and *Anti-Japanese Tribalism* by Young-hoon Rhee deny the coercive nature of the recruitment of 'comfort women.' They argue that the women clearly knew what they were doing at the time of recruitment. Furthermore, both authors claim that there is no evidence that the Japanese military forcibly mobilized 'comfort women.' Even if there was coercion, the authors claim that it was the recruiters' responsibility.

According to Japanese official documents, both the Japanese military and government were directly or indirectly involved in the mobilization, from planning to recruitment to transportation of women. This fact was acknowledged in the Kono Statement of 1993.

The Japanese military and government knew that the women were being mobilized illegally, but they did nothing about it. They were accomplices to this organized crime and ultimately controlled the entire enterprise.

On the Claims that 'Comfort Women' Were Part of the Legalized Prostitution System in Japan

In his book, *Anti-Japanese Tribalism*, Young-hoon Rhee argues that there was a legalized prostitution system at that time, so it should not have been a problem for the military to use the existing system. However, there have been many criticisms of the legalized prostitution system in Japan since the 1920s. In a petition titled "Petition for the Abolition of Legalized Prostitution" submitted by professors including Isou Abe (安部磯雄) of Waseda University in January 1924, they stated that "the legalized prostitution system is fundamentally a bad system that involves brutal human trafficking and cruel enslavement of women." They also argued that "it is a form of slavery that involves two major crimes, namely human trafficking and unlawful detention." Despite the claims that prostitution was legal and unproblematic, the majority of women placed under the system were mobilized through human trafficking, and were actually sexual slaves bound by "advance payment." Between 1930 and 1941, 13 kens in Japan abolished legalized prostitution and 14 kens declared their plan to abolish it. Moreover, not all countries in the world had a system of legalized prostitution. China, for example, abolished it in 1907. In the first trial of the Busan 'comfort women' lawsuit, the Yamaguchi (山口) District Court, in its ruling issued on April 27, 1998, strongly criticized as follows.

> "Just as the 'comfort women' plaintiffs experienced, they [the defendants] coerced and deceived underage girls in the colonies and occupied territories, and took them to comfort stations against their will. Furthermore, the former Japanese military intervened directly and indirectly in the establishment of the comfort stations by participating in the policy-making and system-building that forced the women to have sexual intercourse with former soldiers. Even when viewed in the context of mid-20th century civilization, it is evident that these acts were inhumane and abhorrent. At the very least, as a so-called first-class nation, Imperial Japan's involvement in such acts was unacceptable. Nevertheless, both the former army and the government of Imperial Japan participated in these activities, resulting in serious human rights violations and grave harm...."

5) Transportation of 3,000 'comfort women' through cooperation between the police and the military police

Nagasaki was the first port of disembarkation for the 'comfort women' to Shanghai. Japan had long used the port of Nagasaki to transport goods and people to China. Especially since 1932, when the Japanese Navy stationed a large number of troops in Shanghai, Japanese-style entertainment establishments began to appear around the Hongkou(虹口) district. The Japanese who wanted to work in restaurants, cafes, and other entertainment businesses flocked to the city of Nagasaki, and a direct channel was established between Nagasaki and the Shanghai Consulate.

Those who knew the local situation in Shanghai held informational meetings for women, in cooperation with Nagasaki police. They told the women that they could "make a lot of money," that "only soldiers will be customers," and that "food and lodging will be provided by the military." No one suspected that the jobs guaranteed by the Japanese police were essentially exclusive military "rape centers." During these sessions, the recruiters collected 70 women, and sent them to Shanghai on an army ship escorted by the military police without any special procedures.

In Osaka, the police guaranteed the identification of the recruiters and provided considerable conveniences, allowing the first departure to be completed on January 3, 1938. In addition, women between the ages of 16 and 30, recruited from Ibaraki-ken (茨城県) and Miyagi-ken

Travel Permit

Original Address: ○○○○
Current Address: ○○○○
Occupation: Comfort Station Business

1. Destination: Taiwan, Kaohsiung
2. Purpose: to recruit and transport the 'comfort women'
3. Period: June 27 - September 26, 1940
4. Place of departure: Qinzhou
   Date of departure: June 30, 1940
5. Other information
   This is to confirm that the permit holder will travel as stated above.

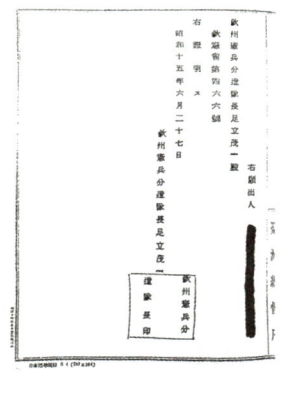

Attention: Adachi Shigeichi (足立茂一),
Commander of Qinzhou Military Police
Qinzhou Alert No. 466
Confirmed as above

June 27, 1940
Adachi Shigeichi,
Commander of Qinzhou Military Police
(Seal here)

(宮城県), among other regions, were transported to Shanghai. Many women were also recruited in Joseon. Some of the Joseon people traveled from Busan to the Kansai region of Japan, and finally to China.

Those who were mobilized as 'comfort women' could enter China without visas if they had travel permits issued by the Chinese police. However, if the local police station and consulate were far away, they could not obtain the permits. After 1940, however, a permit from the head of the local military police was all that was needed to move the 'comfort women.' All forms and procedures were simplified in order to transport the 'comfort women.'

What happened to the 'comfort women' when they arrived in Shanghai with the recruiters? They were received by military officials. They underwent physical examinations, especially tests for STDs. Then it was decided where to deploy the 'comfort women' based on the size of the stationed forces. They were sent to places ranging from combat zones like Nanjing to non-combat areas, according to the military's needs.

Luring and Kidnapping by the Military and Government Officials

The war crimes trials held after the war revealed that the Japanese military or government officials had kidnapped or lured women and turned them into 'comfort women.'

▪ **November 1, 1948 Guilin Trial**

The Japanese army continued to advance southward toward Guilin (桂林) and Liuzhou (柳州) in Guangxi-sheng, China. The Japanese troops occupying Guilin raped, pillaged, and committed all kinds of atrocities. The women, recruited under the pretext of building factories, were forced to work as prostitutes for the Japanese army. Before the Japanese army withdrew from Guilin in July 1945, they organized arson squads and set fire to all of Guilin's commercial districts.

- **Documents submitted as evidence of the Guilin case at the Tokyo Trial**

  Prosecution of Guilin Citizens 1

(...) During their one-year occupation of Guilin, the enemy committed rape and looting, among other atrocities. Captain Naganawa, a Japanese from Fukuoka-ken, was in charge of rebuilding the area. He dominated the propaganda newspapers and cultural organizations, and turned them into the central institution for seducing and enslaving the people. He used fake members to advertise the establishment of factories, gathered women from all over, dragged them out of Lizerman, threatened them and used them as prostitutes to serve the sexual desires of the army like beasts. (...)

- **Documents investigated and released by the Dutch government in 1994**

At the height of the invasion and the beginning of the occupation, rape by Japanese soldiers was common in Tarakan, Manado, Bandung, Padang, Flores, and other areas of Indonesia. In some cases, the Japanese military severely punished the perpetrators. In Blora, near Semarang on the island of Java, about 20 European women were held in two houses. For three weeks, at least 15 women, including a mother and daughter, were raped several times a day as the regiments passed through the area.

Victims of Japanese military comfort stations sued the Japanese government. In 8 out of 10 lawsuits (35 plaintiffs: 10 Koreans, 24 Chinese, and 1 Dutch) demanding an apology and compensation, the Japanese court acknowledged that the plaintiffs became 'comfort women' against their will and were forced to have sexual intercourse with the soldiers while deprived of their freedom.

▪ **BC Class Batavia Trial Case No. 5**

The Indictment

Defendant Aoji Washio (青地鷲雄)

The defendant was a citizen of the enemy country, Japan. It is believed that he committed war crimes in Batavia from September 1943 to September 1945, although the period is not clear. He was the manager of the "Sakura Club," an establishment for the general public of Japan that violated the laws and customs of war, and recruited women to serve the Japanese customers. When the recruited women asked to be released from his business, he threatened them directly or indirectly by mentioning the military police. He forced the women into prostitution by making them stay in a hut on the premises of the club. He did not allow the women to leave the club and forced the women who were his acquaintances to engage in prostitution for Japanese customers.

The above facts fall under Article 4 of the Statue Book Decree of 1946 in Dutch Indonesian official gazette. Therefore, the prosecution intends to punish the defendant accordingly.

(...)

Judgement

(some omitted)

Among the witnesses who testified, the following witness mainly testified as follows:

1. Katarina Poteherr

From May 6 to September 1944, the witness worked as a prostitute (i.e., a 'comfort woman') at the Sakura Club. This was done voluntarily at the suggestion of Rhys Beahorst. The witness told Rhys Beahorst that she wanted to quit twice, but gave up because of the threat of the military police. The witness tried to escape from the Sakura Club, but was caught by the military police and held in solitary confinement at the police station for a week. During that time, the military police told her twice that she had to work at the Sakura Club.

4. Pretirica Caroline Perustitztu van der Curey

From April to December 1944, she worked as a prostitute (i.e., 'comfort woman') at the Sakura Club. The witness accepted the work voluntarily, on the condition that she would accept only one customer a day. But soon she was forced to serve every customer. At the club, the Japanese person, Aoji, was at the top, and Rhys Beahorst was below him.

The witness tried to cover up for the 14- and 15-year-old girls who worked there. This led to a big fight with Rhys, and he told Aoji and his mother. They beat up the witnesses in front of others. The Sakura Club originally had three businesses: a hostess club, a bar, and a brothel.

Women came to the club to work as hostesses or bar staff, but were eventually forced into prostitution. Some of them were 14- to 16-year-old girls who knew nothing about the realities of life. When the women wanted to quit, they were either taken to a police officer or threatened by Rhys Beahorst. They also informed the military police that she was trying to get a boyfriend outside the club. The women of the Sakura Club lived in a fenced-in shack on the club grounds. This was their duty.

(Testimony omitted below)

In light of these facts, the Military Tribunal Council decided that 10 years' imprisonment was appropriate for the defendant's crimes. In addition to the law already considered, the court paid attention to Article 4 of the Official Gazette No. 45, and the court found that Aoji Washi's wrongdoings were in clear violation of the law. Therefore, the court declares that he committed the war crime of "forced prostitution" and sentences him to 10 years in prison.

Lawsuits by the Japanese Military 'Comfort Women' and Judicial Recognition of Damages

Country	Title of Litigation	Year of Litigation Final Decision	Number of Plaintiffs	Judicial Recognition of Damages
Korea	Compensation Claim Case for Korean Victims of the Asia-Pacific War	1991/2004	9	Y
	Claim Case for Official Apology of Busan 'Comfort Women' Women Labor Volunteer Corps	1992/2003	3	Y
	Claim Case for Official Apology and Compensation of 'Comfort Women' among Korean Residents in Japan	1993/2003	1	Y
The Philippines	National Compensation Claim Case for Philippine 'Comfort Women'	1993/2003	46	N
The Netherlands	Compensation Claim Case of Dutch POW・Civilian Internees	1994/2004	1	Y
China	Compensation Claim Case of Chinese 'Comfort Women' (1st)	1995/2007	4	Y
	Compensation Claim Case of Chinese 'Comfort Women' (2nd)	1996/2007	2	Y
	Compensation Claim Case of Sexual Violence Victims of Shanxi-sheng	1998/2005	10	Y
	Compensation Claim Case of Wartime Sexual Violence Victims of Hainan Dao	2001/2010	8	Y
Taiwan	Claim Case for Apology and Compensation of Taiwanese 'Comfort Women'	1999/2005	9	N

2-2
Comfort Stations Established and Managed by the Japanese Military

There were three types of comfort stations: brothels run directly by the Japanese military, those supervised and controlled by the military, and private facilities contracted by the military. Among them, the private comfort stations contracted by the military were mainly located in China and Southeast Asia. The military supervised and controlled private contractors and 'comfort women.' The regulations on the management of comfort stations and the cases of private contractors clearly show how the military established and managed comfort stations.

After the Sino-Japanese War in 1937, the Japanese army occupied Chahar-sheng (察哈爾省), Suiyuan-sheng (綏遠省), Hebei-sheng (河北省), Shandong-sheng (山东省), Shanxi-sheng (山西省), Jiangsu-sheng (江蘇省), Anhui-sheng (安徽省), parts of Henan-sheng (河南省), Hubei-sheng

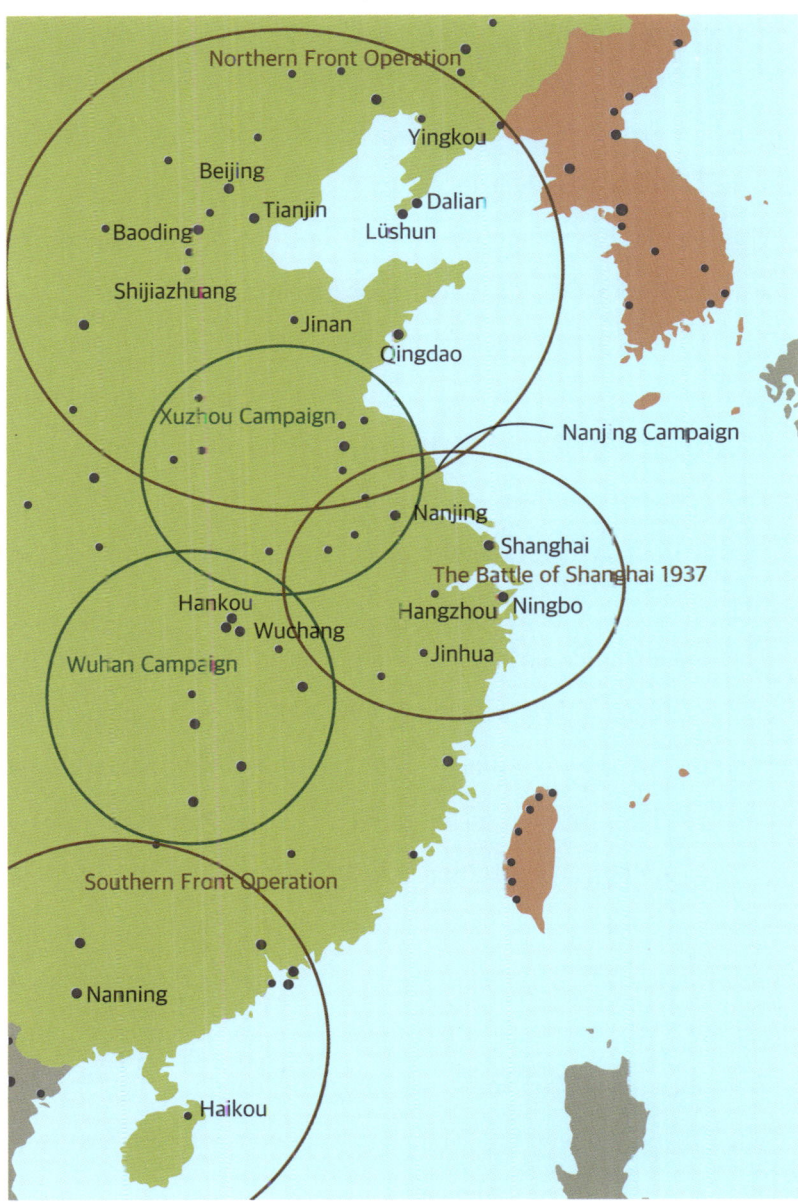

Areas in China Under Japanese Invasion in 1937

(湖北省), Jiangxi-sheng (江西省), and parts of Guangdong -sheng (廣東省). The occupied area was about 2.8 times the size of Japan's territory. Major sea routes and railroads in China were blocked. Chiang Kai-shek retreated to Chongqing after the fall of Nanjing.

The Internal Regulations of the 2nd Battalion of the Independent Heavy Artillery Army stationed in Changzhou, which was located between Shanghai and Nanjing, included various duties, orders, and official business guidelines on newsletters and secrecy protection. Among them was an item on the need for 'comfort women.' The Changzhou Garrison Internal Affairs Regulations (商州駐屯間內務規定) of March 1938 contain extensive details on the operation of comfort stations.

The 2nd Battalion arrived in Changzhou on December 25, 1937. There were two brothels in the area. One was run by the quartermaster and the other by a military unit under the direct control of the Ministry of Defense. The spread of STDs among the soldiers was a very serious problem at that time. The field diary of January 26, 1938 records that a soldier raped a 9-year-old girl, and that the girl was infected with an STD. The field diary states that the quartermaster must check the STD certificate of prostitutes. The document proves that STDs were a major problem for the troops stationed in Changzhou.

The troops stationed in Changzhou were notorious for their brutality. They committed violence against civilian women and many other misdeeds in the comfort stations. For this reason, the internal regulations of the Changzhou garrison consisted of 17 chapters with 100 items, including the use of comfort stations.

The rules for the comfort stations consisted of eight paragraphs, such as policies, facilities, unit prices and time, inspections and precautions in using the facility, the responsibilities of the supervisors, and other matters. They separated the officers from the enlisted men and set the visiting day for each unit. The visitation day fell on the unit's holiday. On that day, each unit used the facility under the direction of officers. These days were not individual holidays. Rather, they were for visiting 'comfort women.' The 'comfort women' were Koreans, Chinese, Japanese, and other nationalities, and the prices varied according to the women's ethnicity. Every Monday and Friday, a doctor at the field hospital conducted an STD test. The military police were responsible for supervision.

Among the precautions to be taken when using the comfort station was the rule that no violence could be used against the owner. Compared to other regulations, there was only one rule on the use of force. As will be explained later, the victims of the Japanese military sexual slavery system found the violence of the soldiers very difficult. The women were considered nothing more than expendable military items, and the soldiers abused them in various ways in order to relieve the stress of the war situation. According to the testimonies, a small act of resistance out of dissatisfaction subjected the women to even harsher punishment. In one case, the woman struggled in

Internal Regulations during the Changzhou Garrison Deployment[21]

2nd Independence Siege Artillery Battalion

This document prescribes internal regulations during the Changzhou Garrison Deployment
March 16, 1938
Battalion Commander, Major Manami (萬波)

(omitted)

Chapter 9 Regulations for the Use of Comfort Stations

Article 59 Plan
Contribute to military discipline through the comfort station.

Article 60 Establishment
The comfort station shall be established within the wall on the south side of the Ilhwa Hall, and the buildings shall be divided into the Ilhwa Hall Annex, one for noncommissioned officers and another for soldiers. The entrance for sergeants and soldiers should be the south gate. The shopkeeper must provide disinfectant for the sake of hygiene. The date of use for each unit is as follows.

Hoshi Unit	Sundays
Kuriiwa Unit	Mondays and Tuesdays
Matsumura Unit	Wednesdays and Thursdays
Narita Unit	Saturdays
Ichiwa Unit	Fridays

The use of other temporary garrison units will be announced separately.

---

21 商州駐屯間內務規定

Article 61 Unit Price and Hours
1. For NCOs and soldiers, it is available from 9 a.m. to 6 p.m.
2. Price per unit
   The usage time is limited to 1 hour per person.

Chinese	1 Yen
Korean	1.5 Yen
Japanese	2 Yen

The above is for NCOs and soldiers. The officer level is double the amount. (A gas mask will be provided)

Article 62 Medical Examinations
Medical examinations occur every Monday and Friday. Friday is the regular day for syphilis testing. The examination time is from 8 a.m. to 10 a.m. The chief examiner will be a medical officer of the 4th Field Hospital, and the medical staff of the Logistic Reserve Hospital and each unit will assist him. The chief inspector shall report the results to the unit referred to in paragraph 3.

Article 63 Instructions for the Use of the Comfort Station
1. Drinking is forbidden in the comfort station.
2. The payment of fees and time keeping are to be strictly observed.
3. Consider all women as poisonous. Users must do everything possible to prevent the spread of poison.
4. Users must not use violence against business owners.
5. Anyone showing signs of drunkenness is not allowed to enter.

Article 64 Miscellaneous
1. A business operator shall not accept Chinese as guests.
2. A business operator is not allowed to provide entertainment such as alcohol and snacks, as well as refreshments.
3. A business operator may not go out except to specially authorized places.
4. Every businessman must have a syphilis test certificate.

Article 65 Supervision
The military police in the respective areas shall be responsible for supervision.

Article 66 Supplement

1. The rest day of the unit is Thursday. On this day, the officers patrol each unit during the time allowed for use.
2. Each unit must be escorted when entering and leaving the comfort station. It is possible to remove the leggings.
3. The 15th of every month is a holiday for the comfort stations.

(omitted)

第九章　慰安所使用規定

第一　方針
漢口慰安所ハ道ヲ挟ンテ軍紀蘧正上前記第八中隊ノ故ヲ以テサンズヰヲ左ニ慰備ス
慰安所ハ日華親善園壁内ニ設ケ日華會館附属建物トシ下士官、兵、軍属ニ区分シ衛生上ノ楗主ニ有故設備ヲナシテ道フ各院、使用ヲ左ノ如ク定ム

星部隊　日曜日
栗岩部隊　月火曜日
松村部隊　水木曜日
成田部隊　土曜日
阿知波部隊　金曜日

第二　其他臨時至急部隊ノ使用ハ別ニ示ス
實貰慰賞ヲ時間
1 下士官兵營業時間ヲ午前九時ヨリ午后六時迄トス
2 草償　使用時間ハ二人一時間ヲ限度トス
支邦人　一月〇〇錢
半島人　一月五〇錢
内地人　同ク如ク定ム

第三　以上ノ下士官、兵ニ對シ膀胱（里耻合）ニ括顎ヲ付ス（防毒面ヲ持ス）
検査　毎週月曜日及金曜日ヲ定例検徴日トス
検査時間　午前八時ヨリ午前十時迄トス

3

第四　検査主任官ハ第四野戦病院医官トシ兵站予備病院並各院医官ハ之ヲ補助スルモノトス、検査主任官ハ其ノ結果ヲ第三項部隊ニ通報スルモノトス
慰安所利用ノ注意事項左ノ如シ
1 慰安所内ニ於テ飲酒スル事ヲ禁ス
2 金額支拂ヲ時間ヲ厳守ス
3 女ニ蠻ノ有害行為又ハ暴力ヲ行フ者ニハ方全ノ期ヲ以テ防遇ス
4 營業者ニ對シ粗暴ヲ行為アルヘカラス
5 酒類ヲ帯ヒタル者ノ出入ヲ禁ス
6 營業者ニハ探シタルヘカラス

第五　親件
1 營業者ニ支邦人ヲ密トシテ探ルコトヲ許ス
2 營業者ハ酒煮茶菓ヲ饗應ヲ禁ス
3 營業者ハ特ニ許シタル場所以外ニ出スル事ヲ禁ス
4 營業者ハ週ヲ検徴ノ結果合格証ヲ所持スルニ限ル

第六　監督擔任
監督擔任部隊ハ寛共分遣隊トス

第七　附加事項
1 部隊ハ慰安所ニ遣ラ當日ニ各隊ヲ使用時限トス
2 幹部ハ木曜日ニ各隊ニ毎ニ引率セシム
3 毎日十五日ニ慰安所ハハ休日トス
但シ卷膀胱アリテ様ニ慰安所ハ慰安所ハ

4

the midst of an officer's violence and lost consciousness. She was stabbed in the thigh with a bayonet. Yet the officer did not stop assaulting her. There were numerous cases in which the military police caught soldiers assaulting women.

The regulations of the comfort stations show that the establishment and management of the facility was part of the military's duties. In other words, the Japanese military sexual slavery system existed within the official structure of the military.

Due to the prolonged war with China, the 35th Division was assigned to maintain public order and security in 1939. The 35th Division was incorporated into the 12th Army with the primary task of maintaining order and security in Shandong-sheng. The Regulations on Outside Facilities of the 35th Division described in detail how to operate and supervise the facilities outside the barracks. It was a comprehensive list of regulations based on the 12th Army Staff's Guidelines for the Development of Outside Facilities and was issued by the divisional headquarters for the construction, management, and supervision of the use of these outside facilities. Outside facilities included off-base facilities such as off-base kiosks, special comfort stations, kaikosha,[22] and military recreation facilities established by local sponsoring organizations.

The regulations for comfort stations are contained in Articles

---

22 偕行社, An organization for active-duty commissioned officers and warrant officers in the Imperial Japanese Army for mutual aid, friendship, and academic research

18 through 24, and the regulations for special comfort stations are contained in Articles 19 through 24. Garrisons of company size and above could open special comfort stations for soldiers, depending on local conditions. The military could operate the facilities directly or subcontract the work to other parties. Basic necessities such as food and medicine were provided by field kiosks. The installation of the special comfort stations was discussed and decided by the head of the administrative unit in charge of the garrison, the head of the accounting department, and the head of the military medical department. The head of the administrative unit was responsible for the overall operation, management, direction, and supervision. The head of the security unit of each district controlled the special comfort stations in his area. On the last day of each year, a report on the establishment, management, and use of the outdoor facilities was submitted to the division commander. Matters concerning comfort stations for senior officers were also included in the regulations.

Japan's rightists claim that the military did not directly establish or manage comfort stations. However, according to the Regulations on Outside Facilities, it is very clear that it was impossible to set up a comfort station without consulting the head of the division's administrative unit, the head of the division's accounting unit, and the head of the military medical unit. In other words, the comfort stations were established and managed as part of the military establishment.

Out-of-Barrack Facility Rules[23]
Issued after July 1942

1. General Provisions

Article 1 These regulations are based on the Guidelines for the Development of Out-of-Barrack Facilities, 仁集參密 (인집참밀) No. 294 of July 1942. The Division shall carry out activities such as construction, management, use and supervision of out-of-barrack facilities in accordance with this regulation. The regulation covers the construction of Out-of-Barrack Facilities, the provision of goods, the supply and distribution of food, hiring employees, and the surveillance in the facilities, etc. When unspecified matters arise, refer to the Regulations for Construction and Repair, the Field Kiosk Regulations and other related laws.

Article 2 The term "Outside Facilities" in this regulation refers to kiosks outside the barracks, special comfort stations, kaikosha, or other military comfort facilities established by local sponsoring organizations.

Article 3 Except as provided in this Regulation, the senior unit commander and the head of the administrative unit shall be responsible for the operation and supervision of the Outside Facilities.

(Omitted)

3. Special Comfort Stations

Article 19 If necessary, garrisons of company size and above may open special comfort stations for soldiers that are hygienic and affordable, depending on local conditions.

Article 20 The special comfort stations shall be managed directly by the unit or operated by subcontractors.

Article 21 In the case of a special comfort station building, the head of the accounting department shall treat it as a separate expense and the head of the administration shall lend it to the commander free of charge. The recipient shall be responsible for the subsequent maintenance of the building.

---

23 營外施設規定

Chapter 2 Japan's Invasion War and the Japanese Military 'Comfort Women' System   101

Article 22 Goods, beverages, and other items necessary for the operation of special comfort stations may be sold as field supplies. The details shall be determined by the head of the Military Medical Department.

Article 23 Drugs, protective equipment, etc. necessary for the operation of special comfort stations may be supplied as government goods. The details shall be determined by the head of the Military Medical Department.

Article 24 The provisions of the preceding paragraphs shall apply to the supervision and management of special comfort stations at divisional headquarters. Otherwise, other provisions shall be observed.

(Omitted)

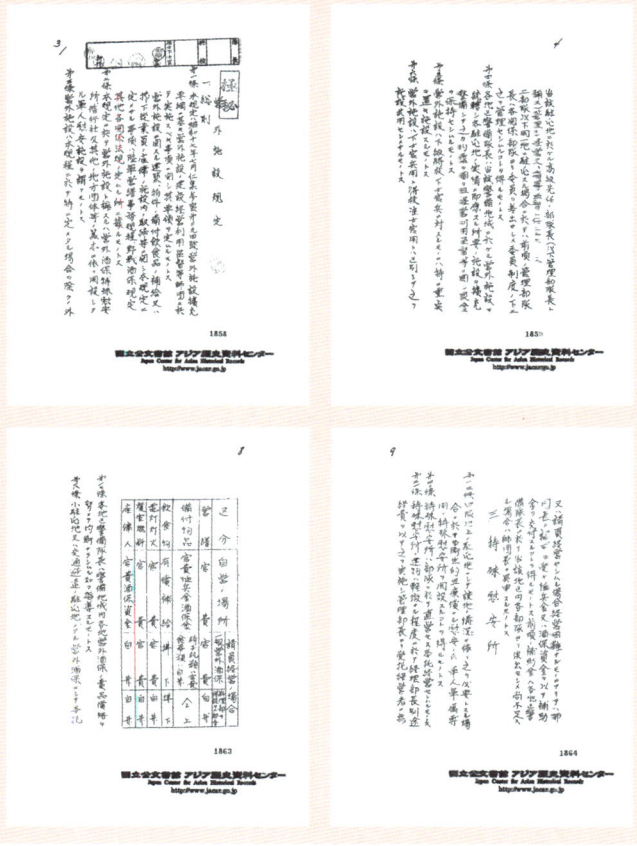

In December 1941, Japan declared war on the United States and other Allied powers. Beginning with the occupation of Singapore in February 1942, it took over Indonesia on March 12, 1942. Java, Indonesia, was under the control of Japan's 16th Army on November 5, 1941. The Japanese navy took control of the Malay Peninsula and adjacent islands. Military government was the direct rule of a region by an army commander. The General Military Government was based at the Southern Military Headquarters, where the Chief of General Staff of the Southern Military also served as the Head of the General Military Government.

Most of the comfort stations in Southeast Asia were run by civilians appointed by the military. For this reason, the Japanese right wing argues that the military simply used these facilities directly managed by private companies. However, related documents clearly show that the Japanese military established and directly managed the comfort stations as part of its support facilities. The following will take a closer look at how the military controlled private enterprises by examining the Compliance Rules for Comfort Facilities and Inn Business,[24] which appeared in the Military Regulations of Malaysia in November 1943.

According to the Compliance Rules for Comfort Facilities and Inn Business, it is clear that private contractors were under the control of the

---

24　慰安施設及旅館營業遵守規則

Compliance Rules for Comfort Facilities and Inn Business

Article 1 Operators of comfort facilities and inns shall abide by these regulations unless otherwise ordered by the military and the military government.

Article 2 Operator of comfort facilities shall display the attached Form No. 1 in a conspicuous place in front of the facility according to the type of business. However, this shall not apply to non-military establishments.

(Omitted)

Article 9 Operators and employees shall undergo medical examinations as prescribed by the provincial minister. Professional women shall be tested for syphilis in addition to the diseases specified in the preceding paragraph.

Article 10 Operators and employees shall obey military sanitary patrols when warned.

Article 11 Professional women shall not work without a work permit. A person who is found to be infected with syphilis may not work until she is completely cured.

Article 12 Operators and employees may not change their occupation and employment without the permission of the military.

(Omitted)

Article 16 Operators (except for military guesthouses) should prepare daily income and expense reports in appropriate forms, along with necessary supplementary books.

Article 17 Except for the business operators of special comfort station facilities, the following balance sheets should be submitted to the military government through the respective branch of the police department.
    1. The attached Form No. 5 'Statement of revenues and expenses' (monthly)
    2. The attached Form No. 6 'Asset and Liability Statement' (every 6 months)

Article 18 Operators of special comfort station facilities shall prepare the attached balance sheet, Form No. 7, on a monthly basis and submit it by the 10th day of the following month.

Article 19 Operators shall, in addition to this Regulation, abide by the instructions and orders of the local minister.

Addendum

This regulation is effective as of December 1, 1943.

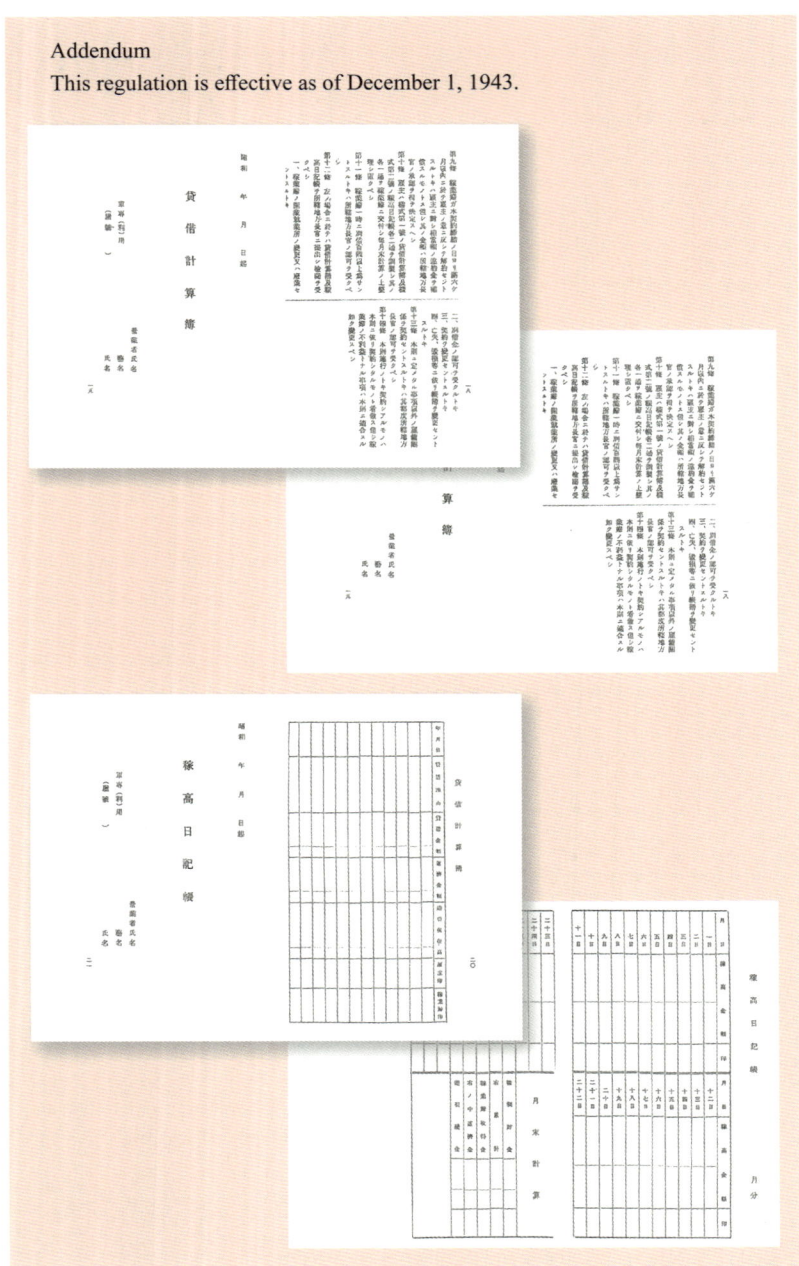

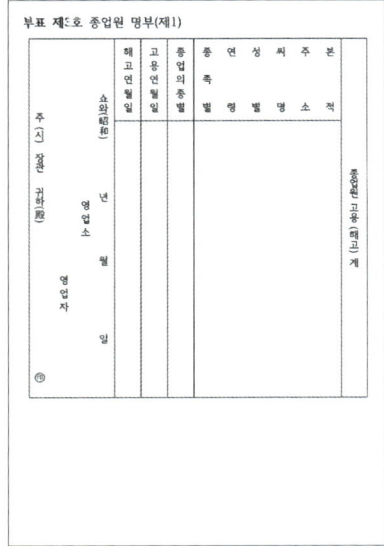

Attached Form No.7, Statement of Revenues and Expenses

Attached Form No.3, List of Employees (1st.)

military. Business owners and employees could not leave their 'comfort women' jobs or find other employment without the military's permission (Article 12). Owners, except for those appointed by the Supply and Logistics Unit of the military, had to submit daily cash books in an appropriate form and prepare supplementary books with information on daily income and expenses (Article 16). In addition, Article 18 stipulated that the owners of the comfort stations should submit a monthly balance sheet to the military government officials through the police department in their jurisdiction in the prescribed form (form No.7) by the 10th of each month. The business owners also had to keep a list of employees and submit the list of new hires and dismissals to the regional minister.

The lists of employees and the balance sheets show that the Japanese military tightly controlled the employment contracts and income of the 'comfort women' business. The list of employees included personal information such as name, residence, address, sex, age, race, occupation, and dates of employment and dismissal. The balance sheet also detailed total income from prostitution and income from entertainment, as well as expenses such as wages, allowances, and other payments. While the management of the comfort stations was the responsibility of the business owners, the Japanese military was able to monitor and control the situation based on the information received on a regular basis. *The Diary of a Japanese military Comfort Station Manager*[25] also describes that private contractors submitted daily business reports, monthly business reports, and monthly account balances to the Japanese military.

The military also conducted tests for STDs. The Military Police Department's Iloilo Miscellaneous File (Iloilo is the name of a region in the Philippines) was compiled on September 29, 1942, after the bacterial test results were released. It was written by the Iloilo Military Dispensary. The data included the names of the Japanese military 'comfort women,' the diagnosis result of STD, and the name of the

---

25 『일본군 위안소 관리인의 일기』, Translated by Byeong-jik An (published by Esoope in 2013)

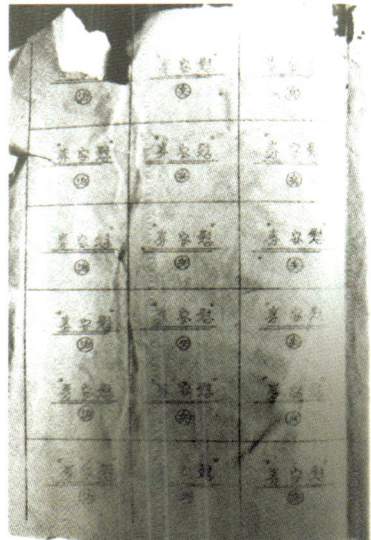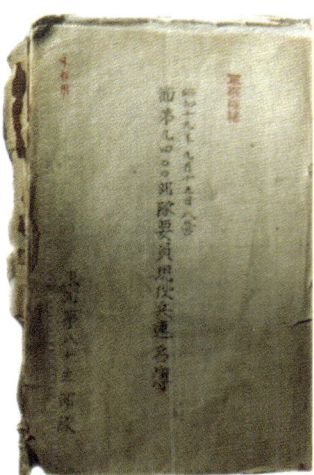

Tickets Issued to Soldiers Who Wanted to Use the Comfort Station.
"Overnight" is for officers who are allowed to stay overnight, "Soldier" is for enlisted men, and "Staff" is for staff sergeants.

disease. Six out of 15 were found to have STDs.

In addition to these data, many sources confirm that the Japanese military directly or indirectly administered the comfort stations. For example, the military bulletin mentioned the establishment of comfort stations and fees. The headquarters directly issued tickets for the comfort stations.

Iloilo Miscellaneous File

(Omitted)

Bacteria test results

September 29, 1942

Iloilo Military Dispensary

With respect to the previous title, the notice reads as follows.

Name	Age	Positive/Negative	Diagnosis	Name	Age	Positive/Negative	Diagnosis
	18	N	Endocervix intumescence			P	
	31	P				N	Endocervix intumescence
	16	P				P	
	17	N	Gonorrhea			P	
	16	P				N	Gonorrhea
	18	P				N	Gonorrhea
	18	P				N	Cervicovaginitis
	16	P					Results for Comfort Station #1

Name	Age	Positive/Negative	Diagnose	Name	Age	Positive/Negative	Diagnose
	25	P			19	Menstruation	
	26	P			22	N	Vulvar intertrigo
	31	Rest			24	P	
	25	N			26	Menstruation	
	25	P			26	P	
	21	P			22	P	
							Results for Comfort Station #2

(omitted)

* Names have been redacted from the original document to protect personal information.

2-3
Unimaginable Abuses and Inhumane Treatment of Women in Comfort Stations

The Japanese right wing argues that the 'comfort women' system was simply the incorporation of licensed prostitution into a part of the military establishment, and that the 'comfort women' were not sex slaves. They also claim that the women's income was sometimes even higher than that of military generals.

It is true that the Japanese military used licensed prostitution. But unlike prostitutes in the licensed brothel system, Japanese military 'comfort women' were denied the freedom to close their businesses, choose their clients, move out of their businesses, and take vacations. As the rules of the comfort stations clearly show, the 'comfort women' were not free to leave the comfort stations. Even when they were allowed to go out, the areas they could visit were strictly controlled. The comfort stations were patrolled 24 hours a day by the military

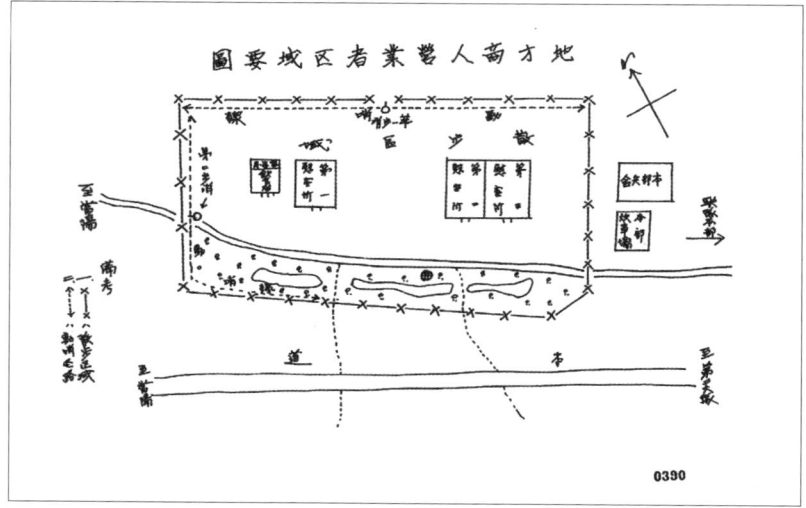

3rd Independent Artillery Regiment - Takamori Unit - A Special Comfort Station Area

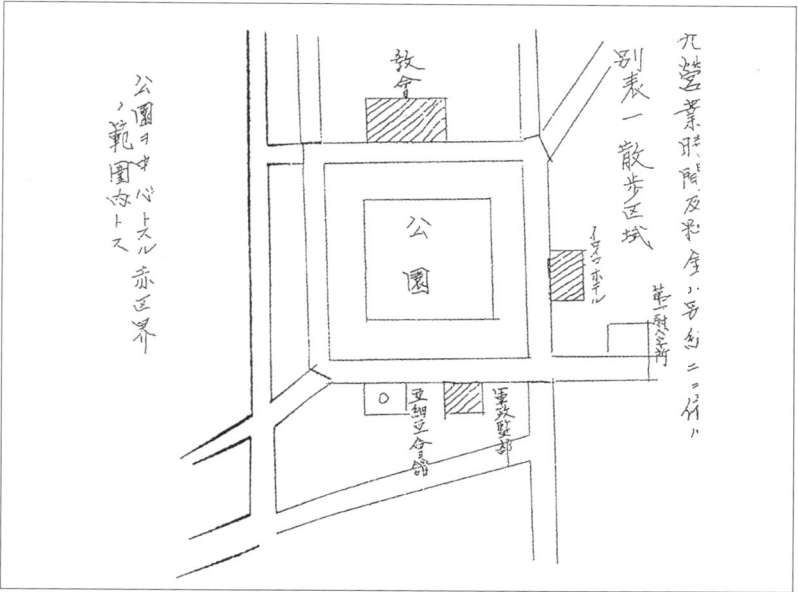

The Japanese Military 'Comfort Women's Walking Area: Attached to the Regulations on the Establishment of Comfort Stations in the Iloilo Troop Dispatch Unit (November 22, 1942)

police. Such close surveillance was supposed to protect residential areas, but in reality, it meant imprisonment.

The women trusted the owners' words that they would no longer starve and that they could make a lot of money. Most of them were very poor and had no experience of living outside their hometowns. They dreamed of a new world and endured the perilous journey in hopes of making money. But what awaited them were the Japanese soldiers. The women had to endure all kinds of brutality while confined to a small room. They ate when they were allowed to eat, slept only when they were allowed to sleep, and were beaten when they were sick or pregnant. They could not escape their miserable life day after day.

Shin-do Song, a victim of the Japanese military 'comfort women' system, was also assaulted and even stabbed by soldiers. She testified that on many days she had to deal with 40 to 50 soldiers a day and did not have enough time to eat or sleep. The 'comfort women' suffered from STDs, irregular menstruation, and genital diseases. They were literally sex slaves. The skin of their vaginas was always in a state of tearing, bleeding, swelling, and deformation due to their prolonged sexual slavery. Victims testified that many women committed suicide by biting their tongues after suffering repeated assaults by multiple soldiers.

Victims of the Japanese military 'comfort women' were sent to all areas where Japanese soldiers were stationed. Okinawa comfort station victim Bong-ki Bae described her life as "hell." Okinawa is the only place in Japan where the ground war took place. In March 1944, the Okinawa Guard was established to strengthen the defense of Southeast Asia. It was expanded to defend the mainland after the fall of Saipan in July of the same year. Bong-ki Bae, the victim, was mobilized to Okinawa in the late fall of 1944. Japan set up comfort stations amid daily bombing by the U.S.A. The Japanese soldiers, fearing death, attacked, assaulted, and raped the Japanese military 'comfort women.' Bong-ki Bae also suffered severe violence that broke her entire body and mind. She suffered from depression and nervous breakdowns for the rest of her life.

In her book, *Comfort Women of the Empire*, Yu-ha Park wrote that the 'comfort women' of the Japanese military from Korea felt comradeship with the Japanese soldiers, and the women's "comforting role" made them proud. There may have been some who saw the Japanese soldiers as comrades or felt a sense of shared destiny. Even if that was the case, the essence of the Japanese military 'comfort women' problem is that many women were forced to live the life of sex slaves against their will. Nothing can absolve the Japanese military and government of their responsibility for mobilizing women as tools to serve their war aims. The reason we remember the harm done by the Japanese military 'comfort women' system is because it was sexual assault against women during the conflict. This is still happening around the world. The argument that soldiers and 'comfort women' shared camaraderie cannot provide a constructive solution to the sexual violence occurring today.

According to the testimony of one victim, Bong-ki Bae, Japanese soldiers shot at the women, brandished knives, and assaulted them. The Japanese military police tried to crack down on this violent behavior, but most of the assailants were only admonished, disciplined, and grounded in the end. This remains a fact in the document. According to the "Military Information Report on Comfort Stations" sent by Seijiro Saijo (chief of the military police) to Sakurada (chief of the general staff) on July 6, 1940, the atrocities committed by the soldiers at the Qinzhou (欽州) Comfort Station in Nanning in June 1940 are recorded as follows.

1. Drinkers
(1) While very drunk, 2 officers fired guns into the comfort station and the surrounding area. They also pulled out a knife and injured two female employees.
(2) While very drunk, 2 petty officers and 3 soldiers committed violence in the comfort station.
(3) While very drunk, 1 soldier and 1 army civilian left the military unit without permission and were not properly dressed.

2. Business Manager
A manager of a military comfort station abused his employees. He was ordered to strictly follow the rules.

Regular testing for STDs was also humiliating for the victims. Most of them remember that the physical examinations were extremely embarrassing. If they were found to have an STD, they were verbally abused by the administrators.

Jan Ruff O'Herne, a Dutch woman taken from Indonesia to a Japanese military comfort station, grew up in a relatively well-off family. However, the tragedy began with the Japanese occupation of Java in 1942. The Japanese army separated Indonesians from other nationalities and imprisoned them separately. Of the Dutch women between the ages of 17 and 28, 16 were selected and sent to the comfort stations against their will. She was one of them.

From the moment the victims were thrown into the comfort stations, regardless of their hometowns or nationalities, they were mentally disturbed. They all said, "I went crazy in the comfort station." They had to provide sexual services to more than four Japanese soldiers a night and more than 10 soldiers a day. As time passed, they could not even move their legs because it hurt so much. If they refused the soldiers, they were punched and kicked, leaving the women too terrified to even glance at the soldiers' faces.

The victims also had a hard time returning home from the war. The Japanese soldiers who had been with them suddenly disappeared one day. According to testimonies, some of the abandoned women in China and the Philippines were beaten because they were 'comfort women.' They had to leave the comfort station without help or possessions and did not know how to return home. If they were captured by the Allies as prisoners of war, they could stay in a concentration camp and return home. In other cases, they did not know where they were or how to return to their hometowns. Some people wandered around and ended up staying where they were. For example, Bong-ki in Okinawa and Keum-ah Im in Wuhan, China, had to live there as stateless people.

The cessation of the war did not mean the end of their misery. Even after liberation, the victims continued to suffer. Even when the women returned to their hometowns, they lived in constant fear of being exposed as 'comfort women' serving the Japanese military. Every day was overshadowed by anxiety as they struggled with the lingering burden of fear and shame. While their formative years should have been filled with cherished memories, these victims were forcibly taken to unfamiliar places and condemned to a lifetime of torment. It wasn't until the 1990s that they heard the words, "It wasn't your fault; the wrongdoing was on the part of Japanese imperialism," when Hak-soon Kim, one of the victims, testified. However, by then, they were in their seventies. They had no choice but to bury that deep pain in the passage of time.

This map is based on official documents discovered so far, testimonies of victims and former Japanese soldiers, and witnesses. It has been confirmed that Japanese military comfort stations were established in 22 countries (e.g., Russia, China, North Korea, South Korea, Japan, Taiwan, Vietnam, Cambodia, Thailand, Myanmar, Philippines, Malaysia, Brunei, Singapore, East Timor, Papua New Guinea, Micronesia, Pharaoh Republic, Solomon Islands, and Indonesia). Among the locations where Korean victims were mobilized, China had the highest number of cases.

Distribution of the Japanese Military Comfort Stations
Locations of Japanese Military Sexual Slavery, Confirmed by Testimony and Official Documents
[Provided by Northeast Asian History Foundation, Women's Active Museum on War and Peace (https://wam-peace.org).]

Chapter 2 Japan's Invasion War and the Japanese Military 'Comfort Women' System 117

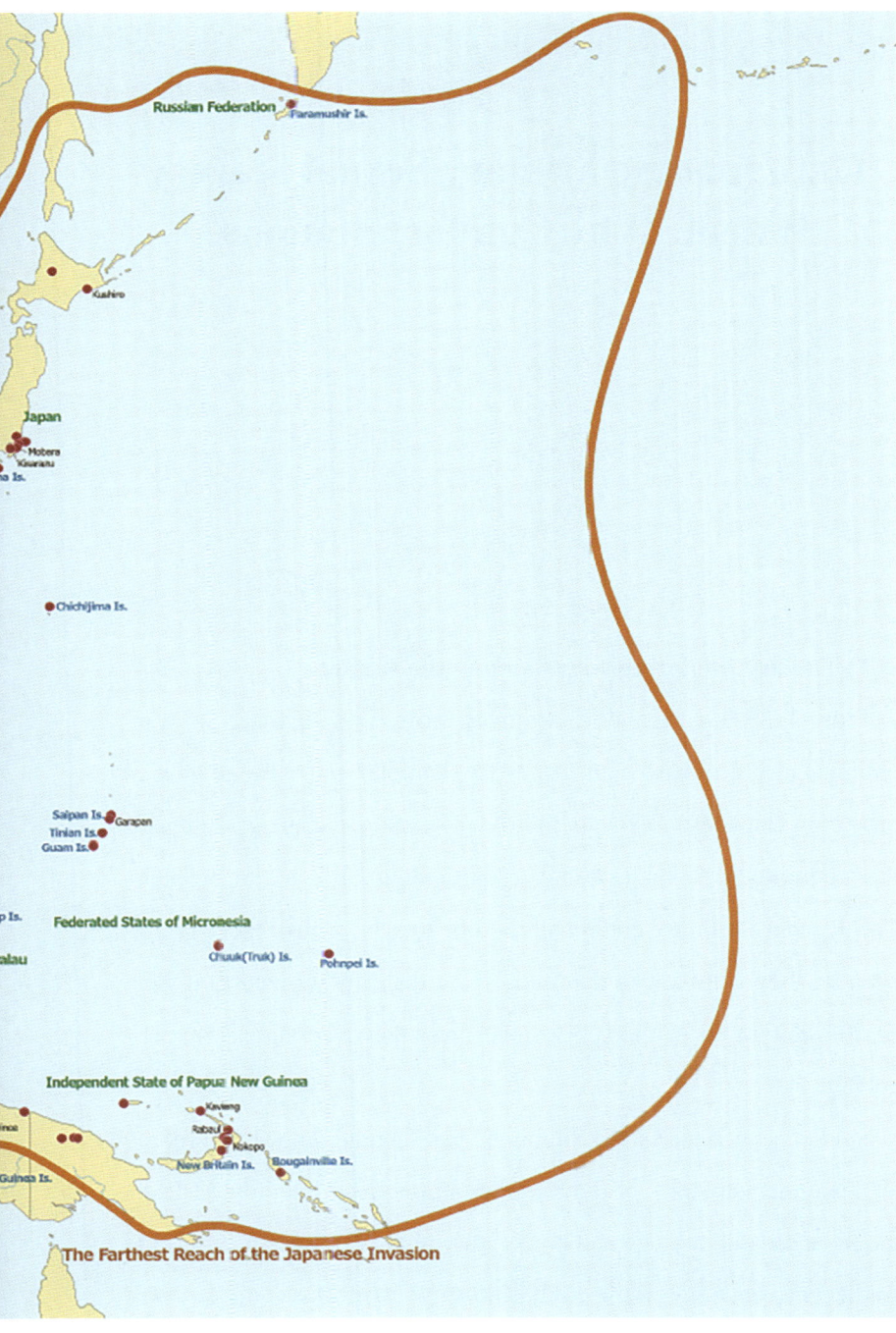

2-4
The Japanese Military Sexual Slavery System: Why Comfort Stations?

1) The accumulating stress among the soldiers

From 1931, the Japanese Kwantung Army was stationed in Manchuria. Later they also sent troops to Shanghai under the pretext of protecting Japanese residents there. However, the crimes of the soldiers continued. Sexual assault, in particular, was a major problem. The Japanese military command did not strictly control these crimes because they were afraid that addressing them might lead to dissent or riots among the soldiers, given the stress they were already experiencing.

Soldiers experience stress simply by participating in war. In order to alleviate the war stress of the clear and imminent possibility of death, the Japanese military deemed it necessary to provide sexual comfort to soldiers and encouraged the establishment of comfort stations.

Recently, there have been many distasteful rumors about soldiers snooping around looking for women. (Omitted) It is deemed appropriate to actively establish facilities and explore various solutions to resolve the sexual needs of soldiers.

(Provided by Naozaburo Okabe's Diary, March 14, 1932)

The most urgent matter for the Japanese military stationed in Manchuria is to provide comfort for the soldiers. (Omitted) Even upon their return, if they find only dilapidated barracks and a lack of material comfort, their hearts are apt to become hardened.

(Provided by Inspection Report of Northern China and Manchuria, March 1934)

The prolonged suppression of soldiers' sexual desires during the war naturally led to assaults on Chinese women. Concerned about this, the military authorities promptly established comfort stations in China. The main purpose was to satisfy the sexual needs of the troops and prevent acts of rape that would undermine the dignity of the military.

(Provided by Dorao Harao, a member of the army hospital, from The Special Phenomenon of the Battlefield and Its Countermeasures, June 1939)

Article 2. The establishment of special comfort stations is intended to alleviate and regulate the harsh morale of the troops, thereby contributing to a heightened spirit.

(Provided by Regulations for Special Comfort Work of Morikawa Unit,

November 14, 1939)

For the Japanese military command, women's sexuality was seen as a mere tool for carrying out the war. As a result, women's human rights were not respected, and they were considered subordinate to the purpose of waging war. In other words, the recognition of women's sexuality was limited to being a means to enable soldiers to continue the war. This reveals the flawed sexual attitudes and violence ingrained in the Japanese government and its military personnel.

Japanese Soldiers Waiting Outside a Comfort Station

2) Establishment of exclusive military comfort stations: An essential element to maintain public order in the occupied territories

From the beginning of the Sino-Japanese War in 1937, the Japanese army sent a large force to occupy Shanghai and to invade Nanjing, the capital of the Nationalist government. In Nanjing, the Japanese army massacred men with bayonets and sexually assaulted women. These atrocities committed in the city are called the Nanjing Massacre. The Japanese army's atrocities were not limited to Nanjing. Unimaginably heinous crimes were committed wherever they set foot, causing great insecurity in the regions. Already defeated in the war and wounded in their pride, the Chinese people were further enraged by the atrocities committed by the Japanese army. The Japanese army faced the dual challenge of fighting fiercely with the Chinese armed forces and dealing with the resistance of the Chinese civilians. They were very concerned about the international public opinion and the lack of discipline among their soldiers.

The Army Group in northern China primarily fought in and occupied Shandong and Henan-sheng. Military officials expressed difficulty in maintaining public security in the occupied areas. They were particularly concerned about rape crimes committed by soldiers. They saw that the rape crimes against Chinese women were leading to anti-Japanese activities among the local people. Naozaburo Okabe, Chief of Staff of the Army Group in northern China, issued a memorandum

Precautions for the Conduct of Soldiers and the Army Toward the Civilian Population

June 27, 1938

Naozaburo Okabe (岡部直三郎)
Chief of staff of the Army Group in northern China

1. Although the security situation in the occupied military area has temporarily improved with the rotation of troops in Shijiazhuang, the destruction of transportation routes in Shandong-sheng has intensified recently. The activities of the guerrilla forces in the western area of the northern Jinghan have also spread through the north of Beijing to the previously peaceful border area of Jidong*. This indicates a reversal of the situation. It is expected that there will be many obstacles to the restoration of security.

2. One of the main reasons for the delay in the restoration of security is the shortage of troops responsible for the security of the rear area, coupled with the unlawful actions of soldiers and military personnel, which have increased the resistance among the local people. Taking advantage of this situation, the anti-Japanese communist faction is inciting the local people and causing serious negative effects on security. According to various sources, the rapid growth of anti-Japanese sentiment is attributed to the spread of incidents of rape committed by Japanese soldiers in various regions.

3. Beginning in Shandong and spreading to Henan (河南) and southern Hebei (河北), organizations such as the Red Spear Society** and the Big Swords Soci-

---

* The Jidong (冀東, East Hebei) Autonomous Government was a regime that existed in Hebei-shenge, China, from 1935 to 1938. According to official Japanese records at the time, it was established under the leadership of Yin Ju-keng (殷汝耕) in response to popular demands for local autonomy. However, China argues that it was a puppet regime set up by the clandestine operations of Japanese special agencies.

** The Red Spear Society (紅槍會) was a secret armed self-defense organization formed by rural peasants in the Huabei (華北) region of China during the late Qing Dynasty. They were called the Red Spear Society because they attached red tassels to the spears they used as weapons. It is considered a secret society that followed the lineage of

ety***, along with similar self-defense groups, have vehemently opposed military plunder and rape for several decades. Especially in the case of rape, it was customary for the residents of various regions to take revenge even at the cost of their lives (referring to the customs of the Red Spear Society as described by the Japanese Army on October 6, 1937). Therefore, the frequent occurrence of rape in various regions is not only a criminal offense but also a treasonous act that undermines the general military operations and causes serious damage to the nation. Those in command should instill a sense of vigilance in those around them and ensure that such acts never occur again. If there are commanders who turn a blind eye to such acts, they can only be regarded as disloyal subordinates.

4. It is crucial to strictly control the above-mentioned actions of individual soldiers, while at the same time promptly providing adequate facilities for sexual comfort to prevent unintended behaviors resulting from the lack of such facilities.

---

the Big Swords Society, which was an underground organization that used sorcery for security. They not only resisted warlords and local insurgents, but also actively participated in the anti-Japanese resistance. Their influence in rural communities was so great that even political forces such as the warlords, the Kuomintang, and the Communist Party could find it difficult to gain control over the local society without involving the Red Spear Society.

*** The Big Swords Society (大刀會) was a civilian underground organization that formed primarily in Shandong-sheng during the late Qing Dynasty in China. It later became an armed self-defense group of rural peasants in the Huabei region, including Henan and Jiangsu-sheng, who suffered under the oppression of European imperialism and the Qing Dynasty. In the late 19th century, the Big Swords Society participated in anti-Christian riots that resulted in the killing of foreign missionaries. They actively participated as a prominent force in the Boxer Rebellion against imperialism, which took place in the Huabei region from November 1899 to September 1901. They not only rejected foreign influence, but also actively resisted warlords and local insurgents, and participated in the anti-Japanese resistance in Manchuria. The Red Spear Society, which also armed itself with red-tasseled spears and practiced sorcery, was considered a secret organization following in the footsteps of the Big Swords Society.

自昭和十三年七月一日
至同　　　七月廿一日

陣中日誌

歩兵第九旅團

七月廿一日
一、警備隊司令部ノ福森少佐ハ
　京浦ノ報告ニ依リ張家圍ニ(佐橋
　西北方大約)附近ニ駐屯シテ居ル不二産瓦(東北方大約)王庄(佐橋
　西北方大約)附近ニ到ラントセリ
　百八里廟方面ノ得ハ佐リ
　瀬口少佐ヨリ電報リ
　北支派遣軍参謀長ヨリ軍人　軍隊ノ駐屯民行為
　ニ關スル注意左記ノ通リ通牒アリ
　軍人　軍隊ノ駐留民行為ニ關スル注意(其ノ一)
　昭和十三年八月十七日
　北支那派遣軍参謀長　岡部直三郎

一、軍占據地域中ノ治安ハ徐州會戰ノ結果一時好轉セリ

而シテ諸情報ヲ綜合スルニ新タニ強烈ナル反日意識ヲ敵
國モトシ原因ノ八九ハ日本軍人ノ強姦事件
ニ在リト謂フヘク而カモ之カ影響ノ及ホス所廣ク深刻ニシテ
住民ノ抗日意識ヲ煽動シ反抗的分子ノ氣勢ヲ助長シ
刀金甌ヲ傳播シ重大ナル惡影響ヲホシコシツツアル
ヲ以テ治安工作ニ實ニ憂慮スヘキ問題ナリトス

兩軍討情報ヲコトニ新タニ如ク強烈トシ及日意識ヲ敵
國セシメ原因ノ八九ハ日本軍人ノ強姦事件
ナリト謂フヘク

七月四日北支那派遣軍ノ指示ヲ以テ各地ニ
紅槍會ノ集團ヲ設クルト共ニ(昭和十三年
十月十日北支那派遣軍司令部参照)
實施セラレタルモノニシテ
住民ハ對日親近ヲ以テ一般ニ信頼ヲ致シタリ紅槍會ノ大刀會
等ハ在リテハ概ネ一致協力抗日ノ爲團結シ古來ヨリ軍隊ノ侵害　強姦
　行爲ニ反抗シヌ土圧ヲ以テ
　ニ住民ノ死ヲ以テ最後ヲ遂ケントシ

山東山東河南河北南部等ニ在リ紅槍會大刀會
ヲ傳ヘテ謂フ
山東山東河南河北南部等ニ在リ紅槍會大刀會
ヲ傳ヘテ謂フ

十月十日北支那派遣軍ノ指示ヲ以テ各地ニ
紅槍會ノ集團ヲ設クルト共ニ
従來各地ニ於テハ軍隊ノ強姦行爲ニ(軍紀上甚タ憤慨ノ事)
ヨリ益ス反抗心ヲ煽リ全局ニ亘リ
ニ反日意識ヲ刺戟スルニ至レリ此ノ事實ニ鑑ミ
ル抗日意識ヲ刺戟スルニ至レリ此ノ事實ニ鑑ミ
不闡ノ大ナル指揮官トシテ
右ノ如キハ個人行爲ト雖國軍
國家ニ反逆スル軍ト國家ノ名
ル者ニシテ其ノ罪　死ヲ以テ
心ヲ抱クノ他ナシ然レトモ戒
ルコト不可能ナリ故ニ此ノ種行爲ヲ防止スルニハ
右ニ對シテハ之レヲ嚴重取締ルト共ニ一面ニ於テハ
速カニ性的慰安ノ設備ヲ整ヘ設備ノ無キ爲不憾ニ

entitled "Precautions for the Conduct of Soldiers and the Army Toward the Civilian Population" to each unit.

This document clearly conveys the above-mentioned concerns. Okabe Naozaburo identified rape crimes as one of the causes that intensified the anti-Japanese sentiments among the Chinese people. He pointed out that "it is not only a criminal offense, but also a treasonable act that undermines the general military operations and causes serious damage to the nation." This was because "the residents were ready to resist to the death against sexual violence." He ordered strict control over individual misconduct and the establishment of comfort stations. It is noteworthy that this document recognized rape crimes as unintended acts that occurred due to the lack of comfort facilities.

Did the establishment of comfort stations, aimed at satisfying the sexual desires of soldiers, eliminate sexual violence against women in the occupied territories?

The comfort stations were not a fundamental solution. They were a complete failure. The measure of confining women to satisfy the sexual desires of the soldiers actually increased their sexual desires. Despite the establishment of comfort stations, sexual violence did not decrease. The problem of sexual violence against women in the occupied territories was not limited to China, but also occurred frequently in Southeast Asia. Setsuzo Kinbara (金原節三), director of the Medical Department in the Medical Service Bureau, wrote in a bulletin on May 9, 1942, that out of 237 crimes committed in the southern regions, including the Philippines and Indonesia, a significant number were cases of sexual violence.

Another reason for the establishment of the comfort stations was to maintain security. It was a precautionary measure to prevent the possibility of soldiers from developing relationships with women in brothels and potentially leaking confidential information.

3) Establishment of comfort stations to prevent STDs among soldiers

In 1939, Tesuo Aso (麻生徹男), a doctor in the Japanese military, wrote a report entitled "Active Preventive Measures against Venereal Disease." At that time, many soldiers in Nanjing and Shanghai were infected with STDs. He believed that it was strategically fatal not to be able to send soldiers to the battlefield during the period of treatment. The report he wrote laid the foundation for the establishment and management of the Japanese military comfort stations. The doctor believed that private brothels frequented by civilians should be banned and that the construction of military comfort stations was necessary to control the spread of STDs. He called military comfort stations "communal toilets for soldiers." The idea was to equate excretion in the toilet with the relief of sexual desire in the comfort station. The term shows how the military perceived women mobilized in comfort stations.

Did the establishment of comfort stations reduce STDs? The

presence of comfort stations actually became a factor that increased STDs, as soldiers infected women while visiting the stations. According to a survey on STDs in the army, there were 11,983 cases in 1942, 12,557 cases in 1943, and 12,587 cases in 1944. It is evident that STDs were rampant among soldiers.

> In general, women's vaginal health tends to be better at younger ages. Soldiers should use military-sanctioned comfort stations. Contracting syphilis as a soldier leads to the same result as wasting military resources. Furthermore, if soldiers go to taverns and consume alcohol, it will increase cases of venereal disease, so alcohol consumption within the military should be minimized. Military comfort stations are not places of pleasure, but hygienic communal toilets for soldiers. It is natural to prohibit the sale and consumption of alcoholic beverages in these facilities, just as alcohol is not sold in the restrooms.
>
> (Provided by *Active Preventive Measures Against Venereal Disease*)

4) Revision of Field Kiosk[26] Regulations: Japanese army prepares legal basis for establishment of 'Rape Center'

Even before the start of the Sino-Japanese War, the need for military comfort stations was raised, and the Japanese Navy set up stations in Shanghai. The army was not directly involved, but when the Sino-Japanese War began, the law was revised to meet the needs of deployed garrisons. The basis for the establishment was the Revision

---

26 野戰酒保, It was a place similar to today's PX (Post Exchange), with recreational facilities and a cafeteria.

Revision of the Field Kiosk Regulations (1937.9.15)

Field Kiosk Regulations (1904.2.9)

Article 1: The Field Kiosk aims to provide soldiers and military personnel on the battlefield with necessary supplies accurately and at reasonable prices.

Proposed Amendment to the Field Kiosk Regulations:

Article 1: The Field Kiosk aims to provide soldiers, military personnel, and other authorized persons in the battlefield or war zones with necessary daily goods, food, and other items accurately and at reasonable prices. The Field Kiosk may also include other necessary comfort facilities.

Reason for Amendment:

To clarify the scope of users for the Field Kiosk and to acknowledge the need for comfort facilities when facing enemy troops.

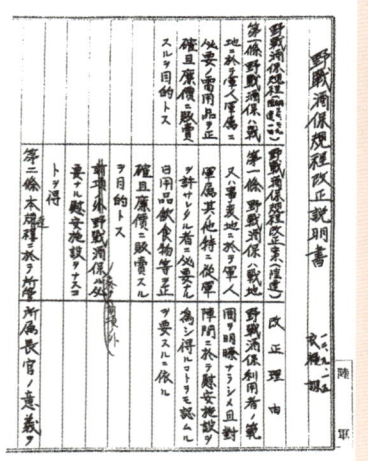
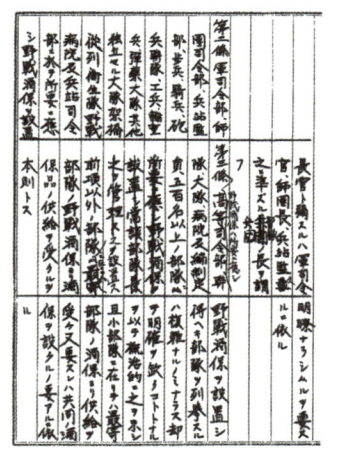

of Field Kiosk Regulations of September 18, 1937.

"Field" means a battlefield, and the kiosks were exclusive military stores set up to provide soldiers and military personnel with necessary goods appropriately and affordably. By amending the regulations for kiosks, provisions were made for the legal establishment of "comfort stations." Professor Kazunaga Nagai (永井和), who discovered this document, argues that it shows that the Japanese military was the entity responsible for establishing comfort stations. While Japanese right-wingers criticize the inclusion of "comfort facilities" in the field kiosk regulations as not explicitly specifying comfort stations, the following evidence clearly indicates that comfort facilities were recognized as comfort stations on the ground.

"Enable the implementation of comfort facilities upon receiving documents from the military in charge."

- December 11, 1937

"A request was made to Lieutenant Colonel Jo, to establish brothels immediately.

- December 19, 1937

[Provided by Diary of Mamoru Inuma, Chief of Staff of the Army Dispatched to Shanghai, from the *Collection of Nanjing War Historical Materials* (『南京戦史資料集』)]

It can be seen that General Inuma, (飯沼守), who served as the Chief of Staff of the Army Dispatched to Shanghai, recognized the "comfort facilities" as "brothels" or "comfort stations." The same recognition can also be found in soldiers' memoirs.

> "On the night of January 8, I heard from the battalion commander about the establishment of comfort stations. Many soldiers were excited about it."
>
> "On January 13th, today, I was suddenly ordered to be in charge of the kiosk. The army on the battlefield is an interesting place. There are only women working in the kiosk. So far, there is only one thing to sell. People who want to buy ○○ are rushing in, and it was very busy from the afternoon until late at night."
>
> (Provided by *Soldier's Diary, 101st Regiment Expeditionary Force in Shanghai*, from *Nostalgic Glaze II*,[27] edited by Tsuneo Tanaka, 1989, p.102)

Article 6 of the Field Kiosk Regulations states, "The operation of the Field Kiosk shall be self-funded. However, under unavoidable circumstances (except for the sale of certain food items), the approval of the relevant minister may be obtained to entrust the operation to civilian contractors. Civilian contractors who accompany and assist in operations in the garrison area (areas where army units are stationed and guarded) shall be treated as military personnel and provided with a special uniform. However, the number of such personnel shall not

---

27 "荻島静夫陣中日記,"『追憶の視線』.

exceed three in infantry, artillery, and mortar battalions, and not exceed two in other units."

The army comfort station was a military service facility that belonged to the field kiosk, and the comfort station operators entrusted with its management were contract merchants with the military. In some cases, they were even given military status.

Chapter 3

How Did the Korean and Japanese Governments Respond?

3-1
Both Countries Stuck in the 1990s: Fact-Finding and Reconciliation Incomplete

1) Unsatisfactory Fact-Finding Efforts

① **Statement by Chief Cabinet Secretary Kato**

Since 1991, the issue of Japanese military 'comfort women' has emerged as a diplomatic problem between Korea and Japan. In June of 1991, the Pacific War Victims' Families Association, consisting of 35 members including three former 'comfort women,' filed a lawsuit demanding compensation from the Japanese government. On December 16, 1991, 25 female lawmakers, including former Social Democratic Party leader Takako Doi (土井多賀子), submitted a petition to the Chief Cabinet Secretary, Kato Koichi (加藤紘一), demanding that the Japanese government apologize to and compensate the Korean victims of Japanese military 'comfort women' who were forcibly abducted during World War II and conduct a detailed investigation. As Japanese Prime Minister Miyazawa Kiichi (宮澤喜一)'s visit to Korea approached, there was a growing wave of criticism from Koreans demanding clarification of the truth about the 'comfort women' issue and seeking countermeasures from Japan. The Korean government also decided to make an official request to the Japanese government to conduct a thorough investigation into the matter.

On December 7, 1991, at a bilateral meeting held in Tokyo at the level of directors, the Korean government demanded the investigation of the truth about the Japanese military 'comfort women' and countermeasures. On December 12, 1991, at the meeting of the Cabinet Secretariat with related ministries, the Japanese government decided to conduct an official investigation of materials on Japanese military 'comfort women' kept by related ministries and agencies.

On January 11, 1992, *the Asahi Shimbun* (朝日新聞) reported that Professor Yoshiaki Yoshimi of Chuo University had discovered documents in the library of the Defense Research Institute of the Ministry of Defense revealing the Japanese military involvement in establishing comfort stations and recruiting 'comfort women.' Immediately after the report, Foreign Minister Michio Watanabe (渡辺美智雄) stated, "Although there is no clear evidence (of the military's direct involvement), it is undeniable that some form of involvement occurred." Chief Cabinet Secretary Kato also said, "We cannot deny the military's involvement at that time." This was the first admission of

Japanese military involvement.

On January 13, 1992, Chief Cabinet Secretary Kato acknowledged the involvement of the Japanese military and issued a statement of apology. Prime Minister Miyazawa also made an official apology for the first time as prime minister regarding the issue of the Japanese military 'comfort women' in his speech to the Korean National Assembly on January 17 during his visit to Korea. The issue of the Japanese military 'comfort women' was first discussed during the summit meeting between President Tae-woo Roh and Prime Minister Miyazawa. Prime Minister Miyazawa promised President Tae-woo Roh that he would make every effort to investigate the facts by mobilizing relevant government ministries and offices.

The Japanese government's investigation focused on whether the Japanese military was involved in the recruitment of Japanese military 'comfort women' and the operation of comfort stations.

On July 6, 1992, Chief Cabinet Secretary Kato released the results of the investigation into the issue of military 'comfort women' from the Korean peninsula.

Kato's statement included the admission of the government's involvement in the establishment of comfort stations, the control of those who recruited 'comfort women,' the construction and reinforcement of comfort facilities, the management and surveillance of comfort stations, the maintenance of hygiene in comfort stations and among 'comfort women,' and the issuance of identification cards and other documents to those associated with comfort stations. In the statement, he apologized and expressed remorse. Further details of the investigation were released by the Cabinet Councilors' Office for Foreign Affairs (内閣官房内閣外政審議室) in a separate report, "On the Issue of the So-Called Military 'comfort women' from the Korean Peninsula." The ministries involved in the fact-finding mission include the National Police Agency, the Defense Agency, the Ministry of Foreign Affairs, the Ministry of Education, the Ministry of Health and Welfare, and the Ministry of Labor. The results were 0 cases from the National Police Agency, 70 cases from the Defense Agency, 52 cases from the Ministry of Foreign Affairs, 1 case from the Ministry of Education, 4 cases from the Ministry of Health and Welfare, and 0 cases from the Ministry of Labor. In terms of content, there were 4 documents on the establishment of comfort stations, 4 documents on the recruitment of military 'comfort women,' 9 documents on the construction and reinforcement of comfort station facilities, 35 documents on the management and supervision of comfort stations and 'comfort women,' 24 documents on hygiene control, 28 documents on the issuance of comfort station identification cards, and 34 documents on the description of comfort stations and 'comfort women.'

The title of the Chief Cabinet Secretary's statement limits the subjects to those from the Korean Peninsula. However, the Japanese government acknowledged that women in China, Taiwan, the Philippines, Indonesia, and elsewhere were also victimized, and provided

Statement by Chief Cabinet Secretary Koichi Kato on the Issue of the So-called "Wartime Comfort Women" from the Korean Peninsula (July 6, 1992)

Since December 1991, the Government has conducted an inquiry as to whether it had been involved in the issue of the so-called "wartime 'comfort women' from the Korean Peninsula into the ministries and agencies which might keep the related materials. I would like to announce the following findings as a result of this inquiry. They are as described in the handouts, and I will summarize the main points here. That is, the inquiry has revealed that the Government had been involved in the establishment of comfort stations, the control of those who recruited 'comfort women,' the construction and reinforcement of comfort facilities, the management and surveillance of comfort stations, the hygiene maintenance in comfort stations and among 'comfort women,' and the issuance of identification as well as other documents to those who were related to comfort stations. Regarding the specific contents of the inquiry, we have outlined each material for those who are interested to read. The Cabinet Councilors' Office on External Affairs will explain in detail later, so that you can ask any questions you have on the contents.

The Government again would like to express its sincere apology and remorse to all those who have suffered indescribable hardship as so-called "Wartime Comfort Women" irrespective of their nationality or place of birth. With profound remorse and determination that such a mistake must never be repeated, Japan will maintain its stance as a pacifist nation and will endeavor to build up new future-oriented relations with the Republic of Korea and with other countries and regions in Asia.

As I listen to many people, I feel truly grieved for this issue. By listening to the opinions of people from various directions, I would like to consider sincerely in what way we can express our feelings to those who suffered such hardship.

an overview of the results of the investigation to governments other than North Korea.

Meanwhile, when asked at the conference if there were any materials showing the forced mobilization of Korean women, Chief Cabinet Secretary Kato replied, "We have not found any materials on recruitment methods." Regarding the issue of compensation for the victims, he said, "The issue of compensation with each country was settled in the San Francisco Peace Treaty. As for 'other measures,' we are considering Korea separately."

In response to Chief Cabinet Secretary Kato's statement, the Korean government issued a comment through a Foreign Ministry spokesperson. It acknowledged Japan's hard work in uncovering relevant documents, but assessed that the full extent of the Japanese military 'comfort women' issue had not been revealed. Victims and organizations such as the Korean Council criticized the absence of any mention of "forced mobilization." They argued that a thorough investigation and disclosure of the truth, including the forced mobilization of 'comfort women,' should be the top priority, and that the discussion of "compensation" mentioned by Chief Cabinet Secretary Kato was premature.

② **Interim Report of Investigation by the Korean Government**
On December 13, 1991, the Korean National Assembly began examining a petition on the issue of Japanese military 'comfort wom-

en.' They heard testimonies from the chief of the Korean Council and from 'comfort women' victims, followed by questions and answers. In January 1992, under the leadership of the Prime Minister's Office, six relevant ministries, including the Ministry of Foreign Affairs and the Ministry of Internal Affairs, examined documents related to Japanese military 'comfort women,' and on July 31, 1992, released the "Interim Report: Investigation into the Status of 'Comfort Women' in the Japanese Armed Forces."

The purpose of the report was to provide an opportunity for a proper clarification of the past, stating that 'Comfort Women' represent the darkest part of our nation's history of suffering under the Japanese occupation. The report is structured as follows: Part 1, Current Status of the Women's Labor Corps Issue; Part 2, Results of the Investigation into the Status of 'Comfort Women' in the Armed Forces under Japan 1) Establishment of Military 'Comfort Women,' 2) Recruitment of ; 'Comfort Women,' 3) Transportation Methods, 4) Deployment, 5) Management of 'Comfort Women,' 6) Transportation, 7) Situation at the End of the War, 8) Situation after the Allied Occupation, 9) Conclusion; Part 3, Testimonies of Military 'Comfort Women'; Part 4, Documents Discovered by the Japanese Government; Part 5, References.

The reference material for the interim report was drawn primarily from the archives of the Japanese government, but also included documents that were not available in Japan. Two of these documents are

"United States Office of War Information/Japanese Prisoner of War Information Report No. 49" and "Report of the Allied Forces Command on Amenities in the Japanese Armed Forces." The Ministry of Foreign Affairs instructed its diplomatic missions in the countries that were allies during World War II and in Southeast Asia to examine documentary sources. The two documents mentioned above were the results of this examination. The Korean government also received cases of 'comfort women' between February 25 and June 25, 1992, and 13 representative cases were included in the report.

Based on the relevant materials and testimonies of the victims, the Interim Report came to the following conclusions on the issue of 'comfort women.'

> "The Japanese military was fully involved in all aspects of the 'comfort women' policy, establishing comfort stations, recruiting, transporting, and managing them. Finally, at the end of the war, they abandoned them. Spared a miserable death on the battlefield, the 'comfort women' continued to live and die in misery, suffering physical pain and mental anguish from illness, and keeping their painful pasts hidden.
>
> The Japanese military implemented the 'comfort women' policy to maintain security and military strength in the occupied territories, claiming that it prevented sexually transmitted diseases and rape, and the 'comfort women' were not recognized

as human beings. These unprecedented crimes against humanity were committed by Japan for the sole functional purpose of maintaining military power. The greatest victims were the innocent unmarried women and some married young women of Korea. The 'comfort women' issue shows the darkest side of our nation's suffering under Japanese colonial rule."

As the title indicates, this report was an interim report, meaning that more thorough investigation is needed to reveal the full extent of the 'comfort women' issue. Until now, however, there has been no official report from the government. In the meantime, large amounts of new data have been collected and research has been conducted. It is necessary to seriously consider releasing an official report at the government level.

③ **Statement by Chief Cabinet Secretary Kono**

After Chief Cabinet Secretary Kato announced the results of the 'comfort women' investigation, Japan accepted Korea's request and began further investigation.

From July 1992, the scope of the investigation was expanded to include all victims of the Japanese military beyond the Korean 'comfort women.' The main body of the investigation was the same as before, centered on the Cabinet Councilors' Office for Foreign Affairs. The Cabinet Office for Foreign Affairs investigated those involved in the

Japanese military 'comfort women.' In cooperation with the "Pacific War Victims' Families Association," they met with the victims from July 26th to 30th, 1992, and listened to their stories in detail.

In February 1993, with the inauguration of the Kim Young-sam government in Korea, efforts to resolve the 'comfort women' issue between Japan and Korea began in earnest. At that time, the issue was politically charged in both countries. President Young-sam Kim took great pride in being the first civilian president and placed "making history right" at the forefront of his administration. Domestically, eliminating the legacy of military rule was a priority, while resolving the issue of Japanese military 'comfort women' was an urgent task in Japan-Korea relations.

The Socialist Party of Japan, on the other hand, believed that the only way for Japan to be completely free of wartime responsibility was to clean up the wartime damage. The 'comfort women' issue was a symbolic reminder of Japan's wartime responsibility.

Members of the Socialist Party of Japan pressured the Liberal Democratic Party (LDP) government through persistent parliamentary inquiries into the issue. By the 1990s, the LDP's domestic support base had faltered, and it was forced to ally with the Socialist Party. The LDP needed the support of the Socialist Party which was active in resolving the issue of Japan's military 'comfort women.'

On August 4, 1993, Chief Cabinet Secretary Yohei Kono issued a statement. It was the result of the Japanese government's second investigation into Japanese military 'comfort women.' Kono stated that 1) the comfort stations were established at the request of the military authorities at the time, and the military was directly or indirectly involved in the establishment and management of the comfort stations and in the transportation of the 'comfort women'; 2) it is clear that there were cases in which the government was directly involved; 3) life in the comfort stations was deplorable under coercive atmosphere; 4) the Korean Peninsula was under Japanese rule, and the recruitment, transportation, and management were carried out under coaxing, coercion, and, generally, against their will.

> **Statement by the Chief Cabinet Secretary Yohei Kono (August 4, 1993)**
>
> The Government of Japan has been conducting a study on the issue of wartime 'comfort women' since December 1991. I wish to announce the findings as a result of that study.
>
> As a result of the study which indicates that comfort stations were operated in extensive areas for long periods, it is apparent that there existed a great number of 'comfort women.' Comfort stations were operated in response to the request of the military authorities of the day. The Japanese military was, directly or indirectly, involved in the establishment and management of the comfort stations and the transfer of 'comfort women.' The recruitment of the 'comfort women' was conducted mainly by private recruiters who acted in response to the request of the military. The Government study has revealed that in many cases they were recruited against their own will, through coaxing, coercion, etc., and that, at times, administrative/military personnel directly took part in the recruitments.

> They lived in misery at comfort stations under a coercive atmosphere.
>
> As to the origin of those 'comfort women' who were transferred to the war areas, excluding those from Japan, those from the Korean Peninsula accounted for a large part. The Korean Peninsula was under Japanese rule in those days, and their recruitment, transfer, control, etc., were conducted generally against their will, through coaxing, coercion, etc.
>
> Undeniably, this was an act, with the involvement of the military authorities of the day that severely injured the honor and dignity of many women. The Government of Japan would like to take this opportunity once again to extend its sincere apologies and remorse to all those, irrespective of place of origin, who suffered immeasurable pain and incurable physical and psychological wounds as 'comfort women.' It is incumbent upon us, the Government of Japan, to continue to consider seriously, while listening to the views of learned circles, how best we can express this sentiment.
>
> We shall face squarely the historical facts as described above instead of evading them, and take them to heart as lessons of history. We hereby reiterate our firm determination never to repeat the same mistake by forever engraving such issues in our memories through the study and teaching of history.
>
> As actions have been brought to court in Japan and interests have been shown in this issue outside Japan, the Government of Japan shall continue to pay full attention to this matter, including private research related thereto.

Unlike the first investigation, the Japanese government sent officials to the United States to examine U.S. documents and conduct on-site research in Okinawa. The investigation expanded to include the National Archives, the Library of Congress, the U.S. National Archives, and the British Library. They conducted interviews not only with victims of Japanese military 'comfort women,' but also with former soldiers, former officials of the General Government of Japan in Korea, former owners of comfort stations, residents near comfort stations, and historical researchers. They examined reports prepared by the Korean government and related organizations such as the Korean Council and the Pacific War Victims' Families Association. In addition to these materials, the testimony book of the victims of the Japanese military 'comfort women' program was also consulted.

The table below summarizes the report released by the Japanese government in March 2013, "On the Results of the Investigation into the So-called Military Comfort Women." There were a total of 217 documents, of which 158 documents had been discovered at the time of the Kono Statement and 59 additional documents were discovered after the statement.

Summaries of Documents Related to Japanese Military 'Comfort Women' by Ministries and Agencies

Ministries/ Bureaus	Number of Documents	Summaries
Defense Agency	96	• Guidelines for the operation of the military units' comfort stations, days and hours of operation, fees, etc. • Business regulations such as supervision and control of comfort station management.
Ministry of Justice	2	• Records of the provisional court in Batavia: Records of a war crimes trial involving a case of a comfort station in Semarang, Java Island.
Ministry of Foreign Affairs	43	• Contents related to the issuance of passports and identification cards for women going abroad. • Descriptions such as "the highest number of passports issued and documents received were attributed to Koreans," based on demographic statistics by entries of Japanese military 'comfort women.'

Ministry of Education	1	• Contents on hygiene management of 'comfort women' and comfort stations, and supervision of comfort stations.
National Police Agency	2	• Explanation of regulations for cracking down on women who travel to China for the purpose of prostitution.
Ministry of Health and Welfare	1	• The Prisoner of War List shows that some wrote 'comfort girl' in the job section.
National Archives of Japan	31	• Amendments to the Law on the Establishment of Comfort Facilities in Manchuria and China and Increasing the Need for the Facilities. • Health examination of Japanese military 'comfort women,' crackdown on people traveling for the purpose of comfort station business, etc.
National Diet Library	18	• ATIS-related documents. - The Reality of Comfort Camps and Japanese military 'comfort women.'
U.S. National Archives/ Photographic Materials	5	• SEATIC (Southeast Asia Translation and Interpretation Center) - In the areas from Mandalay to Myitkyina where the Japanese military was stationed, there were 'comfort women,' mostly Koreans and Chinese. - In addition, there are eyewitness accounts of Japanese troops breaking into Chinese homes to take young girls.
	9	• ATIS (Allied Translator and Interpreter Section) Office. - The Japanese Army Established and Managed Comfort Stations in the Ground War Zone. - The comfort stations were maintained by the military, and the Japanese military 'comfort women' were mostly Koreans. • Guidelines and precautions for comfort stations.
	1	• War Intelligence Agency report on the results of interrogations of 20 Korean 'comfort women' and two comfort station owners. - Japanese military 'comfort girls' is a term for the Japanese military prostitutes who catered to the needs of the soldiers. - Many women applied after being deceived by promises of high incomes, good opportunities to pay off family debts, and easy work. Most of the women were ignorant and uneducated.
	4 Photographs	• Photos of Korean and Japanese 'comfort women' held as prisoners of war.
British National Archives	4	• Rules for the use of comfort stations.

When asked at a press conference whether he recognized that the women had been forcibly detained, Chief Cabinet Secretary Kono said, "There was such a fact. Yes." Asked by reporters if there was evidence of forced mobilization in the documents, he said, "Violence has both physical and mental dimensions. There are many aspects of mental coercion that do not remain in the government's records. We have fully investigated whether there was such a thing or not." Through the testimony of former 'comfort women' of the Japanese military and the testimony of former managers of comfort stations, he continued, "There are many cases where the women were forcibly taken against their will."

Japan's *Asahi Shimbun* and the conservative newspaper *Yomiuri Shimbun* reported that "there were cases in which Japanese government officials such as soldiers and policemen were directly involved in the incidents" and "the Japanese government admitted for the first time that there were cases in which the Japanese government ordered the 'comfort women' to work against their will." The *Yomiuri Shimbun*'s editorial of August 5, 1993 stated, "The government acknowledged the coercive nature, in a broad definition, of the Japanese military 'comfort women' system from the investigation." Except for the *Sankei Shimbun*, all newspapers acknowledged the "coercive nature" of the Kono Statement.

After the announcement of the Kono Statement, the Korean Foreign Ministry responded positively, saying that the Japanese government had generally acknowledged the "coercion" and expressed its determination to face the past in order to draw lessons from it by apologizing to the victims of the Japanese military 'comfort women' system.

However, contrary to the expectations of the Japanese government, victims in Korea and related organizations, including the Korean Council for the Women Drafted for Sexual Slavery by Japan, said that the Kono Statement was "an attempt to evade responsibility while acknowledging the forced mobilization. It is just a hasty announcement." They also claimed that the factual details such as the number of Japanese military 'comfort women' and comfort stations were left out. They also criticized the omission of the details that constituted the core of war crimes.

At the time, the Japanese government failed to convince rightwing politicians of the Liberal Democratic Party in the process of announcing the Kono Statement. They expressed concern about the words "forced detention," arguing that such a term could not be verified. As a result, the words "forced detention" were not included in the statement.

However, the Kono Statement provoked strong opposition from Japanese right-wing groups and politicians. They argued that Japan was giving in to Korea's demands even though there was no evidence of forced mobilization.

After the announcement of the Kono Statement, right-wing activists such as the "Association to Make New History Textbooks" and Yoshiko Sakurai, Japan's leading conservative commentator, vigorously staged campaigns claiming that the facts about the Japanese military 'comfort women' had been distorted. Right-wing lawmakers, including members of the Liberal Democratic Party, demanded that descriptions of Japanese military 'comfort women' be removed from history textbooks.

In the early 1990s, the issue of Japanese military 'comfort women' was a bilateral issue, with Japanese public opinion in favor of Japan's introspection and extension of an apology. However, as the issue has received prolonged attention, it has started to feed anti-Korean sentiments in Japan.

2) Victim Support and Compensation

① Kim Young-sam Government's Policies

The Japanese government first mentioned follow-up measures for the Japanese military 'comfort women' issue after Chief Cabinet Secretary Kato announced the results of the investigation on July 6, 1992.

On March 13, 1993, President Young-sam Kim of Korea said that Korea would not demand material compensation from the Japanese government, and that it would be paid from the Korean government budget. He declared that he would establish a new Korea-Japan relationship on the basis of Korea's moral superiority. At that time, the media argued that Korea should seek Japan's cooperation in reversing the trade imbalance with Japan. In other words, he was under pressure not to provoke a conflict with Japan.

However, President Young-sam Kim's announcement reflected his strong will rather than the influence of public opinion. President Young-sam Kim was proud of being the first civilian president. He set "correcting history" as the task of his administration, and Korea-Japan relations were no exception. He tried to solve the problem of history on the basis of Korea's strong moral position.

On March 27, 1993, the Young-sam Kim government announced that the victims of the Japanese military 'comfort women' would receive a lump sum of KRW 5 million from the Basic Life Protection Fund and KRW 150,000 per month from the same fund. On May 18 of the same year, the National Assembly passed the Victims of Japanese Military 'Comfort Women' Life Stabilization Act. The Ministry of Health and Welfare approved 121 applicants for the government's financial assistance plan. And the victims were granted special rights to national housing with a size of 18 pyeong (about 60 square meters) or less, and rights to public rental housing and permanent rental housing. These were the first assistance measures taken by the Korean government for the victims.

② **Asian Women's Fund Established**

In Japan, after the announcement of the Kono Statement in August 1993, the follow-up measures for the damage caused by the Japanese military 'comfort women' were discussed. On August 31, 1994, Prime Minister Tomiichi Murayama (村山富市) said that the Japanese government would compensate the victims of the Japanese military 'comfort women' by paying compensation money to be raised from private funds. This was the result of agreements among the three parties of the ruling coalition, the Liberal Democratic Party, the Socialist Party, and the New Party Sakigake.[28]

On December 6, 1994, a three-party coalition representative meeting of the "the Sub-Committee to Address the Wartime Comfort Women Issue (Ruling Parties' Project to Deal with Issues Fifty Years After the War)" decided to compensate the victims of Japanese military 'comfort women' through a combination of private fundraising and government funding.

Discussions on the ratio of government budget to private fundraising have been going on since early 1995. Since the Korean government opposed relying solely on private fundraising, the Japanese government discussed ways of increasing financial support from their side. However, the Liberal Democratic Party opposed this. Right-wing politicians in the LDP strongly opposed the idea, arguing that

---

28 新党さきがけ

pooling government funds would be seen as a reward by the Japanese government. After a series of difficult discussions among the ruling coalition parties, Chief Cabinet Secretary Gojo Igarashi (五十嵐廣三) of the Socialist Party proposed in late May 1995 that the operational expenses and support programs of the fund would be covered by the government budget, and the one-time payment would be funded through private fund. There were arguments from the Socialist Party to provide the one-time payment using government funding, but the Ministry of Foreign Affairs and the Ministry of Treasury opposed the idea, saying that "once individual compensation is acknowledged, it can have far-reaching implications on other issues."

On June 14, 1995, the Japanese government announced its plan to distribute monetary compensation to the Japanese military 'comfort women' from private fundraising and to provide medical and welfare assistance with government funds. On July 19, the "Asian Women's Fund (the full title is the National Fund for Asian Peace and Women, and hereinafter referred to as the National Fund)" was officially established.

The people who led the establishment of the fund, including the chairman of the Upper House Bunbei Hara (原文兵衛), viewed themselves as conscientious intellectuals and supported the idea of compensating the victims and establishing a fund. Considering the limited time left for the victims and Japan's political constraints, they thought that the next best way to help the victims was to come up with a workable plan as soon as possible. Professor Haruki Wada

(和田春樹), who played an important role in the establishment and management of the fund, gave a positive assessment of the progress made, saying that the Kono Declaration was announced during the Miyazawa administration and that subsequent measures were made with the Murayama administration although there were clear limitations. Even this approach was a hard-won change in the face of opposition from right-wing conservatives.

In June 1996, the Japanese government decided to send a letter in the name of the Prime Minister expressing apology and remorse for the 'comfort women' when distributing compensation money *tsugunaigin* (償い金, atonement money) from private funds. For victims in three countries, Korea, Taiwan, and the Philippines, it was decided to pay a lump sum of 2 million yen (about 20,000 USD) and 3 million yen per person for medical and welfare support.

Beginning on January 11, 1997, compensation payments were made to the victims. However, on January 6, 1998, the Japanese government placed an advertisement in a Korean daily newspaper to explain the activities of the National Fund and promote the procedures for receiving compensation. In response, the Korean government strongly protested the National Fund advertisement and demanded that it be stopped. On May 1, 2002, the project to compensate Korean victims was terminated. In South Korea, it is reported that 61 victims have received compensation.

③ Criticism of the Asian Women's Fund

When the Asian Women's Fund, or the National Fund, was officially established in July 1995, the Korean victims and support organizations, such as the Korean Council, criticized the fund, created by private organizations, for being a way for the Japanese government to evade its legal responsibility. This shows that intergovernmental consultations do not carry much weight if victims and support groups cannot accept their agreements.

Since then, the Korean government has changed its position and indicated that it cannot accept the National Fund as a way to solve the problem. The lesson is that the outcome of diplomatic negotiations may not be acceptable if there is no domestic consensus.

The core points of contention in the issue of the Japanese military 'comfort women' revolved around the Japanese government's thorough "clarification of the truth" and "apology," as well as the emphasis on Japan's "legal responsibility." In 1996, according to the Korean media at that time, the term "legal responsibility" appeared prominently. As compensation through private funds began to take shape, despite opposition from victims and civil society groups, the Japanese government's legal responsibility became the focus of discussion.

When the National Fund began making payments to Korean victims in December 1996, the issue of Japanese military 'comfort women' again became a diplomatic issue. The Korean government demanded an apology from the Japanese government for unilaterally paying the 'comfort women,' but the Japanese government refused. The situation was also discussed at a meeting between the foreign ministers of South Korea and Japan. The South Korean government demanded the abolition of the National Fund, but the Japanese government said it was a private organization. The Tokyo government, however, insisted that it would continue the payment plan if the victims wished to receive it.

Criticism of the National Fund has also been voiced in Japan. Conservative lawmakers who held a majority in the Japanese Diet, including the Ministry of Finance and the Ministry of Foreign Affairs, strongly opposed state-funded compensation and reparations. They also criticized that the fund established by the Murayama administration could be considered a form of government-led compensation.

Opposition to the Asian Women's Fund was also voiced abroad. In the Philippines, 211 victims accepted it, but Tomasa Sarinog demanded national compensation to the end. When her claim was rejected by the Tokyo District Court, she said, "I wanted to die on the spot because it was shameful." She continued, "I cannot accept the Asian Women's Fund because it cannot compensate for my father's death and my future and dreams."

Most Dutch victims have accepted the National Fund. However, Jan Ruff O'Herne, the victim of the Smarang incident,[29] refused to

---

29 At that time, Indonesia was a colony of the Netherlands, and there was a large population of Dutch nationals residing in Sumatra. The Japanese military forcibly

accept the medical welfare aid because the responsibility of the Japanese government was unclear. She said, "The National Fund is humiliating. I am not asking for their charity. I am asking for legitimate legal compensation from the Japanese government."

In Taiwan, the Taipei Women's Rescue Foundation (hereinafter referred to as the TWRF) was established to support the victims, and in 1992 the foundation began investigating the damage caused by the Japanese military 'comfort women' system. At first, the Taiwanese victims were extremely reluctant to reveal their names and faces. In 1996, the National Fund consulted with the TWRF but from the beginning, the TWRF demanded compensation from the Japanese government and opposed the National Fund. The TWRF filed a lawsuit on July 14, 1999, demanding an official apology and compensation from the Japanese government. In December 2016, they opened the Ama Museum (阿嬤家) in a building of Taipei. The Ama Museum (Women's Human Rights Hall of Peace) moved to a new location and reopened in 2021.

In Indonesia, the compensation project took the form of "elderly care." The problem was that while this process was going on, the victims did not know about the bilateral talks between Japan and Indo-

---

recruited Dutch women as 'comfort women' and established the "Sakura Club" where they were coerced into engaging in sexual activities. In the Batavia (now Jakarta) Military Tribunal held in Indonesia, eight officers involved in this incident were sentenced to 7 to 20 years of imprisonment, while the interpreter was sentenced to 2 years.

Ama Museum

nesia. Victims of the Japanese military 'comfort women' and support groups protested against Japan, but both governments only repeated that all problems had already been solved by the National Fund.

There were also survivors of Japanese military 'comfort women' in China, North Korea, and East Timor. However, the National Fund has not implemented its project in these regions.

On the website of the Japanese Ministry of Foreign Affairs, there is a statement that Japan has fulfilled its moral obligation on the issue of Japanese military 'comfort women' through the National Fund.

The fact is, though, that it only applies to a few regions. Even in those areas, the National Fund has been criticized and rejected by the victims. The claim that the Japanese government has fulfilled all its responsibilities through the National Fund ignores this reality.

3-2
Two Crucial Incidents in 2011 and 2015: A Constitutional Court Decision and a Korea-Japan Agreement

1) The Japanese Military 'Comfort Women' Issue Settled for the Time Being

In order to close the bilateral diplomatic matter over the National Fund, the South Korean government asked the Japanese government to temporarily suspend the controversial fund. At the April 1998 meeting of State Council, the issue of whether to demand compensation from the Japanese government for the victims was discussed in order to defuse domestic disputes. Some argued that compensation should be demanded, but in view of Korea-Japan relations, tthe South Korean government followed the decision of its former Kim Young-sam government. In a statement, the Korean government said it had decided not to demand compensation for each victim of the Japanese military 'comfort women,' but that it would urge the

Japanese government to apologize for the past.

The victims' organizations such as the Korean Council strongly opposed the Korean government's decision not to seek compensation from the Japanese government. They also insisted that the Korean government must demand that the Japanese government accept the recommendations of the UN Human Rights Commission, such as thorough investigation, compensation, and punishment of those responsible.

Anti-Japanese sentiment in Korea peaked after Japan abrogated the Korea-Japan Fishing Agreement. Simultaneously, criticism of the Korean government for its weak stance towards Japan increased. Despite the opposition, the Korean government judged that the compensation claim was an additional burden to improve Korea-Japan relations. The decision not to seek compensation from Japan reflected the will of President Dae-jung Kim. In April 1998, the Korean government decided to distribute KRW 4.88 billion (about USD 3.8 million) in state subsidies to 155 victims. To reach the compensation proposed by the Japanese National Fund, the government provided a total of 38 million won per person, of which 31.5 million won came from the state and the rest from the private sector. The South Korean government announced its plan to provide financial support to the victims of the Japanese military 'comfort women' first, and then later reclaim the compensation from the Japanese government when it is paid.

At a meeting of State Council, there were also objections to the idea of the Korean government paying compensation. It was pointed out that the legal nature of the subsidies under the "Livelihood Stabilization Support Act for the Japanese Military 'Comfort Women'" was ambiguous, and that the Korean government could be perceived as giving up on demanding compensation from Japan. Additionally, it was said that related organizations, including the Korean Council, may express opposition to it. However, the cabinet decided to provide grants first so that victims would not be lured by the Japanese National Fund. In fear of backlash from victims and civic organizations, the Korean government also made it clear that the decision was not intended to relieve Japan of its historical or moral responsibility or to refrain from demanding an apology.

These measures were aimed at resolving the issue of reparations triggered by Japan's National Fund while avoiding the source of the fundamental bilateral disputes that hinder the Korean government's efforts to restore Korea-Japan relations. As a result, the issue of the National Fund fell below the surface, at least at the diplomatic level.

The victims and related organizations, however, still had a problem with such an arrangement and continued to argue for the Japanese government's legal responsibility for war crimes, demanding that Japanese government acknowledge its past wrongs and provide compensation.

In the 1990s, the Korean government believed that the issue of

Japanese military 'comfort women' was a matter between the Korean victims and the Japanese government. The Japanese government, on the other hand, tried to exclude the victims and pursue negotiations as a bilateral diplomatic issue. In the process, there was insufficient communication between the Korean government and the victims' groups. In addition, there was no discussion within the Korean government on how to deal with a situation where Japan refused to accept legal responsibility and pursue compensation for the victims.

2) A Korean Constitutional Court Decision in 2011

The Japanese government claims that the issue of compensation for the victims of Japanese military 'comfort women' has been fully resolved legally. The Japanese government argues that it has established a fund in cooperation with citizens to alleviate the pain and suffering of the victims and has provided medical and welfare support in the form of *tsugunaigin*.

On August 26, 2005, the Korean government announced that through the decision of the "Civil-Government Joint Committee on Follow-up Measures related to the Disclosure of Documents from the Korea-Japan Summit," its right to hold the Japanese government legally responsible for Japan's anti-humanitarian illegal acts is still intact. However, the Roh Moo-hyun government did not put the issue on the agenda of Korea-Japan diplomatic talks. It continued the policy of the Kim Young-sam government.

On August 30, 2011, the Korean Constitutional Court ruled that while the Korean government was obliged to pursue the difference in legal interpretation with the Japanese government under Article 3 of the Claims Agreement, it took no action to resolve this situation, which was ruled unconstitutional.

In accordance with Article 3 of the Korea-Japan Claims Agreement, the Korean Constitutional Court regarded the duty to proceed with dispute settlement procedures as a constitutional requirement. The Korean government had to cooperate with and protect its citizens whose human dignity and values were seriously undermined by the systematic and organized illegal activities of the country of Japan. Furthermore, it was ruled that the basic rights of the victims guaranteed by the Constitution were violated by the failure of the Korean government to fulfill its obligations.

Following the Constitutional Court decision, the Korean government twice requested bilateral consultations with the Japanese government under Article 3(1) of the Claims Agreement in September and November 2011. However, Japan did not respond to the request. At the Korea-Japan summit in December 2011, President Myung-bak Lee urged the Japanese government to make a decision to resolve the issue of Japanese military 'comfort women.' But Japan only reiterated its position that the 1965 Agreement settled all issues.

**Challenge against the Act of Omission Involving Article 3 of
"Agreement on the Settlement of Problem concerning Property
and Claims and Economic Cooperation between
the Republic of Korea and Japan"
Final Decision: Upheld (Unconstitutionality Confirmed)**

(Constitutional Court Decision Date: August 30, 2011)

[Summary of Decisions]

According to the Preamble, Article 2 Section 2, and Article 10 of the Constitution and Article 3 of the Agreement, the respondent's duty to pursue dispute settlement procedures under Article 3 of the Agreement stems from the constitutional request to assist and safeguard the people who had their dignity and value seriously compromised by Japan's organized, continuous unlawful acts in their filing of claims against Japan. As the fundamental rights of the complainants may be significantly undermined if the respondent fails to fulfill its duty to proceed with dispute resolution, the respondent's obligation to act in this case originates from the Constitution and is stipulated in law.

In particular, although not in direct infringement of the fundamental rights of 'comfort women' victims, the Korean government is nevertheless liable for causing disruption in settling the payment of claims by Japan and in restoring the victims' dignity and value in that it signed the Agreement without clarifying details of the claims and employing a comprehensive concept of "all claims." Taking note of such responsibility on the part of the Korean government, it is hard to deny that the government has the specific duty to pursue elimination of the disrupted state in settlement of claims.

Whether this omission to act by the respondent to initiate dispute settlement procedures infringes on the complainants' fundamental rights and is therefore unconstitutional will depend on whether such act stays within the scope of a government institution's legitimate leeway consistent with its duty to protect people's rights, which is determined through overall consideration of the significance of fundamental rights concerned, urgency of the risk of rights violation, effectiveness as a remedy of rights and whether undertaking the dispute settlement procedure runs counter to the genuine interest of the nation.

In fact, the claims of 'comfort women' victims against far-reaching anti-humanitarian crimes committed by Japan are part of the property rights guaranteed by the Constitution. And the payment of claims would imply post-facto recovery of dignity, value and personal liberty of those whose rights had been ruthlessly and constantly violated. In this sense, preventing the settlement of claims would not just be confined to the issue of constitutional property rights but would also directly concern the violation of dignity and value as human beings. Hence the resulting infringement of fundamental rights would be of great implication. At the same time, the victims of 'comfort women' are all aged, which means, if there is an additional delay in time, it may be permanently impossible to do justice to history and recover the victims' dignity and value as human beings through settlement of claims. Therefore, considering that the victims' claims serve as an urgent remedy for violation of fundamental rights and given the background and circumstances of signing the Agreement as well as domestic and foreign developments, it is not so unlikely that this case may result in an effective judicial remedy.

With all the aforementioned factors taken into account, pursuing dispute settlement under Article 3 of the Agreement would be the only rightful exercise of power consistent with the state's responsibility to protect fundamental rights of citizens. As the failure of the respondent to intervene has resulted in serious violation of fundamental rights, the omission to act is in violation of the Constitution.

3) The Kono Statement Reviewed by the Abe Administration

On March 16, 2007, the Abe Cabinet of Japan issued a statement, "Among the materials which were studied in research and investigation, the Government did not find a description which directly proves that there was so-called coercive recruitment by the military or government authority."[30] The United States publicly expressed its concern over this revisionist view of history. The Abe cabinet's decision in 2007 was instrumental in prompting the U.S. House of Representatives to pass a resolution in July 2007, four months later, urging Japan to resolve the issue of Japan's military 'comfort women.' Thomas Schieffer, the U.S. ambassador to Japan, said in 2012 that revising the Kono Statement would harm Japan's national interests.

Criticism of the Kono Statement by Japanese conservative factions became fierce after the Korean Constitutional Court decision. Before Abe's second cabinet took office in December 2012, Prime Minister Abe argued during the Liberal Democratic Party presidential election that the official Kono Statement should be revised. On October 16, 2013, the *Sankei Shimbun* revealed the results of an investigation into 16 former Korean 'comfort women,' who provided testimony that served as the basis of the Kono Statement. The conservative newspa-

---

30 Answer from the Cabinet to Representative Kiyomi Tsujimoto's Question, Larry Niksch, "Japanese Military 'Comfort Women' System," Congressional Research Service Memorandum, April 3, 2007.

per claimed that their testimonies were hardly trustworthy, and that no investigation had been conducted to verify their testimonies. The newspaper claimed that the grounds of coercion acknowledged in the Kono Statement had collapsed. The review of the Kono Statement began with the attacks by the *Sankei Shimbun* and Japanese right-wing lawmakers.

On June 20, 2014, the Japanese government released the details underpinning the Kono Statement in a review report entitled "Details of Exchanges Between Japan and the Republic of Korea (ROK) Regarding the 'Comfort Women' Issue - From the Drafting of the Kono Statement to the Asian Women's Fund" (hereinafter referred to the review report).[31] The review report raised suspicions that the facts were distorted during the negotiations between the two governments. The Abe government promoted the idea that there was no coercion in the recruitment of Japanese military 'comfort women' by claiming that there were no documents that proved coercion in the recruitment process.

Following the release of the review report on the Kono Statement in 2014, Japanese government officials began to deny "sexual slavery" to the international community. On September 5, 2014, Chief Cabinet Secretary Yoshihide Suga (菅義偉) told the United Nations Human Rights Committee (UNHRC) in Geneva, Switzerland, that

---

31 https://www.mofa.go.jp/files/100136721.pdf

the term "sexual slavery" was very inappropriate. Since the 2004 review report on the drafting of the Kono Statement, the Japanese government has made official remarks at the UN that the terms "sexual slavery" and "forced mobilization" were inconsistent with the facts.

The following remarks by Prime Minister Abe to the Budget Committee of the House of Representatives on October 3, 2014, epitomize the Abe cabinet's perception of the Japanese military 'comfort women.'

"The groundless slander that Japan operated a system of sexual slavery is now spreading around the world.... As the government, we believe that forming a correct historical perception based on objective facts will enable Japan's response to receive a fair evaluation from the international community. Therefore, we need to strengthen our international promotion strategically beyond the current level."

4) Korea-Japan Agreement of 2015 on the 'Comfort Women' Issue

After the inauguration of the Park Geun-hye administration in February 2013, Korea and Japan had a sharp confrontation over the issue of Japanese military 'comfort women.' The two countries agreed to resolve the issue through diplomatic channels as it affected diplomacy as a whole. On April 16, 2014, the two countries initiated director-general consultations. From February 2015 to December 2015, a total of 12 director-general consultations and 8 high-level consultations were held. On November 2, at the Korea-Japan Summit, the leaders of the two countries agreed to discuss the issue of Japanese military 'comfort women' as soon as possible in order to resolve the issue. President Geun-hye Park expressed her strong desire to reach an agreement before the end of the year. On December 23, 2015, an agreement was finally reached at the 8th high-level consultative meeting. The foreign ministers of the two countries met in Seoul on December 28, 2015 and held a press conference to announce the contents of the agreement.

The Korean government stated that the average age of the victims was now over 90. The Seoul government added that the agreement was reached based on its judgment that missing the opportunity to resolve the issue of Japanese military 'comfort women' would lead to an eternal impasse. As the issue became the biggest diplomatic agenda between Korea and Japan, the relations between the two countries were reduced to extreme deterioration and confrontation, to the point no summit meeting between the two countries was possible. And the fact that the United States, out of concern that the Korea-Japan conflict would create rifts in the trilateral security cooperation (Korea, the U.S., and Japan), also exerted pressure on both countries, had an impact on the agreement.

After the Korea-Japan Agreement, Foreign Minister Fumio Kishida (岸田文雄) said at a press conference in a downtown Seoul hotel, "This is a historic and groundbreaking achievement. It has made it possible for Korea-Japan relations to enter a new, forward-looking era. Security cooperation among Korea, the U.S. and Japan now has a chance to move forward, and it will greatly contribute to peace and stability in the region."

The following is a summary of the content of the joint press conference held by the foreign ministers of the two countries, based on the website information provided by the ministries of foreign affairs of Korea and Japan.

Comparison of Website Information Provided by the Ministry of Foreign Affairs of Japan and the Ministry of Foreign Affairs of Korea

Website of the Ministry of Foreign Affairs of Japan	Website of the Ministry of Foreign Affairs of Korea
Foreign Minister Kishida	**Foreign Minister Kishida**
(1) The 'comfort women' issue was caused by the involvement of the military at that time, which left a deep scar on the honor and dignity of many women. In this regard, the Japanese government is responsible. As the Prime Minister of Japan, Prime Minister Abe would like to apologize from the bottom of his heart and express his deep remorse to all those who have been deeply hurt with hard-to-heal scars in mind and body for having caused much pain and suffering as 'comfort women.'	(Same as Japan's website)
(2) The Japanese government has been working sincerely on this issue. Based on this experience, the Japanese government will take measures for the psychological healing of all	(Same as Japan's website)

former 'comfort women,' using the budget of the Japanese government. Specifically, the Korean government will establish a foundation for the purpose of supporting the former 'comfort women,' and the Japanese government will provide the lump-sum payment of funds from its government budget. The governments of the two countries will work together to restore the honor and heal the hearts of all the former 'comfort women.'	
(3) Together with the above, and on the premise that the measures in (2) will be steadily implemented, we confirm that the issue will be settled in a final and irreversible manner through this announcement. In addition, the Japanese government, together with the Korean government, will refrain from criticizing each other regarding this issue in the international community, such as the United Nations.	(3) With the above statement by the Japanese government, and on the premise that the Japanese government will steadily implement the above measures, we confirm that the issues will be finally and irreversibly resolved through this announcement. In addition, the Japanese government, together with the Korean government, will refrain from criticizing each other on this issue in the international community, such as the United Nations. Furthermore, the aforementioned budgetary measures will amount to about 1 billion yen. The above statement is the result of consultations conducted in accordance with the instructions of the leaders of Japan and Korea, and we are confident that the Korea-Japan relationship will enter a new era.
Korean Foreign Minister Byung-se Yun	**Korean Foreign Minister Byung-se Yun**
(1) The Korean government acknowledges the intentions expressed by the Japanese government and the steps it has taken up to this announcement. On the premise that the Japanese government will steadily implement the measures mentioned in 1-(2) above, we with the Japanese government, confirm that this issue will be finally and irreversibly resolved through this announcement. The Korean government will cooperate with the measures to be taken by the Japanese government.	(1) The Korean government acknowledges the intentions expressed by the Japanese government and the steps it has taken up to this announcement. On the premise that the Japanese government will steadily implement the measures it previously mentioned, we, with the Japanese government, confirm that this issue will be finally and irreversibly resolved through this announcement. The Korean government will cooperate with the measures to be taken by the Japanese government.

(2) The Korean government acknowledges the concerns of the Japanese government regarding the Statue of Peace in front of the Japanese embassy in Seoul from the perspective of maintaining the composure and dignity of the diplomatic mission. As the Korean government, we also make efforts to find an appropriate resolution through consultations with relevant organizations, considering all possible response options.	(Same as Japan's website)
(3) On the premise that the Japanese government will steadily implement the announced measures, the Korean government will join the Japanese government in refraining from criticizing each other in the international community, including the United Nations.	(Same as Japan's website)

This was a joint announcement, but there was a slight difference between the websites of the Korean and Japanese foreign ministries. The Japanese government states that the core of the Korea-Japan Agreement includes the Japanese government's recognition of historical facts (the degradation of the honor and dignity of many women with the involvement of the military at the time), an apology in the name of the prime minister, an expression of remorse and an attempt to heal the wounded hearts of the victims, the establishment of a foundation for the implementation of the agreement and the contribution of 1 billion yen from the Japanese government budget, efforts to relocate the Statue of Peace in front of the Japanese embassy, and refraining from mutual criticism on the issue in the international community. However, instead of elaborating on the details of the agreement, the

Japanese government emphasized that the issue of Japanese military 'comfort women' had been finally and irreversibly resolved.

The Japanese government did not disclose the fact that they were taking a budgetary measure of 1 billion yen on the website. In addition, regarding the implementation of the agreement, the emphasis was placed solely on Article (2), by stating "on the premise that the measures in (2) will be steadily implemented," which resulted in the omission of Prime Minister Abe's apology and emphasized only the allocation of the Japanese government's budget. By comparing this wording to that of the Korean Ministry of Foreign Affairs, which included not only (2) but also (1) in the "measures previously mentioned," the position of the Japanese government is clearly revealed. In other words, the Japanese government is limiting the measures they must implement to a budget of 1 billion yen. Despite the agreement between the two governments, the measures for psychological healing of the victims and restoring their honor and dignity were not mentioned at all.

The method of apologizing through Foreign Minister Kishida's verbal statement also became an issue. It is said that on the evening of December 28, Abe apologized only in a telephone conversation with President Geun-hye Park. In other words, he never apologized publicly as the Prime Minister of Japan. Abe refused the Korean government's demand for a letter of apology, saying it was not included in the agreement.

The moment one decides to resolve the issue of Japanese military 'comfort women' through diplomatic negotiations, one cannot expect for 100% of the victims' demands to be met. Diplomacy is inevitably limited because it involves making compromises with counterparts. However, claiming that the resolution of the pain suffered by the victims is "irreversible" and "final" raises concerns.

The victims' suffering is irreversible in the sense that it cannot be undone. However, the use of the words "irreversible" and "final" portrayed a sense of absolution, as if the past atrocities committed by the Japanese military and government could not even be questioned or examined. It was seen as providing a way to absolve them from any responsibility. This once again caused pain to the victims.

Only the victims can forgive the perpetrator. No one can do it on their behalf. That is why the Korean government needed to have close consultations with the victims and related organizations. It was the victims and related organizations who first raised the issue of the Japanese military 'comfort women,' and they have been raising their voices for decades.

The resolution proposal agreed upon by the victims is the recommendation made to the Japanese government during the 12th "Asian Solidarity Conference on the Issue of Military Sexual Slavery by Japan" on June 2, 2014. This proposal demanded that the Japanese government first acknowledge historical facts, then apologize in an irreversible, clear, and official manner, and provide compensation to

Recommendations to the Government of Japan: For Resolution of the Japanese Military 'Comfort Women' Issue

(The 12th Asian Solidarity Conference on the Issue of Military Sexual Slavery by Japan, on June 2, 2014)

The international community is now urging the Japanese government to resolve the Japanese military 'comfort women' issue, a grave violation of human rights against women. Resolution of this issue is the first step towards normalization of relations with neighboring countries, and a necessary foundation in order to contribute to world peace. Furthermore, the first step towards "resolution" can only be taken after presentation of a proposal which can be accepted by the survivors themselves.

<u>What then, would be an acceptable proposal to the survivors? An apology is one of the important elements of the resolution sought by the survivors. The key issue here is for the perpetrating country to accurately recognize who conducted which kind of violating acts, to acknowledge responsibility, to clearly and unambiguously express this apology both domestically and internationally, and take continuing measures to make it credible and sincere. Only then will the survivors be able to accept it as a genuine apology.</u>

Now that the survivors, who have been forced to continue to suffer both physically and mentally in the post-war period without recovery, are becoming older, the time remaining for Japan to resolve this issue is short. We, the victims and supporters who participated in the 12th Asian Solidarity Conference, demand that the Japanese government preserve and further develop the "Kono Statement" and, upon recognizing the following points, take the necessary measures.

In order to resolve the Japanese military 'comfort women' (sexual slavery) issue, the Japanese Government should:

1. Recognize the following facts and responsibilities:
- That the Japanese Government and Military proposed, established, managed and controlled military facilities known as "comfort stations."
- That the women were forced to become "comfort women / sexual slaves" against their will, and were kept in coercive circumstances in the "comfort stations."
- That there were various forms of victimization of women from the colonies, occupied areas and Japan who suffered sexual violence by the Japanese military, that the scale of victimization was extensive, and that the suffering continues today.
- That it was a serious violation of human rights which contravened a variety of both domestic Japanese as well as international laws of the time.

2 Take the following measures for reparation:
- Apologize to the individual victims in a manner that is clear, official, and can not be overturned.
- Make compensation to victims as proof of apology
- Accounting of the truth:
- full disclosure of all documents possessed by the Japanese Government
- further investigation of documents within Japan and internationally
- hearings of survivors and other related persons within Japan and internationally
- Measures to prevent further occurrence:
- Implementation of school and social education including references in textbooks used in compulsory education
- Implement commemorative activities
- Prohibit statements by public figures based on incorrect historical recognition, and clearly and officially rebut similar kinds of statements etc.[32]

---

32 https://wam-peace.org/main/wp-content/uploads/2014/07/20140602_EN.pdf

the victims as evidence of the apology. When comparing this proposal with the agreement between Korea and Japan, the limitations of the bilateral agreement become evident.

The "Report on the Review of the Korea-Japan Agreement of December 28, 2015 on the Issue of 'Comfort Women' Victims" revealed that the bilateral agreement was not a strategic response by the Korean government. Instead, the Japanese government's historical revisionist remarks have continued to pour in with the passage of time, and the Japanese government is still shirking its legal responsibility.

The "Reconciliation and Healing Foundation" was established to deliver Japan's 1 billion yen to the victims as part of the follow-up measures after the Korea-Japan Agreement. A project to pay 100 million Korean won (about 10 million yen) to the surviving victims of Japanese military 'comfort women' and 20 million won to the bereaved families of the deceased was promoted. Although a project to heal the wounds of the victims was promised, only the payment of money was made. Victims and related organizations demanded the dissolution of the foundation immediately after its establishment.

After the Korea-Japan Agreement was reached, there was a lack of discussion on how to implement the agreed agenda. The Reconciliation and Healing Foundation operated from July 28, 2016 to December 27, 2017. During this period, 34 out of 46 surviving victims of Japanese military 'comfort women' applied for 100 million won in compensation, and 31 of the 34 applicants were paid. In addition, 68 out of 199 bereaved families of the deceased victims expressed their intention to accept it, and 58 of them received 20 million won each.

The 2015 Korea-Japan Agreement on Japanese military 'comfort women' and the Reconciliation and Healing Foundation have left us with much to think about. In particular, diplomatic negotiations to resolve historical issues such as the Japanese military 'comfort women' have proven to be an impossible task. Furthermore, it has become an opportunity to reconsider how to perceive and handle the issue of Japanese military 'comfort women' problem.

In 2014, the Northeast Asian History Foundation invited former Prime Minister Tomiichi Murayama to hold a seminar on the issue of Japanese military 'comfort women.' Professor Chin-sung Chung of Seoul National University, who attended the seminar, argued that the issue of Japanese military 'comfort women' should be handled in a way that adheres to principles.

Professor Chung pointed out that "it's just an excuse by the negotiators that we need to resolve this quickly because there are not many days left for the victims." She stated that the late victims would not simply wish for a quick resolution. In order to restore all the victims' honor and heal their wounds, it is essential to establish the truth through historical investigation and pursue a principled resolution. Perhaps the victims' wish is not for the government to hastily compromise with Japan but to thoroughly and properly address the issue, even if it takes time. Listening to the voice of the victims means not only paying attention to those who are still alive but also considering the intentions left behind by those who have passed away.

5) Violation of the Agreement by the Japanese Government

After the Korea-Japan Agreement, the Japanese government claimed that the 1 billion yen from the Japanese national budget was not compensation in nature, and that the issue of Japanese military 'comfort women' had been settled by the agreement. However, the conservative forces that formed the base of the Abe administration criticized the agreement as a humiliating distortion of historical facts. In order to deflect criticism from its own support base, the Abe administration adopted a policy of active denial of forced mobilization and sexual slavery at home and in the international community. The main statements made by Japanese government officials after the agreement are summarized below.

Statements by Japanese government officials

Date	Person making the statement	Place of the statement	Main point of the statement
2016. 1.18	Prime Minister Abe, Foreign Minister Kishida	The House of Councilors Budget Committee	The 2007 Cabinet decision remains firm in its stance that there is no evidence indicating direct involvement of the Japanese military and government agencies in supporting the so-called coercive mobilization.

	Foreign Minister Kishida	The House of Councilors Budget Committee	The term "sexual slavery" is an inappropriate expression that lacks factual basis, and the Japanese government holds the view that it should not be used.
2016. 1.18	Prime Minister Abe	The House of Councilors Budget Committee	Regarding the phrase "with the participation of the military at that time" in the joint statement: It means that "the comfort stations were established at the request of the military authorities, and the Japanese military was directly or indirectly involved in the establishment and management of the comfort stations, including the transportation of the 'comfort women.' But it was the contractors who mainly recruited the 'comfort women' at the request of the military."
2.16	Deputy Foreign Minister Sugiyama	UN Committee on Elimination of Discrimination against Women (CEDAW)	According to the Japanese government's investigation, the so-called forced mobilization by the government and military was not confirmed. Seiji Yoshida's fabricated argument about forced mobilization was spread as fact by *the Asahi Saimbun*. (omitted) The claim that 200,000 women were mobilized as 'comfort women' is also unfounded, and (omitted) the term "sexual slavery" goes against the truth.
2.17	Chief Cabinet Secretary Suga	Press Conference	(The denial of the forced mobilization of 'comfort women') does not violate the The 2015 Korea-Japan Agreement on the 'comfort women' issue.
3.8	Foreign Minister Kishida	Press Conference	Regarding the final report of the UN CEDAW, which stated that "… the perspective of the victims' was not adequately reflected," has been criticized as "regrettable" and "far from the views of the international community."

Date	Person	Venue	Content
3.11	Chief Cabinet Secretary Suga	Press Conference	In a speech at the UNHRC, Zeid Al Hussein, the UN High Commissioner for Human Rights, referred to the Japanese military 'comfort women' as "sexual slaves" and criticized the contents of the agreement made by the foreign ministers of Japan and Korea regarding the 'comfort women' issue. In response to this, Suga criticized that there is a "gap with the international community's perception" and expressed deep regret.
3.14	Nakasone, A member of the Liberal Democratic Party (Special Commission Chairman)	Special Commission of the LDP to Restore Japan's Honor and Trust	On the final opinion of the UN CEDAW, which pointed out that the Japanese government's measures for resolving the issue of Japanese military 'comfort women' were inadequate, he stated that the commission will examine the verification of the circumstances of such an opinion.
10.3	Prime Minister Abe	The House of Representatives Budget Committee	Regarding sending a letter of apology to victims of Japanese military 'comfort women,' he said, "We are not considering it at all."
2017. 2.22	The Japanese government	U.S. Supreme Court	The Japanese government submitted an amicus brief to the U.S. Supreme Court regarding the lawsuit to remove the Statue of Peace in Glendale. In the amicus brief, they argued that the explanation of the Statue of Peace in Glendale contradicts the facts and poses a significant obstacle to Japan's diplomatic efforts.
2018. 8.17	Japanese Ambassador to the UN, Otaka Masato (The Ministry of Foreign Affairs)	UN Committee on the Elimination of Racial Discrimination (CERD) in Geneva	A strong objection was raised against the use of the term "sexual slavery" as it is not based on facts and is considered inappropriate.

On February 16, 2016, Deputy Foreign Minister Shinsuke Sugiyama (杉山晋輔), representing Japan at the United Nations Committee on the Elimination of Discrimination Against Women (CEDAW), made a statement that epitomizes the Japanese government's historical perception of the Japanese military 'comfort women.' He said that: 1) Since the early 1990s, when the issue of Japanese military 'comfort women' became a political and diplomatic issue between Korea and Japan, the Japanese government conducted a comprehensive investigation into the issue. But according to the documents found by the relevant ministries, the so-called forced mobilization by the military and government agencies could not be confirmed; 2) The perception that the Japanese military 'comfort women' were forcibly mobilized became widely recognized when, in 1983, Seiji Yoshida (吉田清治) fabricated the false fact in his book that he was ordered by the Japanese military to hunt women on Jeju Island, South Korea; 3) *The Asahi Shimbun* published the reports as if they were true, which had a great impact on the opinions of the international community as well as those of Korea and Japan; 4) The newspaper later admitted that the reports were untrue and officially apologized to its readers while acknowledging the inaccuracy of the figure of 200,000 women; 5) The expression of "sex slaves" was inconsistent with the truth, and 6) Japan's position is that all postwar issues were legally settled based on the San Francisco Peace Treaty and other relevant bilateral treaties and economic agreements. Nevertheless, Japan created the

National Fund to help the victims through the national budget and private fundraising. Sugiyama's statement has become a representative phrase for the Japanese government's stance.

Makiko Takita (田北真樹子) of the *Sankei Shimbun* supported Sugiyama's remarks at the UN CEDAW. She saw Sugiyama's statement as a Japanese government's official position at the UN contradicting the Kono Statement. Takita also mentioned that it expressed the Japanese government's determination to rectify the international community's perception of the Japanese military 'comfort women' issue. On February 19, both the *Yomiuri Shimbun* and the *Sankei Shimbun*, in an article and an editorial, positively assessed the Japanese government's active response to the issue in the international community. Both media acknowledged that such activities would clear the international community of misunderstandings and restore Japan's image tarnished by the Japanese military 'comfort women' issue. Both newspapers argued that it was probably too late for the Japanese government to deny "sexual slavery" and "forced mobilization," but it was positive that the Kono Statement, which caused an allegedly wrong perception of the Japanese military 'comfort women' issue, should be corrected and the relevant facts should be spread to the international community.

The Asahi Shimbun clarified that it was not true that the perception of the Japanese military 'Comfort Women' being forcibly mobilized was spread internationally by *the Asahi Shimbun*. The newspaper expressed regret to the Japanese government for this misconception. It also stressed that the Japanese government's active response at the UN CEDAW, denying "forced mobilization" and "sexual slavery" to the international community, was not the will of the Foreign Ministry, but the order of the Prime Minister's Office. The Ministry of Foreign Affairs had previously taken a position of not providing detailed responses based on the Korea-Japan Agreement. However, it has been revealed that instructions were given by the Prime Minister's Office, stating that it was undesirable for Japan's reputation to be damaged by the international spread of misinformation contrary to the facts, and that the Ministry of Foreign Affairs should respond actively.[33]

The Japanese government even submitted an amicus brief to the U.S. Supreme Court on February 22, 2017, regarding the lawsuit demanding the removal of the Statue of Peace in Glendale, USA. *The Asahi Shimbun* expressed concern about the Japanese government's direct involvement in the removal of the statue, as it was unusual for the Japanese government to submit an amicus brief. The *Sankei Shimbun*, on the other hand, called for active government involvement, stating that the removal of the statue would be natural and that

---

33 As a result of consultations between the Ministry of Foreign Affairs and the Prime Minister's Office: (1) In the preliminary response, it is explained that the government's investigation did not confirm any cases of forced mobilization by the military or government authorities. (2) Sugiyama attends the committee and explains that he opposes the claim of "200,000 'comfort women' as sex slaves. To avoid affecting the Korea-Japan Agreement, he does not mention "Korea" at all and emphasizes that the past reports published by *the Asahi Shimbun* had an impact on the international community (Asahi Shimbun, February 24, 2016).

there were limitations of right-wing civic groups with proper historical awareness. On March 29, 2017, the *Sankei Shimbun* reported that Chief Cabinet Secretary Yoshihide Suga said, "Overseas movements to install the Statue of Peace are extremely regrettable and incompatible with our government's position."

The true spirit of the statue is to remember the pain of the victims of the Japanese military 'comfort women' and to restore their honor and human rights. But the *Sankei Shimbun* and the *Yomiuri Shimbun* tried to discredit the statue as a means of anti-Japanese propaganda in Korea and distorted the intention of the statue's installation around the world as if it was masterminded by anti-Japanese networks in China and Korea. In this way, the Japanese government is actively intervening in the overseas Statue of Peace issue through its embassies and consulates.

After the Korea-Japan Agreement, the Japanese government and the conservative right-wing organizations have become more active in lobbying the international community. They are demanding revisions to be made to the description of the forced mobilization in American history textbooks, claiming that there is no factual basis for it. This is unprecedented.

In March 2016, the right-wing group Global Alliance for Historical Truth (GAHT, 歴史の真実を求める世界連合会) held a press conference in New York at a hotel near the UN headquarters. They claimed to inform the truth about the Japanese military 'comfort women' issue.

They stated that there was no forced mobilization, and it was not "sexual slavery."

6) Criticism of the Korea-Japan Agreement on the 'Comfort Women' Issue

During the 2017 South Korean presidential election, all candidates criticized the 2015 Korea-Japan Agreement. The Moon Jae-in administration formed a task force to investigate the process of reaching the agreement. The conclusions, which were announced on December 27, 2017, are as follows.

After the task force's investigation was completed, President Jae-in Moon criticized the agreement, saying that a crucial flaw had been found. Debates about whether or not to cancel the agreement continued, but Korean Foreign Minister Kyung-wha Kang announced that no further request for renegotiation would be made to the Japanese government.

However, victims and citizens demanded the dissolution of the Reconciliation and Healing Foundation. On January 9, 2018, the government announced that the future of the foundation would be decided after compiling various opinions, including those of victims and related organizations. On November 21, 2018, ten months after the announcement, the Ministry of Gender Equality and Family made a plan to dissolve the Reconciliation and Healing Foundation. The dissolution process was completed on July 3, 2019. As of the end of

> The victim-centered approach that has become an internationally accepted norm for wartime women's human rights was not sufficiently incorporated in the course of the 'comfort women' consultation process, and the Agreement was reached through give-and-take negotiations as if it were a common diplomatic issue. The Korean government took up the consultations, noting that the issue should be resolved while as many victims were still alive as possible. Nevertheless, the Agreement was concluded reflecting mainly the government's position and without sufficiently listening to, and incorporating, the victims' opinions. As long as a resolution is not accepted by the victims as was the case with the Agreement, the 'comfort women' issue will continue to be raised as an unresolved issue even if the two governments declare that it is "finally and irreversibly resolved."
>
> Finally, communications were lacking among the President, those in charge of negotiations, and the Ministry of Foreign Affairs. As a result, the system of modifying or adjusting the policy directions to accommodate changing environments did not operate properly. The Agreement shows that the policy decision-making process requires seeking a wide range of opinions, close communications, and adequate allocation of roles among relevant authorities.
>
> - Provided by *Report on the Review of the Korea-Japan Agreement of December 28, 2015 on the Issue of 'Comfort Women' Victims* (December 27, 2017)

October 2018, the Ministry of Gender Equality and Family still had an amount of 5.78 billion won (about USD 4.5 million) as the remaining funds of the foundation. It said it would collect opinions from victims and related organizations regarding the remaining funds, in order to come up with a reasonable plan.

Even after the Korea-Japan Agreement, the Korean government

continues to provide support and assistance to the victims. Currently, the government appoints a public servant in victims' area of residence as a one-to-one manager to take care of their health and emotional well-being. In addition to housing improvements and winter heating supplies, they also provide welfare support by addressing individual needs and requests. This support system is stipulated in the "Law on Support for Life Stability and Commemoration Projects for Victims of Japanese Military's Comfort Women."

On August 14, 2018, the Memorial day for 'Comfort Women' was established to restore the dignity and honor of the victims, establish a proper historical perspective among the citizens, and promote women's human rights. It was designated as a national memorial day, 27 years after Hak-soon Kim revealed that she was a victim of the Japanese military 'comfort women' program. The first ceremony was held at the National Mang-Hyang Cemetry on August 14, 2018. President Jae-in Moon also attended the ceremony and commemorated the victims. Additionally, a memorial monument for the victims of the Japanese military 'comfort women,' known as the "House of Leave," was installed at the Moran Graveyard of the National Mang-Hyang Cemetry

The Korean government has included the issue of Japanese military 'comfort women' in the school curriculum since 2017 to educate future generations. The Northeast Asian History Foundation provides various research and content, including the "Truth about the Japanese

Memorial Monument for the Victims of the Japanese Military 'Comfort Women'
(Provided by Ministry of Gender Equality and Family, Republic of Korea)

Military 'Comfort Women' and the Victims' Testimonies," through the Northeast Asian History Network (http://contents.nahf.or.kr/english) to raise awareness among the public.

Reports of 'Comfort Women' Victims in Korea

As of June 25, 2019, there were 240 reported victims of the Japanese military 'comfort women' program. This does not include victims who did not report themselves, such as Bong-ki Bae, who was hiding in Okinawa. Below is the breakdown of the registered victims based on the year they reported their cases, along with the number of victims who have passed away in each respective year.

Status of New Cases and Deaths by Year (As of June 25, 2019, Unit: Number)

Year	1993	1994	1995	1996	1997	1998	1999	2000	2001	2002	2003	2004	2005	2006
New Registration	153	15	5	6	6	5	4	6	6	1	5	3	8	11
Deaths	3	3	9	5	9	6	13	10	5	11	6	8	18	6
Year	2007	2008	2009	2010	2011	2012	2013	2014	2015	2016	2017	2018	June 2019	
New Registration	0	0	0	0	0	2	1	1	0	1	0	1	0	
Deaths	14	15	6	9	15	6	4	2	9	7	8	8	4	

According to the Ministry of Gender Equality and Family, as of June 25, 2019, there were 21 surviving victims. By age, there were 7 people between 85 and 89 years old, 13 people between 90 and 95 years old, and 1 person over 96 years old. The average age of the victims was 91. Their places of residence were as follows.

Area of Residence of the 21 Surviving Victims (as of June 25, 2019, Unit: Number)

Total	Area of Residence							
	Seoul	Busan	Daegu	Gwangju	Ulsan	Gyeonggi-do	Gyeongsangbuk-do	Gyeongsangnam-do
46	4	1	2	1	1	8	1	4

There is no available data that provides the total number of victims of Japanese military 'comfort women.' It can only be estimated based on the total number of Japanese soldiers at that time and the ratio of 'comfort women' per soldier. Prominent researchers estimate the number of 'comfort women' as follows.

Researcher	Year of publication	Total number of soldiers	Ratio of 'comfort women' to soldiers	Conversion rate	Number of 'comfort women'
Ikuhiko Hata*	1993	3 million	1 per 50 soldiers	1.5	90,000
	1999	2.5 million	1 per 150 soldiers	1.5	20,000
Yoshiaki Yoshimi	1995	3 million	1 per 100 soldiers	1.5	45,000
			1 per 30 soldiers	2	200,000
Zhiliang Su	1999	3 million	1 per 30 soldiers	3.5	360,000
				4	410,000

*Ikuhiko Hata estimated 3 million in 1993, but revised his estimate to 2.5 million in 1999.

One clear fact is that the Japanese military 'comfort women' system was the largest-scale human trafficking incident perpetrated by the Japanese military and government.

Chapter 4

How Did the Global Community Respond?

4-1
Universal Values: The Issues of Sexual Slavery and Forced Mobilization

The essence of the Japanese military 'comfort women' issue lies in the problem of sexual violence against women that occurred during wartime. The international community has been very passive regarding the issue of sexual violence against women. Sexual violence, including rape, during war was often regarded as a mere by-product of armed conflict. In the 1990s, during events such as the Bosnian War, the Rwandan genocide, and the Kosovo conflict, many women were subjected to sexual violence and suffered serious human rights violations. These incidents catalyzed discussions within the United Nations on sexual violence against women in armed conflict and wartime sexual abuses. In 1991, the UN Economic and Social Council and the Commission on the Status of Women decided to actively address the issue of violence against women. The UN CEDAW, at its

11th session in 1992, also recommended that member states' reports to the Committee should include information on violence against women, considering it as a form of gender discrimination.

In June 1993, the World Conference on Human Rights, held in Vienna from 14 to 25 June, issued a declaration stating that "violations of the human rights of women in situations of armed conflict are violations of the fundamental principles of international human rights and humanitarian law. All violations of this kind, including in particular murder, systematic rape, sexual slavery, and forced pregnancy, require a particularly effective response." This conference became an important link for the Japanese military 'comfort women' movement in its solidarity with the international women's movements. At the NGO Forum of the World Conference on Human Rights, the Asian Women's Forum was organized together with the Asian Women's Human Rights Council under the theme "War Crimes of Sexual Slavery by the Japanese Military: Unresolved Issues of the Japanese Military 'Comfort Women' in Asia." In 1995, participating countries at the World Conference on Women in Beijing declared that they should thoroughly investigate all forms of violence committed against women during armed conflict, including systematic rape, sex trafficking, and sexual slavery, and hold the perpetrators accountable while providing assistance to the victims.

The issue of the Japanese military 'comfort women' began to be recognized by the international community, albeit slowly. In 1994, the UN Commission on Human Rights appointed Radhika Coomaraswamy as the "Special Rapporteur on Violence against Women," and in 1996, the UN Human Rights Sub-Commission appointed Linda Chavez as the "Special Rapporteur on the Sexual Slavery and Slavery-Like Practices during Wartime" to investigate the Japanese military 'comfort women' issue. In January 1996, Special Rapporteur Coomaraswamy submitted the "Report on the Mission to the Democratic People's Republic of Korea, the Republic of Korea and Japan on the Issue of Military Sexual Slavery in Wartime" to the UN Commission on Human Rights. The 37-page report, based on documents and victims' testimonies, described the background of the establishment of the Japanese military comfort, the mobilization of the 'comfort women,' and the condition in the comfort stations, as well as the positions of the South Korean and Japanese governments. The report aimed to address the issue of the Japanese military 'comfort women' as a form of sexual slavery and similar cases. The main points of the report are as follows.

I. DEFINITION

6. The Special Rapporteur would like to clarify at the outset of this report that she considers the case of women forced to render sexual services in wartime by and/or for the use of armed forces a practice of military sexual slavery.

(Omitted)

8. The Special Rapporteur, however, holds the opinion that the practice of 'comfort women' should be considered a clear case of sexual slavery and a slavery-like practice in accordance with the approach adopted by relevant international human rights bodies and mechanisms. In this connection, the Special Rapporteur wishes to underline that the Sub-Commission on Prevention of Discrimination and Protection of Minorities, in its resolution 1993/24 of 15 August 1993, noting information transmitted to it by the Working Group on Contemporary Forms of Slavery concerning the sexual exploitation of women and other forms of forced labour during wartime, <u>entrusted one of its experts to undertake an in-depth study on the situation of systematic rape, sexual slavery and slavery-like practices during wartime.</u> The Sub-Commission further requested the expert in the preparation of this study to take into account information, including on 'comfort women,' which had been submitted to the Special Rapporteur on the right to restitution, compensation and rehabilitation of victims of gross violations of human rights.

9. Furthermore, the Special Rapporteur notes that the Working Group on Contemporary Forms of Slavery, at its twentieth session, welcomed information received from the Government of Japan on the issue of "women sex slaves during the Second World War" and recommended that such practices as "treatment akin to slavery" be settled through the establishment of a Japanese administrative tribunal.

10. Finally, for the purpose of terminology, the Special Rapporteur concurs entirely with the view held by members of the Working Group on Contemporary Forms of Slavery, as well as by representatives of non-governmental organizations and some academics, <u>that the phrase 'comfort women' does not in the least reflect the</u>

suffering, such as multiple rapes on an everyday basis and severe physical abuse, that women victims had to endure during their forced prostitution and sexual subjugation and abuse in wartime. The Special Rapporteur, therefore, considers with conviction that the phrase "military sexual slaves" represents a much more accurate and appropriate terminology.

(Omitted)

II. HISTORICAL BACKGROUND

A. General

(Omitted)

B. Recruitment

(Omitted)

27. As already mentioned, this information is, however, abundant in the stories of former 'comfort women' and presents a reasonably clear picture. Three types of recruitment are identified: the recruitment of willing women and girls who were already prostitutes; the luring of women with the offer of well-paid work in restaurants or as cooks or cleaners for the army; and, finally, large-scale coercion and violent abduction of women in what amounts to slave raids in countries under Japanese control.

(Omitted)

C. Conditions in the comfort stations

(Omitted)

34. The station itself was usually a one- or two-story building, with a dining or reception area downstairs. The women's rooms were usually located at the back or upstairs, and tended to consist of cramped, narrow cubicles, often as little as 3 feet by 5, with room for only a bed. In such conditions 'comfort women' were expected to serve as many as 60 to 70 men per day. In some front-line locations, the women were forced to sleep on mattresses on the floor and were exposed to terrible conditions of cold and damp. The rooms were separated in many cases only by a tatami or rush mat which did not reach the floor, and so sound travelled easily from room to room.

35. A typical comfort station was supervised by a private operator and the women often taken care of by a Japanese or, in some cases, a Korean woman. Their health checks were carried out by an army doctor but, as many of the 'comfort women' recall, these regular checks were carried out to prevent the spread of venereal diseases; little notice was taken of the frequent cigarette burns, bruises, bayonet stabs and even broken bones inflicted on the women by soldiers. The women, moreover, had very little time off and the free time dictated in many of the existing regulations was often ignored by officers who wished to stay longer or visit at different times. On many days, the women barely had time to wash themselves before the next customer arrived.

(Omitted)

(Provided by Report of the Special Rapporteur on violence Against Women, Its Causes And Consequences, United Nations Digital Library)

The Japanese government did not accept the Coomaraswamy Report. In March 1996, the Japanese government submitted a 42-page government document criticizing the Coomaraswamy Report to the UN Commission on Human Rights, but withdrew it. Japan acknowledged the Kono Statement but criticized the appendix submitted with the UN Special Rapporteur's report as "irresponsible and inappropriate." On the basis of such criticism, the Japanese government argued that the Coomaraswamy Report quoted George Hicks' description of the historical background without verification, while adding a subjective interpretation. The Japanese document also claimed that the report quoted the testimony of Seiji Yoshida (吉田清治), which was somewhat controversial. It also argued that the Coomaraswamy Report accepted and generalized unconfirmed testimonies to deliberately exaggerate the brutality of the Japanese military, while ignoring the complex and difficult situation of the 'comfort women' issue. Regarding the allegation that the Japanese military 'comfort women' was a sexual slavery system, the Japanese government said, "It is very inappropriate to define the so-called 'wartime comfort women' system as that of 'sexual slavery' from a legal point of view."

Japan was the only country in the international community to criticize the Coomaraswamy Report. It is noteworthy that the report defined Japanese military 'comfort women' as military sex slaves and acknowledged the forced recruitment of the women.

Linda Chavez's successor, Gay McDougall, submitted a final

report entitled "Systematic Rape, Sexual Slavery and Slavery-like Practices during Armed Conflict" (hereafter the McDougall Report) in August 1998. The 62-page report included an appendix entitled "An Analysis of the Legal Liability of the Government of Japan for 'comfort women Stations' Established during the Second World War." The main points of the report are as follows:

> **Appendix**
> AN ANALYSIS OF THE LEGAL LIABILITY OF THE GOVERNMENT OF JAPAN FOR "COMFORT WOMEN STATIONS" ESTABLISHED DURING THE SECOND WORLD WAR
>
> **Introduction**
>
> 1. Between 1932 and the end of the Second World War, the Japanese Government and the Japanese Imperial Army forced over 200,000 women into sexual slavery in rape centres throughout Asia. These rape centres have often been referred to in objectionably euphemistic terms as "comfort stations." The majority of these 'comfort women'[34] were from Korea, but many were also taken from China, Indonesia, the Philippines and other Asian countries under Japanese control. Over the past decade, an increasing number of women survivors of these atrocities have come forward to seek redress for these crimes. The present appendix relies exclusively on the facts established in the Japanese Government's own

---

34 This term has obvious derogatory connotations and is used solely in its historical context as the term assigned to this particular atrocity. In many ways, the unfortunate choice of such a euphemistic term to describe the crime suggests the extent to which the international community as a whole, and the Government of Japan in particular, has sought to minimize the nature of the violations.

> review of the involvement of Japanese military officials in establishing, supervising and maintaining rape centres during the Second World War. Based on these admissions by the Japanese Government, the appendix then seeks to evaluate the Japanese Government's current legal liability for the enslavement and rape of women in "comfort stations" during the Second World War. Although numerous grounds for liability may exist, this report focuses specifically on liability for the most egregious international crimes of slavery, crimes against humanity and war crimes. The appendix also sets out the legal framework under international criminal law and examines claims that may be brought by survivors for compensation.
>
> (Provided by systematic rape, sexual slavery and slavery-like practices during armed conflict: final report/ submitted by Gay J. McDougall, Special Rapporteur)

The McDougall Report defined the issue of Japanese military 'comfort women,' involving wartime sexual violence, as a serious human rights violation against women. It called the comfort stations "rape centers." Furthermore, the Japanese military 'comfort women' issue was an obvious violation of international law, which called for compensation for the victims and punishment for those responsible. The Japanese military 'comfort women' issue was discussed in various United Nations human rights treaty bodies, including OHCHR (Office of the High Commissioner for Human Rights; UN Human Rights), CERD (Committee on the Elimination of Racial Discrimination), CESCR (Committee on Economic, Social and Cultural Rights), UNHRC (UN Human Rights Committee), and CAT (Committee against Torture), as well as the ILO (International Labor Organization) Committee of Experts. It urged the Japanese government to acknowledge the historical facts, officially apologize, compensate the victims, and educate future generations.

It took the courageous testimony of victims, international solidarity, and the efforts of civil society groups to bring the issue to a full discussion at the United Nations.

---

title

The State party should take immediate and effective legislative and administrative measures to ensure:

(a) That all allegations of sexual slavery or other human rights violations perpetrated by the Japanese military during wartime against the 'comfort women' are effectively, independently and impartially investigated and that perpetrators are prosecuted and, if found guilty, punished;
(b) Access to justice and full reparation to victims and their families;
(c) The disclosure of all available evidence;
(d) Education of students and the general public about the issue, including adequate reference s in textbooks;
(e) The expression of a public apology and official recognition of the responsibility of the State party;
(f) Condemnation of any attempts to defame victims or to deny the events.

[Provided by International Covenant on Civil and Political Rights (CCPR)/Human Rights Committee/Concluding observations on the sixth periodic report of Japan]

The issue of Japanese military 'comfort women' continues to be discussed at the United Nations for a very long time now. This is because the issue has not been resolved and the Japanese government has not been able to admit its role.

4-2
Japan's Denial and the Global Reaction

In Japan, the right wing denies that Japanese military 'comfort women' were forcibly mobilized and were sex slaves. They took out an advertisement in the *Washington Post* entitled "The Facts."

In March 2007, the advertisement was released in which the Abe government denied the Kono Statement. It sparked a response from the international community demanding an apology from the Japanese government and efforts to resolve the issue. The United States, the Netherlands, Canada, and the EU Parliament passed a resolution calling on the Japanese government to make efforts to resolve the issue.

The U.S. House of Representatives Resolution of July 30, 2007, stated, "Japanese public and private officials have recently expressed a desire to dilute or rescind the 1993 Statement by Chief Cabinet

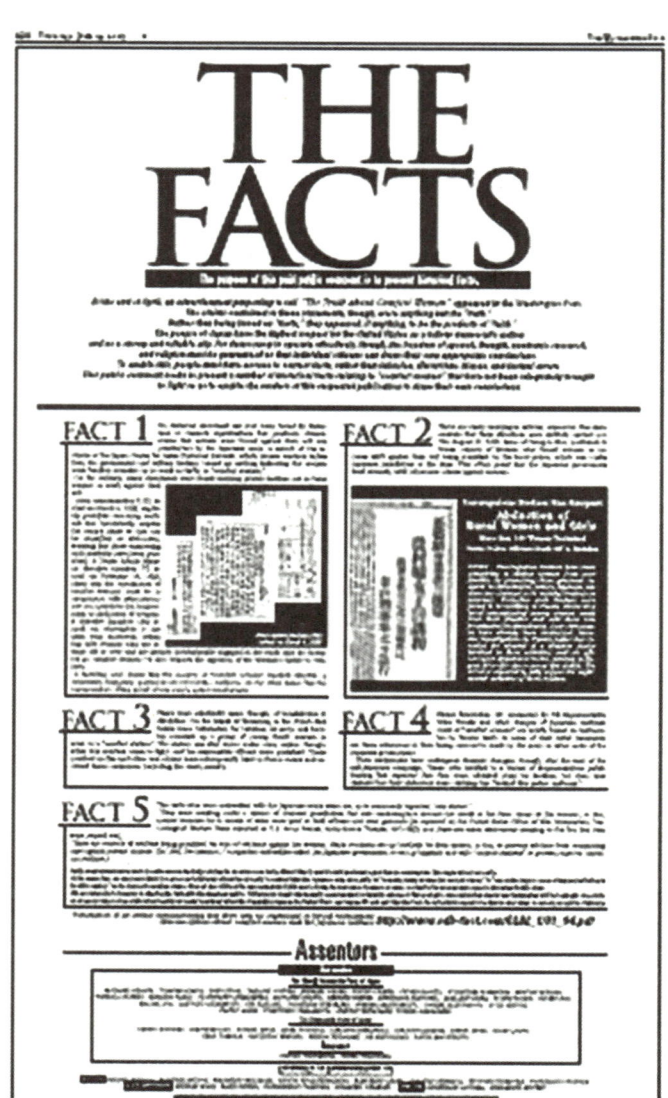

Chapter 4 How Did the Global Community Respond? 209

The Facts

1. No historical document has ever been found by historians or research organizations that positively demonstrates that women were forced against their will into prostitution by the Japanese army. (Omitted)

2. (Omitted) brokers who forced women to become ianfu against their will being punished by the local police, which was under Japanese jurisdiction at the time. (Omitted)

3. There were admittedly cases, though, of breakdowns in discipline. (Omitted) an army unit forcibly rounded up a group of young Dutch women to work at a "comfort station." The station was shut down under army orders, though, when this incident came to light, and the responsible officers were punished. (Omitted)

4. (Omitted) In none of their initial statements are there references to their being coerced to work by the army of other units of the Japanese government. Their testimonies have undergone dramatic changes, though, after the start of the anti-Japanese campaign. (Omitted).

5. The ianfu who were embedded with the Japanese army were not, as is commonly reported, "sex slaves." They were working under a system of licensed prostitution that was commonplace around the world at the time. Many of the women, in fact, earned incomes far in excess (Omitted), two-fifths of the approximately 20,000 ianfu during the war were Japanese women, (Omitted)

Secretary Yohei Kono on the 'comfort women,' which expressed the Government's sincere apologies and remorse for their ordeal." The Lower House of the Dutch Parliament Resolution of November 8, 2007, stated that "The Japanese government acknowledged through the 1993 Kono Statement that it sincerely recognizes the fate of the 'comfort women,' expressed regret for the victims, and took responsibility for it. However, as revealed by the statement made by Prime Minister Shinzo Abe in March and the advertisement placed in the *Washington Post* by Japanese parliament members earlier this year on the same subject, the Japanese government and members of the Japanese legislature have shown actions that are inconsistent with this." These resolutions, which were adopted by the legislatures of various countries, including the U.S. House of Representatives, calling for a resolution of the issue of the Japanese military 'comfort women,' were responses driven by concern over the attempts by the Japanese government and its right wing to revise the Kono Statement.

In the resolutions of various country's legislatures, there is a symbolic representation of the international community's recognition and direction for resolving the issue of Japanese military 'comfort women.' The essence lies in acknowledging historical facts, offering apologies, providing reparations to the victims, and educating future generations.

The following are key excerpts from the U.S. House Resolution 121, the Dutch House Resolution, and the EU Council Resolutions.

U.S. House Resolution 121 (July 30, 2007), reflecting the amendment offered by Representative Lantos of California and Representative Ros-Lehtinen of Florida

Whereas the Government of Japan, during its colonial and wartime occupation of Asia and the Pacific Islands from the 1930s through the duration of World War II, officially commissioned the acquisition of young women for the sole purpose of sexual servitude to its Imperial Armed Forces, who became known to the world as ianfu or 'comfort women';

Whereas the 'comfort women' system of forced military prostitution by the Government of Japan, considered unprecedented in its cruelty and magnitude, included gang rape, forced abortions, humiliation, and sexual violence resulting in mutilation, death, or eventual suicide in one of the largest cases of human trafficking in the 20th century;

Whereas some new textbooks used in Japanese schools seek to downplay the 'comfort women' tragedy and other Japanese war crimes during World War II;

Whereas Japanese public and private officials have recently expressed a desire to dilute or rescind the 1993 statement by Chief Cabinet Secretary Yohei Kono on the 'comfort women,' which expressed the Government's sincere apologies and remorse for their ordeal;

Whereas the Government of Japan did sign the 1921 International Convention for the Suppression of the Traffic in Women and Children and supported the 2000 United Nations Security Council Resolution 1325 on Women, Peace, and Security which recognized the unique impact on women of armed conflict;

Whereas the House of Representatives commends Japan's efforts to promote human security, human rights, democratic values, and rule of law, as well as for being a supporter of Security Council Resolution 1325;

Whereas the United States-Japan alliance is the cornerstone of United States security interests in Asia and the Pacific and is fundamental to regional stability and prosperity;

Whereas, despite the changes in the post-cold war strategic landscape, the United States-Japan alliance continues to be based on shared vital interests and values in the Asia-Pacific region, including the preservation and promotion of political and economic freedoms, support for human rights and democratic institutions, and the securing of prosperity for the people of both countries and the international community;

Whereas the House of Representatives commends those Japanese officials and private citizens whose hard work and compassion resulted in the establishment in 1995 of Japan's private Asian Women's Fund;

Whereas the Asian Women's Fund has raised $5,700,000 to extend "atonement" from the Japanese people to the 'comfort women'; and

Whereas the mandate of the Asian Women's Fund, a government-initiated and largely government-funded private foundation whose purpose was the carrying out of programs and projects with the aim of atonement for the maltreatment and suffering of the 'comfort women,' came to an end on March 31, 2007, and the Fund has been disbanded as of that date: Now, therefore, be it

Resolved, That it is the sense of the House of Representatives that the Government of Japan—

(1) should formally acknowledge, apologize, and accept historical responsibility in a clear and unequivocal manner for its Imperial Armed Forces' coercion of young women into sexual slavery, known to the world as 'comfort women,' during its colonial and wartime occupation of Asia and the Pacific Islands from the 1930s through the duration of World War II;
(2) would help to resolve recurring questions about the sincerity and status of prior statements if the Prime Minister of Japan were to make such an apology as a public statement in his official capacity;
(3) should clearly and publicly refute any claims that the sexual enslavement and trafficking of the 'comfort women' for the Japanese Imperial Armed Forces never occurred; and
(4) should educate current and future generations about this horrible crime while following the recommendations of the international community with respect to the 'comfort women.'

[Provided by H.Res.121 - 110th Congress (2007-2008)]

Dutch House of Representatives Resolution (November 8, 2007)

The Japanese government acknowledged the issue of 'comfort women' in the 1993 Kono Statement, expressing regret for the victims and promising accountability. However, in March of last year, then-Prime Minister Abe Shinzo withdrew the statement, and earlier this year, Japanese parliament members took out an advertisement in the Washington Post on the same issue. In this way, the Japanese government and the House of Representatives have not acted responsibly. The Dutch House of Representatives strongly urges the Japanese government not to distance itself from the Kono Statement and to take responsible action regarding the Japanese military forced prostitution system. The Japanese government should apologize directly to the surviving 'comfort women' for the suffering they endured and take additional measures, such as providing financial compensation. It also demands that the true history of the forcibly drafted 'comfort women' during World War II be included in school textbooks and taught to future generations.

EU Parliament Resolution (December 13, 2007)

The European Parliament,

1. Welcomes the excellent relationship between the European Union and Japan based on the mutually shared values of a multi-party democracy, the rule of law and respect for human rights;
2. Expresses its solidarity with the women who were victims of the 'comfort women' system for the duration of World War II;
3. Welcomes the statements by Japanese Chief Cabinet Secretary Yohei Kono in 1993 and by the then Prime Minister Tomiichi Murayama in 1995 on the 'comfort women,' as well as the resolutions of the Japanese parliament (the Diet) of 1995 and 2005 expressing apologies for wartime victims, including victims of the 'comfort women' system;
4. Welcomes the Japanese Government's initiative to establish, in 1995, the now-dissolved Asian Women's Fund, a largely government-funded private foundation, which distributed some "atonement money" to several hundred 'comfort women,' but considers that this humanitarian initiative cannot satisfy the victims" claims of legal recognition and reparation under public international law, as stated by the UN Special Rapporteur Gay McDougall in her above-mentioned report of 1998;
5. Calls on the Japanese Government formally to acknowledge, apologise, and accept historical and legal responsibility, in a clear and unequivocal manner, for its Imperial Armed Forces' coercion of young women into sexual slavery, known to the world as 'comfort women,' during its colonial and wartime occupation of Asia and the Pacific Islands from the 1930s until the end of World War II;
6. Calls on the Japanese Government to implement effective administrative mechanisms to provide reparations to all surviving victims

of the 'comfort women' system and the families of its deceased victims;

7. Calls on the Japanese parliament (the Diet) to take legal measures to remove existing obstacles to obtaining reparations before Japanese courts; in particular, the right of individuals to claim reparations from the government should be expressly recognised in national law, and cases for reparations for the survivors of sexual slavery, as a crime under international law, should be prioritised, taking into account the age of the survivors;

8. Calls on the government of Japan to refute publicly any claims that the subjugation and enslavement of 'comfort women' never occurred;

9. Encourages the Japanese people and government to take further steps to recognise the full history of their nation, as is the moral duty of all countries, and to foster awareness in Japan of its actions in the 1930s and 1940s, including in relation to 'comfort women'; calls on the government of Japan to educate current and future generations about those events;

10. Instructs its President to forward this resolution to the Council, the Commission, to the governments and parliaments of the Member States, the Japanese Government and Parliament, the UN Human Rights Council, the governments of the ASEAN States, to the governments of the Democratic People's Republic of Korea, the Republic of Korea, the People's Republic of China, Taiwan and Timor-Leste.

[Provided by European Parliament Resolution of 13 December 2007 on Justice for the 'Comfort Women' (sex slaves in Asia before and during World War II)]

Researchers from around the world, including those from Japan, affirmed that the 'comfort women' victims were indeed victims of the sexual slavery system, considering it a historical truth. In addition to the countries that have adopted the aforementioned resolutions, many nations worldwide oppose Japan's revisionist history movement.

The sexual violence against women in the former Yugoslavia and the Japanese military 'comfort women' system are fundamentally the same issue. In the Bosnian War, powerless women and children were continuously subjected to violence and rape. The International Criminal Tribunal for the former Yugoslavia (ICTY), established in 1993, was the first international criminal tribunal to classify rape as a form of torture and an inhumane crime that turns people into sexual slaves.

The arguments made by Prime Minister Abe and other Japanese government officials in the international community, such as "the Japanese military 'comfort women' were not sexual slaves" and "there was no forced mobilization," are the same as claiming that the countless cases of rape and violence inflicted on women during brutal wars were merely tactics to win a war.

The Japanese right wing and the book *Anti-Japanese Tribalism* argue that the 'comfort women' were not in a desperate state of confinement in the comfort stations, and that there are records showing that the women were allowed to go out. They even claim that records should not be selectively tailored to suit one's own preferences and try to downgrade the Japanese military 'comfort women' to mere prostitutes. However, it is not acceptable to obscure the nature of the Japanese military 'comfort women' system with only a few pieces of evidence. Rather, they are the ones who selectively tailor information to fit their own views. While everything that has happened is history, historians do not record everything. It is up to historians to decide which history to record. This process reflects the perceptions of reality.

The problem with the Japanese military 'comfort women' lies in the inherent violence of this system and the significant violation of women's rights. This is also the perception of the international community. Even if there were instances of 'comfort women' who did not personally feel that way, or cases where they saved money and went out, the fundamental issue of sexual slavery remains unchanged.

Even today, sexual violence against women in armed conflicts continues in various parts of the world. War is closely linked to the victimization of women. There are survivors who bear the scars of wartime 'comfort women' victimization. Their pain and suffering should not be downplayed on the pretext that not all victims suffered equally. Historical truth does not come from simply listing all the facts, but from articulating insights that penetrate the essence of history.

Epilogue:
Sharing and Remembering the Courage and Pain of the Victims

On Wednesday, January 8, 1992, a demonstration was held in front of the Japanese Embassy building in Korea. Since then, demonstrations with the same objective have taken place every successive Wednesday, reaching a total of 1,620 occurrences as of Wednesday, November 1, 2023. It is the longest-running single gathering in the world. It demands that the Japanese government acknowledge the forced mobilization of 'comfort women' and seeks an official apology and compensation.

On December 14, 2011, a peace monument known as the Statue of Peace was erected in front of the Japanese Embassy building to commemorate the 1,000th Wednesday Demonstraion in honor of the victims of the Japanese military 'comfort women.' The statue was created by the married couple of sculptors, Eun-sung Kim and Seo-

Wednesday Demonstraions for the Resolution of the Japanese Military Sexual Slavery Issue
(Provided by Yonhap News Agency)

kyung Kim, to urge the Japanese government to resolve the issue of the Japanese military 'comfort women.'

The Statue of Peace depicts a short-haired girl in traditional Korean dress, sitting and staring at the Japanese embassy. A bird is perched on her shoulder. According to the artists, her bobbed hair represents the separation from her parents and hometown. The bird on her shoulder serves as a link between the deceased victims and reality. The girl slightly lifts her bare feet with raised heels, and this bare foot symbolizes the wandering of the victims who could not find a settlement even after the war.

The international solidarity movement for the resolution of the

Epilogue: Sharing and Remembering the Courage and Pain of the Victims 221

The Statue of Peace in Michigan, USA (Provided by Yonhap News Agency)

Japanese military 'comfort women' issue is expanding as a global movement. On August 14, 2019, the 1,400th Wednesday Demonstraion was held simultaneously in 24 cities and 10 countries around the world. This was possible because of the global awareness that the atrocities inflicted on the 'Comfort Women' were wartime sexual violence that violated women's human rights.

The "Statue of Peace" has gained international recognition, extending its presence not only within Korea but also to countries such as the United States, Germany, and China. As of August 9, 2019, it has been installed in 124 locations in Korea and 9 locations overseas. Despite opposition from the Japanese government, the number of "Statues of Peace," modeled after victims from various countries, continues to grow. This is the result of the solidarity of global citizens who share the pain of the victims' heartbreaking history and express their anger.

However, the Japanese government has reacted hypersensitively to the "Statue of Peace." It argues that these statues ignore international practices, demanding their demolition. Using the term "comfort women Statue" instead of acknowledging the term "Statue of Peace," the Japanese government is pressing for the removal of the statues not only in South Korea, but also in other countries.

In the 2015 Agreement between Korea and Japan on the issue of 'Comfort Women,' the Japanese government strongly insisted on the relocation of the "Statue of Peace." When the "Statue of Peace" was erected in December 2016, standing prominently in front of the Japanese Consulate General building in Busan, the Japanese ambassador to Korea and the Consul General in Busan were recalled to Japan. From these events, we can see how sensitive the Japanese government is to the "Statue of Peace."

The Japanese government fails to acknowledge that the "Statue of Peace" serves as a tribute to and a remembrance of those who suffered

The "Statues of Peace" at Shanghai Normal University, a Girl from China and a Girl from Korea

during wartime. It aims to share the pain of the victims, restore their dignity and honor, and convey a spirit of peace, not to chant "anti-Japanese" sentiments.

Let us look at the Hiroshima National Peace Memorial Hall, which commemorates the victims of the atomic bombing of Japan. The memorial poignantly portrays the devastating effects of the atomic bomb, featuring images of individuals charred to an ashen black from the initial blast, people leaping into the river, and melted glass bottles. Visitors do not view this memorial as a symbol of anti-American sentiment. The United States, as the party responsible for dropping the bomb, has never complained about the memorial.

There is also a statute of girls in Okinawa, the southernmost part of Japan. The statue commemorates the Himeyuri students (ひめゆり学徒隊; Himeyuri Gakutotai; Lily Princesses Student Corps; Lily Corps), which were mobilized during the Battle of Okinawa. The statue of the girls represents female students of Himeyuri, and is located at the site of the former Okinawa Teacher Training College.

The missing female students from the classrooms are depicted sitting in the photographs at the Himeyuri Peace Museum. Their school was destroyed without a trace, but the names of the students remain at the museum. Through the Himeyuri statue of schoolgirls, Okinawa aims to recall the horrors of war and emphasize the importance of peace. The "Statue of Peace," which honors the victims of the Japanese military 'comfort women' conveys the same message.

As long as sexual violence against women continues in regions affected by wars and armed conflicts, the issue of the Japanese military 'comfort women' will not end. The issue is not limited to the old history between Korea and Japan. It pertains to the present and future of women's rights.

The "Statue of Peace" has an empty chair. This chair is reserved for all the victims who have died or whose suffering remains hidden. It is also a place for those who strive to ensure that tragedies like the Japanese military 'comfort women' never happen again.

The Japanese right wing portrays the issue of the Japanese military 'comfort women' as "anti-Japanese tribalism," labeling it as a symbol

Himeyuri Statue of Schoolgirls

of anti-Japanese sentiment. They are trying to change the international community's perception of the issue. However, the 'comfort women' issue is a matter of humanity. The issue of the Japanese military 'comfort women,' who were trampled upon by the imperialist military forces, holds a universal significance based on humanism.

I look forward to the day when the "Statue of Peace" will be erected in front of Tokyo Station in Japan, just as the Holocaust Memorial stands in the heart of Berlin to commemorate the Jewish genocide. I hope that this book will hasten the day when the "Statue of Peace" will be erected in Tokyo.

Chronology of the Japanese Military 'Comfort Women' Issue

Chronology of the Japanese Military 'Comfort Women' Issue

No.	Date	Korea	Japan	International Community
1	1990. 1.4~24	Chung-ok Yun, Professor of Ewha Womans University, launched the investigative series, "Report following the footsteps of Volunteer Labor Corps Victims" in the *Hankyoreh newspaper*.		
2	1990. 6.6		A director of the Ministry of Labor denied military involvement in 'comfort women' issue in the Budget Committee of the House of Councillors.	
3	1990. 7.10	The "Korean Women's Labor Corps Research Association" was launched.		
4	1990. 10.17	37 Korean women's organizations sent an open letter to the Korean and Japanese governments.		
5	1990. 11	37 Korean women's organizations established the "Korean Council for the Women Drafted for Military Sexual Slavery by Japan."		
6	1990. 12.10	The representative of the "Pacific War Victims' Families Association" requested for human rights remedy to the Japan Federation of Bar Association (JFBA).	The "Association to Clarify Post-war Responsibility of Japan" was established.	
7	1991. 1.8	The "Korean Council" issued a statement when Japanese Prime Minister Kaifu (海部) visited Korea.		
8	1991. 1.19		At the Kudanshita YWCA in Tokyo, the 'Association for the Remeberane of the Japanese Military Comfort Women' was founded.	
9	1991. 4.24~28		The legal team of the "Association to Clarify the Post-war Responsibility of Japan" visited Korea and conducted an investigation.	

Chronology of the Japanese Military's 'Comfort Women' Issue 229

No.	Date	Korea	Japan	International Community
10	1991. 5.28	The "Korean Council" requested an open letter and an official response from Japanese Prime Minister Kaifu.		
11	1991. 5.31 ~6.2		Women from South Korea, Japan, and North Korea held their first seminar on "Peace in Asia and Women's Role" in Tokyo and Kobe, and jointly demanded compensation.	
12	1991. 8.14	Hak-soon Kim, a victim of 'comfort women' system, made her first statement at a press conference in Seoul.		
13	1991. 8.17 ~20		The "Association to Clarify Postwar Responsibility of Japan" investigated victims in Korea.	
14	1991. 8.24		A citizens' group held a rally in Osaka demanding an investigation and compensation from the Japanese government for the 'comfort women' issue.	
15	1991. 8.27	Foreign Minister Sang-ok Lee emphasized that Korea will continue to carefully review and address the issue of Japanese military 'comfort women.'	Danino (谷野), director of the Foreign Ministry's Asia Bureau, stated at the Budget Committee of the House of Councillors that the issue of compensation for Japanese military 'comfort women' was resolved at the time of the 1965 Japan-Korea Agreement.	
16	1991. 11.6		The Women's Division of the Japan Socialist Party held a symposium titled "Japan's Postwar Responsibility and the Issue of Japanese Military 'comfort women.'"	
17	1991. 11.13		"Woori Network for the Japanese Military 'Comfort Women' Issue" was formed in Tokyo by the Korean women residing in Japan.	

No.	Date	Korea	Japan	International Community
18	1991.12.6		3 Korean former 'comfort women' with 32 other survivors, including former soldiers, filed a lawsuit at the Tokyo District Court.	
19	1991.12.7		Cabinet Secretary Kato (加藤) stated that Korean victims of 'comfort women' program would not be compensated.	
20	1991.12.8		The Japanese government conducted an investigation of 6 ministries and agencies for the possible existence of records related to the government's involvement in the 'comfort women' issue.	
21	1991.12.10	The Korean government, through the Japanese embassy in South Korea, demanded an apology from the Japanese government and a thorough investigation into the truth of historical issues.	The Japanese government stated that the issue of 'comfort women' and Japan are not related.	
22	1991.12.11	The "Korean Council" sent a letter of complaint to Kato (加藤), Chief Cabinet Secretary, through the Japanese Embassy, and decided to hold regular demonstrations in front of the Japanese Embassy.		
23	1991.12.16		25 female members of the Japan Socialist Party, including former chairman Doi (土井), submitted a petition to Minister Kato, demanding that the Japanese government apologize, conduct a thorough investigation, and provide compensation for the Korean victims of the 'comfort women' who were forcibly taken during World War II.	
24	1991.12.25		2 Korean former 'comfort women' and 2 victims of the 'Women's Labor Volunteer Corps' filed a lawsuit with the Shimonoseki Branch of the Yamaguchi District Court, demanding an official apology and compensation from Japan.	

No.	Date	Korea	Japan	International Community
25	1992. 1.8	The first Wednesday Demonstration was held in Seoul.	The Japanese consul in Korea, Kawashima (川島), stated that there was no evidence to prove the Japanese government's involvement in the issue of Japanese military 'comfort women.'	
26	1992. 1.10		Professor Yoshimi (吉見) of Chuo University released discovered documents related to the Japanese military 'comfort women' issue.	
27	1992. 1.11		Foreign Minister Watanabe (渡邊) stated on television, "Although there is no definitive proof, we cannot completely deny the involvement of the Japanese military in the 'comfort women' issue." This was Japan's first acknowledgement of the Japanese military's involvement.	
28	1992. 1.12		Chief Cabinet Secretary Kato stated that Prime Minister Miyazawa (宮沢沢) will explain the Japanese military's role in the mobilization of 'comfort women' during his visit to Korea.	
29	1992. 1.13		Chief Cabinet Secretary Kato stated at a press conference, "The Japanese government deeply reflects on and regrets the immeasurable pain and sorrow experienced by many in Korean Peninsula due to Japan's past actions. Whenever the opportunity arises, we want to sincerely apologize and express our remorse on behalf of the Japanese government to those who endured indescribable suffering as victims of the Japanese military 'comfort women' system."	
30	1992. 1.14	A hotline for reporting cases of Japanese military 'comfort women' victims was established, with the number 110.	13 organizations held a rally in Tokyo demanding an apology and compensation, and launched the "Network for Action on the Japanese Military 'Comfort Women' Issue."	

No.	Date	Korea	Japan	International Community
31	1992. 1.16	President Tae-woo Roh mentioned the 'comfort women' issue during his summit meeting with Prime Minister Miyazawa.	Chief Cabinet Secretary Kato revealed that the Japanese government was considering measures of government-level compensation for the Japanese military 'comfort women' issue.	
32	1992. 1.17		Prime Minister Miyazawa expressed the sentiment of apology and reflection at the Korea-Japan summit meeting.	
33	1992. 1.22	The "Korean Council" announced the filing of a complaint with the United Nations Human Rights Committee.		
34	1992. 2.15	Chang-ha Choi, a Korean pastor residing in Japan, visited the UN OHCHR in Geneva and submitted additional documents on the issue of Korean 'comfort women' during the Japanese military occupation.		
35	1992. 2.17		A lawyer, Totsuka (戸塚), stated at the UN HRC that the case of Japanese military 'comfort women' was a crime against humanity and urged the UN to intervene in the matter.	
36	1992. 2.21			The "Taipei Women's Rescue Foundation" opened an investigation hotline for the Japanese military 'comfort women' issue and received 9 inquiries. In Taiwan's Legislative Yuan, 43 lawmakers proposed compensation claims.
37	1992. 2.25	The Korean government opened the "Victim Centers" in each city and district office to receive case reports and conduct preliminary investigations.		
38	1992. 3.1	The Korean Christian Women's United (KCWU), along with 2 former 'comfort women,' held a memorial service for Ms. Bong-ki Bae in Toksashiki, Okinawa-ken..		

No.	Date	Korea	Japan	International Community
39	1992. 3.9		Watanabe (渡辺), Minister of Foreign Affairs, expressed willingness to address the issue of the Japanese military 'comfort women' during the Foreign Affairs Committee.	
40	1992. 3.13			Taiwan officially demanded apology and compensation, for Japanese military 'comfort women.'
41	1992. 3.16		Prime Minister Miyazawa stated at the Budget Committee of the House of Councillors that the issue of Japanese military 'comfort women' has been resolved at the national level, but the right to file individual lawsuits has not been extinguished.	
42	1992. 3.24		A citizens' group in Fukuoka-ken opened the "Japanese Military 'Comfort Women' Hotline 110" from the 24th to the 25th.	
43	1992. 4.26			Confirmation of the existence of the Japanese military comfort stations in the Philippines during the Pacific War.
44	1992. 4.13	6 Korean victims of 'comfort women' filed a lawsuit in Tokyo District Court.		
45	1992. 5.13			- The UN Human Rights Office's Working Group on Contemporary Forms of Slavery adopted a report requesting information on 'comfort women' to Secretary-General Ghali. - The Working Group on Contemporary Forms of Slavery of the UN Sub-committee on the Elimination of Discrimination requested the Secretary-General to share the information on Japanese military 'comfort women' with Special Rapporteur van Boven.

No.	Date	Korea	Japan	International Community
46	1992. 5.18	Hak-soon Kim and 5 Korean victims of 'comfort women' presented 5 demands, including the establishment of a historical archive, during a meeting with officials from the Japanese Prime Minister's Office.		
47	1992. 7.3	The Korean government confirmed 74 surviving Japanese military 'comfort women' in a survey conducted from February to June.		
48	1992. 7.6	The Korean government remarked, "We expect further factual investigation" regarding Japan's first investigation results on the Japanese military 'comfort women' issue.	- The Japanese government announced the results of its first investigation into the issue of Japanese military 'comfort women' from the Korean Peninsula, releasing 127 pieces of evidence. - Chief Cabinet Secretary Kato acknowledged the Japanese government's involvement and expressed apology and remorse at a press conference.	
49	1992. 7.7	The "Korean Council" issued a statement of protest against the results of the Japanese government's investigation.		
50	1992. 7.9			China's Ministry of Foreign Affairs said it "hopes for a serious and respectful handling."
51	1992. 7.10	Korean government considered independent action.		
52	1992. 7.11		Abe (阿部), president of the JFBA expressed dissatisfaction with the Japanese government's investigation into the 'comfort women' issue, and called for a thorough investigation.	
53	1992. 7.13			The Indonesian government welcomed the Japanese government's response.
54	1992. 7.16			A survivor of Japanese military 'comfort women' in Indonesia gave testimony.

Chronology of the Japanese Military's 'Comfort Women' Issue   235

No.	Date	Korea	Japan	International Community
55	1992. 7.21			The Dutch Ministry of Justice and Security announced the fact that the Dutch Temporary Courts Martial in Batavia had issued guilty verdicts against Japanese military officials involved in the Japanese military 'comfort women' program.
56	1992. 7.31	The Korean government released the "Interim Report on the Investigation of the Status of Military 'Comfort Women' Under the Japanese Colonial Rule," asserting the "existence of forced mobilization," and demanding a "sincere investigation by Japan."		
57	1992. 8			The issue of Japanese military 'comfort women' was raised at the UN Sub-commission on the Prevention of Discrimination and Protection of Minorities.
58	1992. 8.7			Chinese victims of the Japanese military 'comfort women' system delivered a petition to the Japanese Embassy in Beijing, demanding an apology and compensation from the Japanese government.
59	1992. 8.10 ~11	- The Asian Solidarity Conference on the Issue of Military Sexual Slavery by Japan was held in Seoul, with participants from Korea, Japan, Taiwan, and the Philippines. - They confirmed a collective action to demand an apology and compensation.		
60	1992. 8.13 ~14	The 'Investigation Team on Forced Mobilization in Korea" conducted fact-finding missions and held symposiums in Pyongyang and Japan.		The UN Sub-committee on the Elimination of Discrimination adopted a resolution similar to the one on the "Contemporary Form of Slavery" in May.

No.	Date	Korea	Japan	International Community
61	1992. 8.14			- The UN Human Rights Council adopted a resolution to collect information on the issue of Japanese military 'comfort women.' - The "Taipei Women's Rescue Foundation" presented testimonies of Japanese military 'comfort women.'
62	1992. 8.2		369 victims of the Japanese invasion, including 'comfort women' filed a lawsuit for compensation at the Tokyo District Court.	
63	1992. 9.18			Maria Rosa Henson gave her first testimony in the Philippines.
64	1992. 10.5			Maria Rosa Henson sent a letter to the Prime Minister entitled "Include in Textbooks."
65	1992. 10.10			A new former Japanese military 'comfort woman' testified for the second time in the Philippines.
66	1992. 10.16	The president of the "Korean Council" said during her visit to Tokyo that she "opposes measures in lieu of compensation."		
67	1992. 10.22			22 Japanese military 'comfort women' have been identified in the Philippines.
68	1992. 10.23	The Korean Foreign Minister stated in parliament, "We are considering livelihood assistance."		
69	1992. 10.24		At its annual meeting, the Kyushu Bar Association adopted a statement demanding full compensation from the Japanese government for Korean victims of forced labor.	
70	1992. 12		- The scope of the government's investigations was expanded to include the National Diet Library, and official documents from the U.S. National Archives were examined. - The government initiated interviews with former soldiers and former comfort station operators.	

No.	Date	Korea	Japan	International Community
71	1992.12.7	A commemorative rally was held on the first anniversary of the lawsuit, with testimonial gatherings from various regions across the country.		
72	1992.12.8			- Chinese victims of the Japanese military 'comfort women' system testified. - Former Japanese military 'comfort women' testified in Australia and the Netherlands.
73	1992.12.9		An international public hearing on Japan's post-war compensation was held in Tokyo, attended by victims from South Korea, North Korea, the Netherlands, the Philippines, and China.	
74	1992.12.25		Korean victims of the Japanese military 'comfort women' filed a lawsuit with the Shimonoseki Branch of the Yamaguchi District Court, demanding compensation and an apology from the Japanese government.	
75	1993.1.23	.	The "Group Supporting the Comfort Women Trial for Koreans Living in Japan" was established.	
76	1993.1.18			During the 49th session of the UN Human Rights Council, the Korean government called for a thorough investigation into the issue of Japanese military 'comfort women' during World War II and demanded adequate compensation from the Japanese government.
77	1993.2			- The issue of Japanese military 'comfort women' was raised at the UN Commission on Human Rights. - A signature-collecting campaign demanding compensation was conducted on the U.S. West Coast.

No.	Date	Korea	Japan	International Community
78	1993. 3.2			The "Group for the Support of Filipino Victims of the Japanese Military 'Comfort Woman' System" was formed.
79	1993. 3.5	A Korean former Japanese military 'comfort woman,' Shin-do Song(□□□), filed a lawsuit with the Tokyo District Court.		
80	1993. 3.13	According to media reports, President Young-sam Kim stated during a meeting with his chief presidential secretaries, "It is important to uncover the truth without demanding material compensation from Japan. Compensation for the victims of Japanese military 'comfort women' will be provided from the Korean government budget starting next year."		
81	1993. 3.17			In the Netherlands, materials proving the forced mobilization of the Japanese military 'comfort women' were presented.
82	1993. 3.23		The Japan Federation of Bar Association (JFBA) initiated investigations into war victims in various parts of Asia.	
83	1993. 3.27	The Korean government announced a policy to provide the following measures: - One-time grant of KRW 5 million for basic living expenses - Monthly support of KRW 150,000. - Provision of welfare. - Permanent rental of public housing.		
84	1993. 4.2			- 18 Filipino victims of the Japanese military 'comfort women' system filed a lawsuit with the Tokyo District Court. - In Malaysia, 2 people testified that they were Japanese military 'comfort women.'

Chronology of the Japanese Military's 'Comfort Women' Issue 239

No.	Date	Korea	Japan	International Community
85	1993. 4.6		Danba (丹波), director of the Treaties Bureau, indirectly stated at the Foreign Affairs Committee of the House of Councillors that the Japanese military 'comfort women' issue did not violate Article 29 of the International Labour Organization (ILO) Regulations on Economic Coercion.	
86	1993. 4.21		The "Center for Research and Documentation on Japan's War Responsibility" was established.	
87	1993. 4.24			The International Commission of Jurists (ICJ) began investigating the issue of Japanese military 'comfort women.'
88	1993. 5			The UN Working Group on Contemporary Forms of Slavery raised the Japanese military 'comfort women' issue: the Japanese government argued that all claims had been resolved through bilateral agreements.
89	1993. 5.14		The JWRC asked the Japanese government to establish an investigation committee.	
90	1993. 5.15			A victim of the Japanese military 'comfort women' system gave testimony at the UN Commission on Human Rights Council in Vienna.
91	1993. 5.18	The Korean National Assembly passed the Livelihood Stabilization Support Bill for the Japanese military 'comfort women.'		
92	1993. 5.25			The ICJ submitted an interim report on the issue of Japanese military 'comfort women' to the UN Human Rights Council.

No.	Date	Korea	Japan	International Community
93	1993. 6.30	President Young-sam Kim said in a meeting with Japanese Minister for Foreign Affairs, Muto (武藤), "Regarding the 'comfort women' issue, we are not seeking compensation from Japan, but we need to clarify the truth."		
94	1993. 7.24 ~26		The Japanese government listened to the testimonies of the 'comfort women' victims in Korea.	
95	1993. 8			The issue of Japanese military 'comfort women' was discussed at the UN Sub-commission on the Prevention of Discrimination and Protection of Minorities.
96	1993. 8.4	The "Korean Council" criticized the statement by Chief Cabinet Secretary Kono as lacking clear enforceability.	- The Japanese government announced the results of the second investigation into the so-called 'comfort women' issue (statement by Chief Cabinet Secretary Kono). - It acknowledged the coercive nature of the recruitment of 'comfort women' and the involvement of the Japanese government and military.	
97	1993. 8.20			28 Filipino victims of the Japanese military 'comfort women' system filed a lawsuit with the Tokyo District Court.
98	1993. 8.25			The UN Sub-commission on Prevention of Discrimination and Protection of Minorities entrusted Linda Chavez as Special Rapporteur on Systematic Rape, Sexual Slavery, and Slavery-like Practices during Wartime.
99	1993. 8.31	The Ministry of Health and Welfare confirmed support for 121 victims of the Japanese military 'comfort women' and announced detailed support measures.		

Chronology of the Japanese Military's 'Comfort Women' Issue 241

No.	Date	Korea	Japan	International Community
100	1993.9	The Korean government initiated livelihood support for the victims of the Japanese military 'comfort women' system.	The JFBA released a report on investigations into wartime atrocities, including the Japanese military 'comfort women' system, in Asia and overseas.	
101	1993.9.9		Chief Cabinet Secretary Takemura (竹村) told the House of Representatives that the issue of compensation for the Japanese military 'comfort women' had been resolved, but following Prime Minister Kono's statement, the government intended to explore responses beyond compensation.	
102	1993.10.18	Received the list of prisoners of war from the Japanese Ministry of Health, Labor and Welfare (including records with the term 'comfort women' in the Occupation column).		
103	1993.10.25		Doi (土井), the speaker of Japan's House of Representatives, received an investigation report on the Japanese military 'comfort women' from the "Taipei Women's Rescue Fund."	
104	1993.10.28		At the 1st Sub-committee during the 36th Human Rights Conference, the JFBA discussed the issue of post-war compensation.	The Commission on Human Rights (CHR) in Geneva mentioned Japan's discrimination and human rights issues, focusing on post-war compensations, including the Japanese military 'comfort women,' as a topic of deliberation.
105	1993.11.3			24 U.S. lawmakers sent a letter to Prime Minister Hosokawa (細川), urging an investigation into the lawsuit filing related to the issue of Japanese military 'comfort women.'
106	1993.11.7		Numata (沼田), Deputy Minister of the Japanese Ministry of Foreign Affairs, announced the policy of teaching children about the Japanese military 'comfort women' issue in all textbooks starting in 1994.	

No.	Date	Korea	Japan	International Community
107	1994. 1.25			8 Dutch war victims, including one related to the Japanese military 'comfort women,' filed a lawsuit against the Japanese government with the Tokyo District Court.
108	1994. 2.7	The "Korean Council" and 27 former 'comfort women' filed a complaint with the Tokyo Public Prosecutors' Office demanding the punishment of those responsible. (The office declined to prosecute.)		
109	1994. 3.5			- The UNCHR adopted a resolution addressing the punishment of those responsible for the forced mobilization of the Japanese military 'comfort women.' - The resolution discussed the issue focusing on the punishment of those accountable.
110	1994. 4			The UNCHR appointed Radhika Coomaraswamy as the Special Rapporteur on Violence against Women (including the issue of the Japanese military 'comfort women').
111	1994. 5.24	The Japanese military 'comfort women' victims' support group visited Japan to demand compensation.		
112	1994. 6.6		- A 'Citizens's Rally for Post-war Compensation' was held in Tokyo, with former 'comfort women' from South Korea, the Philippines, and Japan. - The leader of the Japan Socialist Party, Murayama, and Hatoyama, a member of the New Party Sakigake, also attended.	
113	1994. 6.7	Korean former 'comfort women' protested in front of the Japanese National Diet.		

No.	Date	Korea	Japan	International Community
114	1994. 7.18	The "Pacific War Victims' Families Association," "KAISA-KA (women's group for Philippino Japanese military 'comfort women')," and "Group Supporting for Comfort Women Trial for Koreans Living in Japan" demanded the complete withdrawal of the Japanese government's proposal for the Asia Exchange Center and Fund.		
115	1994. 7.22	The "Korean Council" criticized Japan's proposal for a fund.		
116	1994. 8.15			A group that promotes successful international arbitration trials to ensure compensation for individuals
117	1994. 8.19		The Japanese government announced that it was considering providing compensation money for Japanese military 'comfort women' from private donations.	The UNCHR appointed two Special Rapporteurs to investigate the mobilization of Japanese military 'comfort women' during World War II. This was the first official investigation by a UN body into the issue of Japanese military 'comfort women.'
118	1994. 8.22			KAISA-KA criticized the Japanese government's proposal to raise funds.
119	1994. 8.31		Prime Minister Murayama, in a speech commemorating the 50th anniversary of the end of World War II, stated, "I would like to explore the path of broad national participation together regarding the issue of Japanese military 'comfort women.'"	
120	1994. 11			The International Commission of Jurists (ICJ) recognized the criminal nature of the 'comfort women' system.
121	1994. 11.9		Established a committee of experts to review the establishment of the "Japan Center for Asian Historical Records" as an advisory body to the Chief Cabinet Secretary.	

No.	Date	Korea	Japan	International Community
122	1994. 11.22	The "Korean Council" proposed to the Japanese government to accept the international arbitration.		- The ICJ's final report stated that the Japanese government had a legal obligation to provide compensation, with a provisional offer of $40,000 per victim. - Special Rapporteur Coomaraswamy submitted a preliminary report on the 'comfort women' issue.
123	1994. 11.24	Korean victims of the Japanese military 'comfort women' system launched a hunger strike protest in front of the Japanese National Diet.		
124	1994. 12.7		The Sub-committee to Address the Wartime 'Comfort Women' Issue of the Japanese ruling party's "Project Team to Deal with Issues on the Fiftieth Years After the War" released its first report on the issue of Japanese military 'comfort women.'	
125	1994. 12.9	Korean victims of the Japanese military 'comfort women' system issued a statement opposing the agreement reached by the Japan's ruling party and ended their hunger strike protest.		
126	1994. 12.12	Cardinal Stephen Sou-hwan Kim sent a letter to Prime Minister Murayama demanding clarification of the truth, compensation, and an apology.		
127	1994. 1.10			UNCHR announced plans to send a team to Japan and Korea in April to examine the issue of Japanese military 'comfort women.'
128	1995. 1.24		The JFBA recommended that the Japanese government apologize and provide compensation through legislation.	

Chronology of the Japanese Military's 'Comfort Women' Issue   245

No.	Date	Korea	Japan	International Community
129	1995. 3		Chapter 8 of the JFBA Report to the 9th UN Commission on Crime Prevention and Criminal Justice, related to the elimination of violence against women, described the 'comfort women' as one of the issues facing Japan in terms of violence against women. It also mentioned early reparations to the victims and legal responsibility as an urgent task with the 50th anniversary of the end of World War II.	The UN Commission on the Status of Women NGO Workshop adopted a resolution in support of women who were victims of the 'comfort women' system.
130	1995. 3.1	The "Pacific War Victims' Families Association" criticized the Japanese government's fundraising plan.		
131	1995. 3.2	The "Korean Council" organized a protest rally against the Japanese government's fundraising plan.	A lawyers' group presented a draft of the 'Foreign Victims' Compensation Act.'	
132	1995. 3.8			The UNHRC adopted a resolution based on Coomaraswamy's provisional report on "Violence Against Women."
133	1995. 3.17		Civic groups held the 3/17 rally to oppose the deceptive private fundraising scheme.	
134	1995. 3.20	The "Korean Federation of Korean Trade Unions" filed a complaint with the ILO against the Japanese government for violating international conventions prohibiting forced labor in relation to the Japanese military 'comfort women' issue.		
135	1995. 4.28			The Working Group on the Contemporary Form of Slavery of the UN Sub-committee on the Elimination of Discrimination, adopted a report that partially mentioned the Japanese military 'comfort women' issue.

No.	Date	Korea	Japan	International Community
136	1995. 5.19		The Asian Women's Fund (the full title is the National Fund for Asian Peace and Women) was established.	
137	1995. 5.22			Linda Chavez met with government officials in the Philippines regarding the Japanese military 'comfort women' issue.
138	1995. 5.23			UNHRC Special Rapporteur Linda Chavez visited Korea to investigate the issue of Japanese military 'comfort women' as an international concern.
139	1995. 5.27 ~5.31			Linda Chavez made a private visit to Japan at the invitation of Japanese lawyers.
140	1995. 6.9		At the plenary session of the Japanese House of Representatives, a resolution was passed to reaffirm efforts for "Peace through History as a Lesson."	
141	1995. 6.14		- Chief Cabinet Secretary Iigurashi (五十嵐) announced the projects of the Asian Women's Fund, including medical/welfare assistance and restoration of women's honor and dignity, financed by private donations and government funds. - The Japanese government announced its plan to establish a private fund with contributions from Japanese civilians to provide cash compensation to victims of the Japanese military 'comfort women' system.	
142	1995. 6.15		- Civic groups issued a statement of protest against Iigurashi's announcement. -Yoshikazu Sakamoto (坂本義和) and others proposed to Prime Minister Murayama to apologize and provide compensation regarding the 'comfort women' issue. - The Osaka Fu Special English Teachers' Union (OFSET) filed a complaint with the ILO against the Japanese government for violating the prohibition of forced labor.	

No.	Date	Korea	Japan	International Community
143	1995. 6.19		The National Fund for Asian Peace and Women was launched.	
144	1995. 6.22 ~6.27			Coomaraswamy, the Special Rapporteur, officially visited Japan for investigating the Japanese military 'comfort women' issue.
145	1995. 7.26		Chief Cabinet Secretary Iigurashi explained to Special Rapporteur Coomaraswamy about the establishment of a fund during their meeting.	
146	1995. 8.3			The UN Sub-committee on the Elimination of Discrimination welcomed Linda Chavez's "Report on Systematic Rape in Wartime" and appointed her as a Special Rapporteur.
147	1995. 8.7			15 Chinese war victims, including 5 victims of the Japanese military 'comfort women' system, filed a lawsuit with the Tokyo District Court.
148	1995. 8.11		The Japanese government made a cabinet decision to provide the cooperation necessary for the implementation of the National Fund.	
149	1995. 8.15		- Prime Minister Murayama delivered a statement on the 50th anniversary of the end of World War II. - Prime Minister Murayama attended a citizens' rally, met with war victims, including former Korean 'comfort women,' and conveyed a message of apology. - Commenced fundraising for the National Fund. - Launched the "National Fund for Postwar Compensation."	

No.	Date	Korea	Japan	International Community
150	1995. 8.18			- The UNHRC adopted a resolution urging the Japanese government to take direct action to resolve the issue of 'Comfort Women.' - The UN Sub-committee on the Elimination of Discrimination adopted a resolution similar to the report of the UN Working Group on Contemporary Forms of Slavery.
151	1995. 8.30			- The NGO Forum on Women was held in Beijing. - The "Korean Council" participated.
152	1995. 9			The 4th World Conference on Women adopted a resolution in support of the victims of the Japanese military 'comfort women'system.
153	1995. 9.4	A joint symposium on "Wartime Violence against Women," organized by the "Korean Council" and various organizations related to the Japanese military 'comfort women' from Japan, the Philippines, and North Korea, issued a joint statement. It expressed opposition to the establishment of private funds, called for the clarification of the truth, and demanded compensation for the victims.		
154	1995. 9.14			During the government-to-government meetings at the World Conference on Women in Beijing, the issue of the Japanese military 'comfort women'emerged as a major concern, and the Japanese government delegation remained silent on the matter.
155	1995. 11.16		The chairman of the group demanding compensation from the Japanese government at the JFBA released a statement.	

Chronology of the Japanese Military's 'Comfort Women' Issue   249

No.	Date	Korea	Japan	International Community
156	1996.1			The Coomaraswamy report was submitted to the UNHRC.
157	1996.2.6		Chief Cabinet Secretary Kajiyama (梶山) mentioned that there was no legal basis for accepting the UN report, expressing the government's position that it could not provide national compensation.	The UNHRC released the report of Coomaraswamy, the Special Rapporteur on Violence against Women, on the issue of the Japanese military 'Comfort Women.'
158	1996.2.16		Prime Minister Hashimoto (橋本) spoke in the Budget Committee of the House of Councillors that there was no room for the Japanese government to accept the Coomaraswamy Report.	
159	1996.2.18	The Republic of Korea opens the Pacific War Victims Resource Center.		
160	1996.3.1			The ILO Committee of Experts on the Application of Conventions and Recommendations (hereinafter referred to as the Committee of Experts) submitted an opinion stating that the Japanese military 'comfort women' system during World War II constituted a violation of the ILO conventions prohibiting forced labor. The Committee urged the Japanese government to take prompt action to address the issue.
161	1996.3.4			- The ILO Committee of Experts expressed the opinion that "if the OFSET's appeal is upheld, they would be entitled to receive wages and other benefits." - A member of Taiwan's Legislative Council submitted a petition to the Prime Minister of Japan, the Speaker of the House of Representatives, and the President of the House of Councillors for compensation for the 'comfort women' of the Japanese military.

No.	Date	Korea	Japan	International Community
162	1996. 3.29			The 4th Asian Women's Solidarity Conference, adopted a resolution urging the establishment of an international tribunal to address crimes related to the Japanese military 'comfort women' issue.
163	1996. 4			The UNHRC adopted a compromised resolution "considering" the contents of the Coomaraswamy Report.
164	1996. 4.9			The establishment of an "International Coalition Supporting Recommendations Against Funding" is announced in Geneva.
165	1996. 4.10	Joon-young Sun, the Korean ambassador to Geneva, urged the Japanese government to accept the recommendations of the UN Special Rapporteur, who called for the implementation of national compensation for the victims of Japanese military 'comfort women' system during the UNHRC session.		The UNHRC, during its deliberations on "Violence against Women," stated, "The South Korean government urged the Japanese government to take the necessary steps immediately and independently to implement the recommendations of the Coomaraswamy Report." China, the Philippines, and North Korea also made statements as Member States.
166	1996. 4.11		During the UNHRC, Chief Cabinet Secretary Kajiyama (梶山) accepted Korea's report to demand compensation for the Japanese military 'comfort women,' but clarified that there would be no individual compensation.	
167	1996. 4.18			Civic organizations from South Korea, North Korea, Japan, the Philippines, Taiwan, and other countries jointly declared their refusal to accept the National Fund.
168	1996. 4.19			The UNHRC adopted a resolution on the elimination of violence against women, but limited its focus to the entirety of the Coomaraswamy Report.

Chronology of the Japanese Military's 'Comfort Women' Issue 251

No.	Date	Korea	Japan	International Community
169	1996. 4.20		137 Japanese intellectuals, including university professors, writers, and journalists, released a statement in connection with the UNHRC resolution. They called on the Japanese government to immediately accept the recommendations of the UN Special Rapporteur, including recognizing the legal responsibility for the 'comfort women' and implementing national compensation.	
170	1996. 5.12		It was revealed that since 1997, Japanese middle school textbooks have included descriptions related to the issue of the Japanese military 'Comfort Women.'	
171	1996. 5.13		Prime Minister Hashimoto made the final decision to send a "letter of apology" to the Japanese military 'Comfort Women.' He also asked for the business community's cooperation in establishing a fund for the 'Comfort Women.'	
172	1996. 6.4		116 members of the LDP formed the "Bright Japan Parliamentarians' Association" headed by former Minister of Justice Okuno (奥野), and criticized the descriptions in the textbooks.	
173	1996. 6.20	191 members of the Korean National Assembly issued a statement demanding that "the Japanese government must provide compensation."		
174	1996. 6.23	During the foreign ministers' meeting between Korea and Japan, the Korean side demanded individual compensation for the 'Comfort Women' issue.	Prime Minister Hashimoto met with President Young-sam Kim on Jeju Island. He expressed "apology and reflection" over the 'Comfort Women' issue during a press conference.	

No.	Date	Korea	Japan	International Community
175	1996. 6.26			The Working Group on Contemporary Forms of Slavery of the UN Subcommittee on the Elimination of Discrimination adopted a report focusing on information about the Japanese government's stance on the 'Comfort Women' issue.
176	1996. 7.19		The National Fund decided to provide a one-time payment of two million yen to each victim of the Japanese military 'comfort women' system from South Korea, the Philippines, and Taiwan, as well as a government-funded welfare support program of 700 million yen.	
177	1996. 8			The UN Human Rights Sub-committee urged the Japanese government to cooperate fully in resolving the issue of wartime sexual slavery.
178	1996. 8.23			The UN Sub-committee on the Elimination of Discrimination adopted a new resolution stating, "We welcome the useful information on the Japanese government's handling of the issue," referring to the report of the Working Group on Contemporary Forms of Slavery.
179	1996. 8.24			The UN Human Rights Sub-committee adopted a resolution for the expeditious establishment of an administrative tribunal.
180	1996. 10.18	The "Citizens' Coalition for the Proper Resolution of the Japanese military 'comfort omen' Issue" was formed, and fundraising activities began in Korea.		
181	1996. 12.11			Taiwanese lawmakers visiting Japan urged the government to legislate national compensation.
182	1997. 1.15		The National Fund reached an agreement on a welfare support program in the Philippines.	

No.	Date	Korea	Japan	International Community
183	1997. 1.24		Prime Minister Hashimoto, said at a press conference after the Korea-Japan summit, "There is no issue that has hurt women's honor and dignity as much as the Japanese military 'comfort women' program. The 'National Fund for Asian Peace and Women' represents the hearts of the Japanese government and the Japanese people, and we hope for the understanding of the South Korean people."	
184	1997. 1.28		The "National Fund for Asian Peace and Women" paid 2 million yen to seven former Korean 'comfort women.'	
185	1997. 5.22		A group of young lawmakers within the LDP, known as the "Association of Young Lawmakers Thinking about Japan's Future and History Education," announced their intention to formally request the government to remove descriptions related to the Japanese military 'comfort women' from textbooks and other educational materials	
186	1997. 6.15	The existence of Hoon, a surviving 'comfort woman' victim in Cambodia, became known to the world.		
187	1997. 7.25			A resolution urging the Japanese government to establish appropriate compensation measures for victims of war crimes was submitted to the U.S. House of Representatives for consideration.
188	1997. 8.5	Hoon returned home.		
189	1997. 8.8			In the UN Human Rights Sub-committee, both government representatives and representatives from NGOs criticized the Japanese National Fund.

No.	Date	Korea	Japan	International Community
190	1997. 8.18	The Korean government and civil society representatives at the UN Human Rights Sub-committee criticized the Japanese government's use of private funds to compensate the victims.		
191	1997. 8.26			The UN Human Rights Sub-committee called for cooperation with relevant UN bodies and organizations on the issue of the Japanese military 'comfort women.'
192	1997. 12.16	Hak-soon Kim, the first 'comfort woman' survivor to come forward passed away.		
193	1998. 1.6		The Japanese National Fund placed advertisements in four Korean newspapers, including *Hankyoreh*, to solicit applications.	
194	1998. 3.28	The government announced plans to provide KRW 4.88 billion in financial assistance to victims of the Japanese military 'comfort women' program.		
195	1998. 4.6			- Special Rapporteur Coomaraswamy, who investigated "violence against women," including the Japanese military 'comfort women,' completed a four-year investigation and submitted a final report. - The report extensively discussed the issue of Japanese military 'comfort women' in the first section on "Violence against Women in Armed Conflict," noting that the Japanese government had not acknowledged its legal responsibility. It was also mentioned that the compensation lawsuits filed by the former 'comfort women' were being closely monitored.

No.	Date	Korea	Japan	International Community
196	1998. 4.14	The spending bill related to the 'comfort women' issue was passed. The Ministry of Foreign Affairs and Trade stated, "The South Korean government will not demand compensation from the Japanese government for individual victims. However, Japan should sincerely reflect on and apologize for its past inhumane actions."		
197	1998. 4.21	- The "Korean Council" welcomed the decision to provide support funds to surviving 'comfort women' victims, but expressed "great regret" that the Japanese government was not asked to provide compensation. - The "Korean Council" also argued that the Korean government should urge Japan to comply with the recommendations of the UNHRC, including clarification of the truth, compensation, and punishment of those responsible. - During a meeting of the State Council, it was decided to provide financial assistance of KRW 4.91 billion to 155 'comfort women' survivors.	The Ministry of Foreign Affairs spokesperson emphasized that the Korean government's decision to provide financial assistance to survivors of the 'comfort women' program was not intended to oppose the activities of the "National Fund for Asian Peace and Women."	
198	1998. 4.27		The Yamaguchi District Court issued the first trial ruling in the lawsuit filed by the former Japanese military 'comfort women' and victims of the Women's Labor Volunteer Corps against the Japanese government. The court clearly recognized the Japanese government's responsibility for compensation in this matter and ordered the government to pay 300,000 yen to each of the three plaintiffs. The claim of the plaintiff of the Women's Labor Volunteer Corps was dismissed.	

No.	Date	Korea	Japan	International Community
199	1998.5.1		Minister of Justice Shimoinaba (下稲葉) appealed to the Hiroshima High Court against the verdict in the 'comfort women' case. The plaintiff of the Women's Labor Volunteer Corps, who received a dismissal verdict, also filed an appeal.	
200	1998.6.11		Hara (原), the president of the National Fund sent a letter to President Dae-jung Kim of South Korea, expressing regret that 7 former 'comfort women' who had received assistance from the Fund and a letter from the Japanese Prime Minister were being criticised in Korea. He asked the Korean government to respect the wishes of the individuals, and provide the governmental compensation regardless of whether they received assistance from the National Fund.	
201	1998.8.13			The McDougall Report, submitted to the Geneva Committee on Human Rights, defined the operation of the Japanese military comfort stations as a system of slavery, wartime sexual crimes, and crimes against humanity. The report emphasized the unlimited responsibility of the Japanese government in this regard.
202	1998.9.17		Ueda (上田), the head of the International Cooperation Division at the Ministry of Foreign Affairs, clarified the Japanese government's position that the resolution adopted by the UN Human Rights Sub-committee on the McDougall Report did not officially recommend any action against Japan.	

No.	Date	Korea	Japan	International Community
203	1999. 3.6	Ministry of Foreign Affairs officials announced their intention to explore ways to address the 'comfort women' issue from the perspective of women's rights and ethics if it becomes a contentious issue at the UNHRC.		
204	1999. 4.16			International NGOs criticized the Japanese government's handling of the 'comfort women' issue during the UN Human Rights Council session held in Geneva, Switzerland.
205	1999. 8.16			During the Human Rights and Protection Sub-committee at the United Nations Headquarters in New York, the representatives of Asian women's organizations and governments strongly condemned the fact that the Japanese government and military forcibly mobilized the 'comfort women' during World War II, as well as the present Japanese government's actions to conceal this fact.
206	1999. 8.26	The Korean Ministry of Foreign Affairs and Trade announced that the UNHRC adopted a resolution stating that the issue of compensation for 'comfort women' cannot be resolved by any means, including peace agreements.		
207	1999. 10.1		On April 5, 1993, a Japanese district court ruled against a lawsuit filed by former 'comfort woman' Shin-do Song seeking an apology and compensation from the Japanese government.	
208	2000. 3.16		The JFBA submitted a statement to the UNHRC calling for a resolution on "Systematic Rape and Sexual Slavery in Armed Conflict."	

No.	Date	Korea	Japan	International Community
209	2000. 4.10		The House of Councillors submitted for consideration a bill entitled "Bill on the Promotion of Resolution of Issues Concerning Victims of Sexual Coercion during Wartime."	
210	2000. 7.28		The House of Councillors submitted the draft of the "Bill on the Promotion of Resolution of Issues Concerning Victims of Sexual Coercion during Wartime."	
211	2000. 9			15 survivors of the Japanese military 'comfort women' system from Korea, Taiwan, and the Philippines filed a lawsuit in the Washington DC Federal District Court under the Alien Tort Claims Act of 1787, seeking redress for illegal acts committed by foreign nationals.
212	2000. 9.18	Victims of the 'comfort women' system who filed a class action lawsuit in U.S. courts held a protest in front of the Japanese Embassy in Washington, D.C.		
213	2000. 10.30		The House of Councillors submitted the draft of a bill entitled "Bill on the Promotion of Resolution of Issues Concerning Victims of Sexual Coercion during Wartime."	
214	2000. 11.30		The Japanese High Court rejected an appeal in the case filed by a 'comfort women' survivor, Shin-do Song, against the Japanese government. The court ruled that although the establishment of the comfort stations constituted a violation of international law at the time, individuals do not have the right to seek compensation directly from a foreign country under international law. It further ruled that the right to claim compensation for ethnic Koreans in Japan had already expired in 1985, 20 years after the signing of the Treaty on Basic Relations between Japan and the Republic of Korea.	

Chronology of the Japanese Military's 'Comfort Women' Issue   259

No.	Date	Korea	Japan	International Community
215	2000. 12.8		A joint North-South Korean team of prosecutors consisting of 9 legal experts indicted 8 individuals, including Emperor Hirohito and Prime Minister Tojo Hideki, for crimes against humanity and violations of the Forced Labor Convention at the 'International Tribunal on Japanese military Sexual Slavery.'	
216	2000. 12.8 ~10			The "Women's International War Crimes Tribunal on Japan's Military Sexual Slavery" was convened.
217	2000. 12.12		The "Women's International War Crimes Tribunal" applied charges of crimes against humanity to hold Emperor Hirohito, the former Emperor of Japan, legally accountable.	
218	2001. 3.2		The JFBA submitted a report on the Japanese government's 2nd report under Articles 16 and 17 of the International Covenant on Economic, Social, and Cultural Rights. The report stated that the National Fund project was not an official apology or legal compensation by the Japanese government, that the victims refused the Prime Minister's letter and the lump sum payments, and that the victims were pursuing legal action against the Japanese government. The report also claimed that the Japanese courts have also failed to recognize the government's responsibility, resulting in no relief for the victims through the legal process.	
219	2001. 3.27		Takasu (高須), head of the International Cooperation Division of the Ministry of Foreign Affairs, told the House of Councillors' Welfare and Labor Committee that the Japanese government disagreed with the opinion of the ILO Committee of Experts, which recommended that the 'comfort women' issue constituted a violation of ILO Convention No. 29 on Forced Labor.	

No.	Date	Korea	Japan	International Community
220	2001. 3.29		The Japanese Supreme Court dismissed the appeal in the case of the 'comfort women' and the Women's Labor Volunteer Corps, upholding the lower court's decision. The plaintiffs in the case of the Japanese military 'comfort women' faced a 'reverse dismissal,' while the plaintiff in the case of the Women's Labor Volunteer Corps faced a 'complete rejection' of the claims.	
221	2001. 4.9	In the UNHRC, Korean government officials raised concerns about Japan's distortion of textbooks, including the issue of 'comfort women.'		
222	2001. 6.7			Despite Japan's opposition, the ILO's Committee on the Application of Standards formally adopted the issue of the Japanese military 'comfort women' for the first time in history.
223	2001. 7			U.S. Congressman Lane Evans introduced Resolution No.195, demanding an apology from the Japanese government.
224	2001. 10			Judge Henry Kennedy dismissed the lawsuit filed in September 2000 in Washington, D.C Federal District Court by 15 survivors of Japanese military 'comfort women' system from Korea, Taiwan, and the Philippines under the Foreign Tort Claims Act of 1787.
225	2001. 11		JFBA Report on the 4th Report of the Japanese Government on the Status of Implementation of the Convention on the Elimination of All Forms of Discrimination Against Women (CEDAW) stated that the Japanese government's report does not meet the recommendations of the CEDAW, and the compensation program of the National Fund does not meet the demands of the victims and the JFBA. The JFBA called for the recognition of Japan's legal responsibility and comprehensive reparations measure for the victims.	

No.	Date	Korea	Japan	**International Community**
226	2001. 12.4			The International Women's Tribunal on Japanese military Sexual Slavery, held in the Hague, Netherlands in 2000, aimed to prosecute the perpetrators of the Japanese military 'comfort women,' demanded a guilty verdict against Japan, as well as compensation for the victims.
227	2002. 2.26			The "Shanghai Korean Women's Labor Association," a list of Korean women who were forcibly mobilized in the Shanghai area, including victims of the Japanese military 'comfort women' system, was discovered.
228	2002. 11.12		Ishikawa (石川), the head of the International Cooperation Division of the Japanese Ministry of Foreign Affairs, told the Cabinet Committee of the House of the Councillors that it was difficult for the Japanese government to verify whether the 'comfort women' case constituted a violation of the Forced Labour Convention of 1932, as pointed out by the ILO Committee of Experts.	
229	2003. 3.26		The Shimonoseki Trial, which had initially acknowledged Japan's national responsibility for the 'comfort women' in 1998, ended with a verdict of dismissal. The ruling stated that the Japanese government had no obligation to pay compensation.	
230	2004. 12.18	'Asia Peace Solidarity,' which involved lawmakers, civic groups, and experts from both Korea and Japan, was launched with the aim of finding new solutions to historical issues between the two countries.		
231	2005. 1.24		Announcement of the dissolution plan for the National Fund in 2007	

No.	Date	Korea	Japan	International Community
232	2005. 2.28		The Democratic Party, the Communist Party, and the Social Democratic Party jointly introduced a bill, "Legislation to Promote the Resolution Concerning Victims of Wartime Sexual Coercion," which stipulated that the Japanese government should take measures, including apologies and compensation, for the Japanese military 'comfort women.'	
233	2006. 10.3		Prime Minister Abe stated in the plenary session of the House of Representatives that the Abe Cabinet intended to uphold the Kono's Statement on the 'comfort women' issue.	
234	2007. 1			U.S. Congressman Mike Honda introduced Resolution No. 121.
235	2007. 2			A hearing was held before the Committee on Foreign Affairs of the U.S. House of Representatives. (Location: Rayburn House Office Building, Room 2172/ Witnesses: Yong-soo Lee, Gun-ja Kim, Jan Ruff O'Herne, Mindy Kotler, Ok Cha Soh.)
236	2007. 3.5		Prime Minister Abe expressed his opinion to the Upper House Budget Committee that he believed the coercion in the 'comfort women' program was due to the economic situation at the time and was committed by the recruiters.	
237	2007. 3.6		In anticipation of the dissolution of the National Fund on March 31, 2007, President Murayama reported on the organization's past activities and achievements and urged the government to continue its efforts to uphold the dignity of women, even after the dissolution of the Fund.	

No.	Date	Korea	Japan	International Community
238	2007. 3.8		- Lower House member Tsujimoto (辻元) submitted Question No. 110 to Prime Minister Abe regarding his awareness of the 'comfort women' issue. - "Group of Lawmakers Thinking about Japan's Future and History Education," submitted a proposal to the Japanese government requesting a review of the forced mobilization of 'comfort women.'	
239	2007. 3.16		The Abe Cabinet made a decision stating that there was no direct evidence of the forced mobilization of 'comfort women.'	
240	2007. 4.27		Prime Minister Abe expressed sympathy and an apology regarding the 'comfort women' issue during a joint press conference with President Bush.	
241	2007. 5.25			"The 'comfort women' Issue" was posted on the website of the Japanese Embassy in the United States. It stated that House Resolution No. 121 contained factual errors and that the resolution, if passed, would harm U.S.-Japan relations.
242	2007. 6.14		The Historical Fact-Finding Committee in Japan placed an advertisement in the *Washington Post* entitled "The Facts." Based on Professor Hata's paper, which argued that there was no organized and forced recruitment of 'comfort women,' the ad claimed that the 'comfort women' were not sex slaves. It also stated that the claims of HR No.121 led by Congressman Honda that the 'comfort women' program was the largest human trafficking operation in the 20th century were a distortion of history.	

No.	Date	Korea	Japan	International Community
243	2007.7			The U.S. House of Representatives passed Resolution No. 121 unanimously.
244	2007.12.12			The European Parliament adopted a resolution regarding the 'comfort women' issue.
245	2008.9		JFBA Report on the 6th Report of the Japanese Government on the Convention on the Elimination of All Forms of Discrimination Against Women (CEDAW) alleged that the Japanese government failed to comply with the recommendations of the Committee on the Elimination of Discrimination Against Women and the Committee on Economic, Social, and Cultural Rights regarding the final resolution of the Japanese military 'comfort women' issue and the pursuit of reparations for victims.	
246	2008.10.5		Prime Minister Aso (麻生) expressed at the Upper House Budget Committee that the Aso Cabinet adheres to the Kono's Statement.	
247	2010.8.20		Foreign Minister Okada (岡田) stated that financial compensation for 'comfort women' had been completed through the "Asian Women's Fund."	
248	2011.8.30	The Korean Constitutional Court ruled that the 'comfort women' issue was in an unconstitutional state caused by government negligence.		
249	2011.9.15		Foreign Minister Yamaguchi (山口) stated that the Japanese government will maintain its legal stance despite the South Korean government's proposal for negotiations following the Constitutional Court's ruling on the unconstitutionality of the 'comfort women' issue.	

Chronology of the Japanese Military's 'Comfort Women' Issue 265

No.	Date	Korea	Japan	International Community
250	2011. 10.14		Foreign Minister Genba (玄葉) stated that the 'comfort women' issue had been completely resolved in the 1965 Korea-Japan Claims Settlement Agreement.	
251	2011. 12.14	The 1000th Wednesday Demonstration rally was held and a "Statue of Peace" was erected in front of the Japanese Embassy in Korea.		
252	2012. 7.25		Prime Minister Noda (野田) responded to a special committee on tax reform of the Social Security Division of the House of Councillors that there was no document indicating organized recruitment by the military or government officials regarding the Kono Statement.	
253	2012. 10.23		When Mayor Hashimoto (橋下) of Osaka made remarks denying coercion in the 'comfort women' system and quoted Professor Yoshimi, Professor Yoshimi publicly protested that the statement was untrue and demanded an apology from Mayor Hashimoto.	
254	2013. 4.12		Shimomura, Minister of Education, Culture, Sports, Science and Technology, told the Lower House Budget Committee while discussing the Kono Statement that the issue of coercion in the 'comfort women' program had been officially denied by the first Abe Cabinet's decision in 2007.	
255	2013. 8.13	Twelve Japanese military 'comfort women' victims, including Chun-hee Bae, filed an application for conciliation against the Japanese government with the Seoul Central District Court, claiming damages of KRW 100 million each, totaling KRW 1.2 billion.	The Japanese government refused to accept the application for conciliation.	
256	2014. 1.2			Authorities in Cupertino, California, USA, officially approved a proposal to erect a 'comfort women' memorial.

No.	Date	Korea	Japan	International Community
257	2014. 1.7			Instead of organizing protests, Korean-American organizations decided to launch a campaign to send letters of thanks to the Glendale City Council for its support of the 'comfort women.'
258	2014. 1.10			A document was discovered in Jilin-sheng, China, revealing that the forced mobilization of 'comfort women' was carried out by the Japanese government.
259	2014. 1.15	The Ministry of Gender Equality and Family stated that it will take steps to apply for the registration of testimonies and records related to the Japanese military 'comfort women' with UNESCO's "Memory of the World" program.	Chief Cabinet Secretary Suga opposed Korea's application for World Heritage status of records related to "comfort women," emphasizing that the issue had been resolved through the Korea-Japan Claims Settlement Agreement.	
260	2014. 1.15			- The 'comfort women' issue was included in a U.S. House of Representatives bill. - China also cooperated in the inclusion of the 'comfort women' issue in Memory of the World Programme. - The 'comfort women' bill was passed by the U.S. Senate.
261	2014. 1.17			- U.S. President Barack Obama signed a comprehensive bill in 2014 that included a provision urging the Japanese government to comply with the 'Comfort Women' Resolution. - The first 'Comfort Women' Resolution Memorial was erected in New York.
262	2014. 1.28	The Ministry of Gender Equality and Family held a special session at the UN Headquarters in Brussels, Belgium, to raise awareness about the issue of Japanese military 'comfort women.'		

Chronology of the Japanese Military's 'Comfort Women' Issue 267

No.	Date	Korea	Japan	International Community
263	2014. 1.29	Foreign Minister Byung-se Yun visited the House of Sharing.	Prime Minister Abe told at the plenary session of the House of Representatives that the UN's criticism was one-sided and based on factual errors, and that the UN's recommendations had no legal binding force.	
264	2014. 1.30			The Ministry of Gender Equality and Family organized a 'Comfort Women' Comics Exhibition in Angoulême, France.
265	2014. 2.1			Ed Royce, Chairman of the U.S. House Committee on Foreign Affairs, laid a wreath at the "Statue of Peace" in Glendale, California.
266	2014. 2.4	A request for judicial cooperation was made to the Japanese Ministry of Justice to secure the appearance of Suzuki, who was charged with the suspected sledgehammer attack on the 'Statue of Peace."		Congressman Mike Honda sent a letter to U.S. Secretary of State John Kerry, urging him to implement the 'Comfort Women' bill.
267	2014. 2.11		Former Prime Minister Murayama attended the "Exhibition of Artworks by Japanese military 'comfort women'" held at the Korean National Assembly Members Building and apologized to the former 'comfort women.'	
268	2014. 2.12	- Cartoonists who participated in the 'Comfort Women' Comics Exhibition at the International Comics Festival in Angoulême attended a Wednesday Demonstration rally.	Former Prime Minister Murayama, in a lecture at the Korean National Assembly Building, urged a "speedy resolution" of the Japanese military 'comfort women' issue through governmental negotiations between Japan and Korea.	The *Washington Post* published an editorial titled "Japan's Denialism" criticizing Japan's distortion of history and comments made by the new president of NHK, Momii (籾井).
269	2014. 2.16		Japanese intellectuals launched the "Connecting Japan and Korea Campaign 2015" proposing to correct Japan's wrongdoings, including the 'comfort women' issue and forced mobilization, in order to improve Japan-Korea relations.	

No.	Date	Korea	Japan	International Community
270	2014. 2.18			Royce, chairman of the U.S. House Foreign Affairs Committee, said that in order to resolve historical disputes between Japan and Korea, it is necessary for Japan to apologize and for Japanese political leaders to make efforts to resolve the 'Comfort Women' issue.
271	2014. 2.21		The Global Alliance for Historical Truth, which included Japanese Americans, filed a lawsuit demanding the removal of the "Statue of Peace" in Glendale, California.	
272	2014. 3.1	President Geun-hye Park urged the Japanese government to immediately address the issue of Japanese military 'comfort women' in her speech commemorating the March 1st Movement.		
273	2014. 3.4		A 'comfort women' exhibition' was held at the Japanese-Korean History Museum in Minato Ward, Tokyo.	Former U.S. Secretary of State Richard Armitage delivered a speech, stating that Japan cannot win in the 'comfort women' debate with Korea.
274	2014. 3.5	Foreign Minister Byung-se Yun criticized the Abe government's stance on the issue of the so-called 'comfort women' during his speech at the regular session of the UNHRC in Geneva.		
275	2014. 3.6	U.S. Ambassador to South Korea Sung Kim said the issue of 'comfort women' and sexual slavery was a serious human rights violation, and hoped Japan would address the issue in a way that would alleviate the suffering.		
276	2014. 3.7		Japanese scholars Yoshimi (吉見), Hayashi (林), and Nishino (西野) held a press conference to express their opposition to the destruction of the Kono Statement. They stated that the forced mobilization of 'comfort women' during the war was carried out only by Japan.	

No.	Date	Korea	Japan	International Community
277	2014. 3.11	Minister Yoon-sun Cho of the Ministry of Gender Equality and Family announced her intention to register 'comfort women' records with UNESCO's Memory of the World program.		A former 'comfort woman,' Jan Ruff-O'Herne, expressed her willingness to participate in the installation of the "Satue of Peace" in Australia.
278	2014. 3.20			The Jilin Provincial Archives in China released documents that provide evidence of the forced mobilization of 'comfort women.'
279	2014. 3.24	The Korea-Japan Joint Parliamentary Group agreed to explore ways to resolve the issue of Japanese military 'Comfort Women.'		- The Jilin Provincial Archives in China additionally released documents related to the recruitment of Korean 'Comfort Women.' - It was revealed that a U.S. Federal government interagency task force concluded in the early 2000s that the Japanese military The 'comfort woman' systemconstituted an organized sexual slavery program.
280	2014. 3.28	The 20-Year History of the "Korean Council"s was announced.		Phumzile Mlambo-Ngcuka, the Executive Director of UN Women, stated that the Japanese government should take legal responsibility for the 'comfort women' issue.
281	2014. 3.29	More than 20 women's and religious organizations from South and North Korea held an international women's conference in Shenyang, Liaoning-sheng, China, to discuss resolving the issue of Japanese military sexual slavery ('comfort women').		
282	2014. 3.30			The Global Alliance for Historical Truth (GAHT), composed of Japanese Americans, demanded the removal of the "Statue of Peace" in Glendale, California, and filed a lawsuit against the city.
283	2014. 4.18			Taiwan's President Ying-jeou Ma urged the Japanese government to actively resolve the issue of Japanese military 'comfort women.'

No.	Date	Korea	Japan	International Community
284	2014. 4.25			- U.S. President Barack Obama criticized the 'comfort women' system during a press conference. - The Jilin Provincial Archives in China released 87 documents related to Japan's invasion of China, including the 'comfort women' and Unit 731 crimes.
285	2014. 4.26			President Barack Obama mentioned the 'comfort women' issue during a joint press conference with South Korean President Geun-hye Park.
286	2014. 5.15			The Global Alliance for Preserving the History of WWII in Asia submitted a statement in a lawsuit related to the removal of the "Statue of Peace" in the United States.
287	2014. 5.30			A memorial ceremony for the 'Comfort Women' Memorial Statue was held at the Fairfax County Government Center in Virginia, USA.
288	2014. 6.10		Chief Cabinet Secretary Suga, requested China to withdraw its application for inclusion in the Memory of the World Programme, asserting that it was based on political motives.	China's Foreign Ministry spokesperson Chunying Hua (华春莹) announced plans to apply for the inclusion of historical documents related to the 'comfort women' system and the Nanjing Massacre in UNESCO's Memory of the World Programme.
289	2014. 6.12	Vice Foreign Minister Tae-yeol Cho spoke about the 'comfort women' issue at the international conference in London aimed at eliminating sexual violence in conflict areas.		Biqiang Guo (郭必强), deputy inspector of China's Second Historical Archives Inspection Office, revealed the contents of documents related to the Nanjing Massacre and the 'comfort women' issue that China submitted as part of its application for inclusion in UNESCO's Memory of the World Programme.

No.	Date	Korea	Japan	International Community
290	2014. 6.16	- The "Korean Council" submitted a resolution to the UNHRC, urging the resolution of the 'comfort women' issue. - A production briefing for the musical "Flower Shoes," which deals with the issue of Japanese military 'comfort women,' was held.	Osaka Mayor Hashimoto claimed that even the U.S. military used French women as 'comfort women.'	
291	2014. 6.20	The U.S. Senate delivered a copy of a letter urging the resolution of the 'comfort women' issue to the House of Sharing in Korea.	The Abe Cabinet produced a review report indicating that both the South Korean and Japanese governments had made prior adjustments during the drafting process of the Kono Statement.	
292	2014. 6.25	122 South Korean women who served as 'comfort women' for the U.S. Military in Korea filed a lawsuit against the Korean government seeking compensation.		Filipino organizations representing 'comfort women' victims criticized President Benigno Noynoy Aquino for not addressing the 'comfort women' issue during his visit to Japan.
293	2014. 6.27			A U.S. congressman sent an official letter to the Japanese ambassador criticizing the Japanese government's verification of the Kono Statement.
294	2014. 7.3	The term 'comfort women' first appeared in an annex to the South Korea-China summit.		The Chinese newspaper Huanqiu Shibao released on the Internet documents containing confessions written by Japanese war criminals during World War II.
295	2014. 7.7			The Taiwanese government announced plans to build a "Japanese military 'comfort women' History Museum" in cooperation with civilian organizations.
296	2014. 7.8			The Foundation of Japanese Honorary Debts, a Dutch NGO, protested in front of the Japanese Embassy in Hague, the Netherlands, expressing their opposition to the verification of the Kono Statement and demanding an apology and compensation from Japan.

No.	Date	Korea	Japan	International Community
297	2014. 7.15			- The UN CCPR (Civil and Political Rights) in the Human Rights Committee initiated an evaluation of the Japanese military 'comfort women' system and hate speech against Koreans. - The CCPR also criticized Japan and called for the use of the term "enforced sex slaves" instead of 'comfort women.'
298	2014. 7.17			The UN Human Rights Committee at the European headquarters in Geneva, Switzerland, criticized Japan's response to the 'comfort women' issue, stating that Japan should use the appropriate term "enforced sex slaves" instead of the indirect term 'comfort women.'
299	2014. 7.18			An English play entitled *Comfort Women: A New Musical*, which deals with the issue of the Japanese military 'comfort women,' was performed on Broadway in the U.S.
300	2014. 7.21	Victims of the Japanese military 'comfort women' system visited the United States to highlight the unfairness of the verification of the Kono Statement.		
301	2014. 7.22	Hee-jung Kim, the Minister of the Ministry of Gender Equality and Family, announced that she would register the records of the Japanese military 'comfort women' as national records.		
302	2014. 7.24			The UN CCPR recommended that the Japanese government publicly apologize to the women who were victims of 'comfort women' and provide compensation.
303	2014. 7.25		The Japanese Ministry of Foreign Affairs responded to the UNHRC's demands regarding the 'comfort women' issue with a rebuttal.	

Chronology of the Japanese Military's 'Comfort Women' Issue   273

No.	Date	Korea	Japan	International Community
304	2014. 7.29	An exhibition on the Japanese military 'comfort women,' entitled *Dream of Butterflies*, was held at the Atelier Gallery in Euljiro 4-ga, Seoul.		
305	2014. 7.30			The White House, along with officials from the State Department, held a private meeting with the victims of the Japanese military 'comfort women' system.
306	2014. 8.4			The unveiling ceremony of the "Japanese Military 'Comfort Women' Memorial" took place in New York.
307	2014. 8.5	In Daegu, construction of the "Japanese Military 'Comfort Women' History Museum" began.		The California court in the United States dismissed the lawsuit against the removal of the "Statue of Peace" in Glendale by a Japanese organization.
308	2014. 8.6	A Japanese individual who damaged artwork related to the Japanese military 'comfort women' was placed under investigation by police without arrest.		The UN High Commissioner for Human Rights, Navi Pillay, issued a statement assessing Japan's failure to adequately address the issue of wartime sexual slavery and criticizing the continued violation of the human rights of 'comfort women' survivors.
309	2014. 8.13			The Supreme Court of the Philippines dismissed the lawsuit filed by 'comfort women' survivors in the Philippines against their own government.
310	2014. 8.14	- World 'Comfort Women' Memorial Day: 1.56 million signatures from around the world. - Speaker of National Assembly Eui-hwa Chung visited the House of Sharing. - 'Comfort women' survivor Oksun Lee participated in a protest held in Berlin, Germany.		

No.	Date	Korea	Japan	International Community
311	2014. 8.16			- The Chinese-Canadian citizen group '아시아 제2차 대전 사실 (史實) 보호회,' joined the worldwide petition campaign initiated by the "Korean Council," aiming to collect 100 million signatures for the resolution of the 'comfort women' issue. - The unveiling ceremony of the "Statue of Peace" was held in Southfield, Michigan, USA.
312	2014. 8.18	Pope Francis, during his visit to Korea, offered consolation to the women who were victims of the Japanese military 'comfort women' system at a Mass at Myeongdong Cathedral.		
313	2014. 8.19	Ambassador Ho-young Ahn, South Korea's ambassador to the United States, said during a forum in Washington D.C. that there is sufficient evidence of the forced mobilization of "comfort women."		
314	2014. 8.21		Japan's Liberal Democratic Party demanded the government to issue a new statement on the 'comfort women' issue and the Kono Statement in 2015.	The UN Committee on the Elimination of Racial Discrimination criticized the Japanese government's stance on the issue of the Japanese military 'comfort women,' noting that despite international condemnation, Japan was sidelining the issue. They also called for legal regulation of hate speech and protests.
315	2014. 8.31			The UN High Commissioner for Human Rights, Navi Pillay, strongly urged the Japanese government to thoroughly investigate the issue of the Japanese military 'comfort women' and to punish those responsible.
316	2014. 9.11		Fukui City opposed the erection of a "Statue of Peace" in its sister city, Fullerton, USA.	

No.	Date	Korea	Japan	International Community
317	2014.9.13		Japanese writer Shiono (塩野) wrote an article in the monthly magazine *Bungeishunjū* (文藝春秋) denying the forced mobilization of the Japanese military 'comfort women.'	Zainab Hawa Bangura, the UN Special Representative on Sexual Violence in Conflict, emphasized that Japan and South Korea should engage in dialogue to resolve the issue of Japanese military 'comfort women.'
318	2014.9.15			A "Statue of Peace" was unveiled in China before the release of a movie about the Japanese military 'comfort women.'
319	2014.9.18			Ted Poe, a Republican member of the U.S. House of Representatives, publicly criticized Japan, urging it to fully acknowledge past wrongdoings, including the forced mobilization of 'comfort women' and the coercion of sexual slavery.
320	2014.9.19			An exhibition on the Japanese military 'comfort women' was held at the Canadian Museum for Human Rights.
321	2014.9.24	President Geun-hye Park mentioned the 'comfort women' issue for the first time at the UN General Assembly.		
322	2014.10.3			Minister of Foreign Affairs of the Netherlands, Frans Timmermans, said that coercion in the 'comfort women' system was a clear fact.
323	2014.10.6		In connection with the threat incident against the former *Asahi Shimbun* journalist, citizens including writer Natsuki Ikezawa (池澤夏樹) formed a citizens' group called "Don't Give In, Hokusei! Group" to encourage the university to resist the threats.	
324	2014.10.15	Choong-hee Hahn, Deputy Ambassador to the UN, urged the Japanese government to resolve the 'comfort women' issue.	The Historical Science Society of Japan issued a statement countering the Abe Cabinet's denial of the forced mobilization of "comfort women."	

No.	Date	Korea	Japan	International Community
325	2014.10.16		Suga, the Chief Cabinet Secretary, asked Radhika Coomaraswamy to withdraw certain parts of the Coomaraswamy Report of the UN Human Rights Commission.	Radhika Coomaraswamy refused the Japanese government's request to withdraw some contents of the Coomaraswamy Report.
326	2014.10.21	Kwan-jin Kim, the Chief of the National Security Office, met with Yachi (谷内), the head of Japan's National Security Council (NSC), and asserted that resolving the 'comfort women' issue was the most important and urgent matter.		- Critic and commentator Tony Marano, known as 'Texas Daddy,' criticized the "Statue of Peace" in the Glendale City Council in California, USA. - The Johns Hopkins University School of Advanced International Studies (SAIS) in the U.S. held a seminar on the topic of "The Tragic Stories of Chinese 'comfort women.'"
327	2014.10.23	Prime Minister Hong-won Chung stated that Korea would strengthen its public diplomacy on issues such as 'comfort women,' Dokdo, and the naming of the East Sea. He also mentioned plans to expand networking with foreign think tanks and opinion leaders.		
328	2014.10.24	President Geun-hye Park said during a meeting with Japanese lawmakers that the 'comfort women' issue is the first step in resolving relations between Korea and Japan. She emphasized that avoiding repetitive actions that hurt the feelings of the victims and Korean citizens is crucial to building trust between the two countries.	Chief Cabinet Secretary Suga mentioned that efforts were being made to promote understanding in various countries to clear up misunderstandings arising from former Chief Cabinet Secretary Kono's Statement about "forced recruitment."	
329	2014.10.25	- The Korea-Japan Parliamentarians' Union held a joint meeting in Seoul and adopted a joint statement to work for the restoration of the honor of the 'comfort women' victims. - National Assembly Speaker Euihwa Chung said that resolving the issue of Japanese military 'comfort women' requires Japan's sincere self-reflection.		

Chronology of the Japanese Military's 'Comfort Women' Issue 277

No.	Date	Korea	Japan	International Community
330	2014. 10.28	The Ministry of Foreign Affairs claimed that crimes against humanity such as the comfort women' program involving the government and military authorities cannot be considered settled under the Claims Settlement Agreement.	The city of Mishima in Shizuoka-ken refused to sponsor a civic event it had supported for 20 years, citing the inclusion of performances related to the Japanese military 'comfort women.'	
331	2014. 11.2		The Japanese government and political circles raised issues regarding the content of the history textbook jointly produced by Korea and Japan that dealt with the 'comfort women' issue.	
332	2014. 11.14		Japanese civic group "Japan Nationwide Action for the Resolution of the Japanese Military 'Comfort Women' Issue" confirmed that the Japanese Ministry of Justice examined documents containing information about forced mobilization and prepared internal internal reports.	
333	2014. 11.17		The *Hokkaido Shimbun* canceled previous reports about Japanese military 'comfort women.'	
334	2014. 11.18		Foreign Minister Kishida (岸田) announced the government's request for correction of content of the world history textbook regarding Japanese military 'comfort women' to McGraw Hill Publishing Co. in the USA.	
335	2014. 11.23			McGraw-Hill Publishing Co. rejected Japanese government's request to change content of the world history textbook.
336	2014. 11.25	The "Korean Council for the Women Drafted for Military Sexual Slavery by Japan," held an art exhibition in Washington D.C. with the theme of "Grief and Hop of the Japanese Military 'comfort women.'"	The Liberal Democratic Party decided to include denial of forced mobilization of the 'comfort women' in their pledge for the House of Representatives election.	

No.	Date	Korea	Japan	International Community
337	2014. 11.26	The "Korean Council" held Wednesday Demonstrations in Paris, France.		
338	2014. 12.7			China submitted an 8-minute documentary on Japanese military 'comfort women' to UNESCO.
339	2014. 12.14		Consul General Kusaka (草賀) of New York, USA, wrote a rebuttal to the *New York Times* editorial which criticized the Abe government over the issue of Japanese military 'comfort women.'	
340	2014. 12.15	The Northeast Asian History Foundation and the Jilin Provincial Archivessigned a MOU on joint study of the Japanese military 'comfort women' issue.		
341	2014. 12.18		The city council of Kiyose in Metropolitan Tokyo withdrew its statement of opinion demanding an apology and compensation from the government.	Mike Honda, a U.S. representative, told the Korean reporters that it is nonsense to argue that there was no coercion in the 'comfort women' program.
342	2014. 12.19		Funabashi City Council adopted a statement of opinion that there was no forced mobilization in the Japanese military 'comfort women.'	
343	2014. 12.22		*Asahi Shimbun*, in the Third Party Committee report, admitted that the conveyance of misinformation on 'comfort women' issue and delayed retraction of it could be a betrayal of readers' trust.	
344	2014. 12.24			Horinouchi (堀之内), Japanese Consulate General in Los Angeles, California, wrote an opinion piece in the local newspaper that he opposes the erection of "Statue of Peace."
345	2014. 12.25	National Archives designated additional 1,065 records related to the Japanese military 'comfort women' program as national records.		

No.	Date	Korea	Japan	International Community
346	2014. 12.26		President Watanabe of *Asahi Shimbun* apologized for erroneous reports about Japanese military 'comfort women' issue. The "Society for Dissemination of Historical Fact" sent booklets to the U.S. Congress, which described victims of the Japanese military 'comfort women' system as "prostitutes."	
347	2015. 1.9		Former *Asahi Shimbun* reporter Uemura (植村) filed a lawsuit against *Shukan Bunshun* (週刊文春) and Professor Nishioka (西岡) of Tokyo Christian University.	
348	2015. 1.26		8,700 Japanese right-wingers filed a lawsuit against *Asahi Shimbun*, claiming that there is no evidence of forced mobilization of the 'comfort women.'	
349	2015. 2.8			19 American historians issued a statement criticizing Abe's historical revisionism.
350	2015. 2.11		Special Advisor to the President of the Liberal Democratic Party, Uda Hagi (萩生田) said "There are no war criminals in Japan."	
351	2015. 3.17		19 Japanese far-right scholars demanded revisions to the U.S. McGraw Hill textbook, arguing that the 'comfort women' were "prostitues."	
352	2015. 3.30			The U.S. State Department defined the issues of Japanese military 'comfort women' as "the trafficking of women for sexual purposes."
353	2015. 4.8		Discovered a document showing that a Japanese military unit commander ordered forceful mobilization of 'comfort women.'	

No.	Date	Korea	Japan	International Community
354	2015. 4.27		Japan's Prime Minister Abe called the Japanese military 'comfort women,' "victims of human trafficking" during a lecture at Harvard University (denial of sexual slavery and its responsibility on the part of Japanese government maintained).	
355	2015. 5.16			187 historians across the world issued a collective statement urging Japanese Prime Minister Shinzo Abe's right historical perception.
356	2015. 5.25			China upgraded the document *'Comfort Women': Japanese military Slavery* to national level historical record.
357	2015. 8.12	Former Japanese Prime Minister Hatoyama (鳩山) visited the Seodaemun Prison in Seoul and apologized.		
358	2015. 8.14		Japanese Prime Minister Abe delivered a "70th Anniversary of the End of World War II Address."	
359	2015. 9.22			San Francisco, USA, passed a resolution to build a memorial monument for Japanese military 'comfort women.'
360	2015. 11.2	President Geun-hye Park mentioned the issue of Japanese military 'comfort women' in her keynote speech at the U.N. General Assembly in New York.		
361	2015	Korea-Japan summit was held in Seoul for the first time in 3 years and 5 months.		
362	2015. 12.1			The first 'comfort women' memorial, the Nanjing Lijixiang 'Comfort Women' Memorial, opened in Nanjing, China.
363	2015. 12.5	Heeum Japanese Military 'Comfort Women' History Hall in Daegu opened.		

No.	Date	Korea	Japan	International Community
364	2015. 12.28	At the Korea-Japan Foreign Ministers' Meeting in Seoul, a bilateral agreement was made on the issue of Japanese military 'comfort women.'		
365	2015. 12.29			Taiwan's Foreign Minister called for consultation with the Japanese Government on Japanese military 'comfort women' issues.
366	2016. 1.14		Sakurada (櫻田), a member of the House of Councillors of the Liberal Democratic Party of Japan, said, "The comfortwomen were professional prostitutes."	
367	2016. 1.28	A lawsuit was filed by the 'comfort women' victims.		
368	2016. 2.16		Sugiyama (杉山), a representative of the Japanese Foreign Ministry said, "There was no forced mobilization of Japanese military 'comfort women'" at the United Nations Committee on the Elimination of Discrimination Against Women in Geneva, Switzerland.	
369	2016. 2.24	- The movie *Homecoming* based on the testimony of the victims of the Japanese military 'comfort women' was released - The "Korean Council" declared March 1 as National Action Day for the invalidation of the Agreement on the Japanese military 'comfort women.'		
370	2016. 2.27	- Groundbreaking ceremony for the Exhibition Hall and House of Sharing Memorial Hall was held. - Ministry of Gender Equality and Family provided 500 million KRW for their construction.		
371	2016. 2.29	Lawyers for a Democratic Society filed a lawsuit requesting disclosure of information on negotiation documents on the Japan-Korea Agreement on the Japanese Military 'Comfort Women' (2015.12.28).		

No.	Date	Korea	Japan	International Community
372	2016. 3.1	- Demonstrations against the bilateral agreement on the Japanese military 'comfort women' were held throughout Korea. - Korean college students completed a sit-in 62 day protests to protect the "Statue of Peace." - 50 local governments across the country announced a plan to erect the "Statue of Peace" in overseas sister cities.		
373	2016. 3.7		- Japan's Ministry of Foreign Affairs posted Sugiyama's remarks at the UN Committee on the Elimination of Discrimination against Women, which denied forced mobilization of Japanese military 'comfort women' on its website.	The UN Committee on the Elimination of Discrimination against Women urged the Japanese government to stop avoiding responsibility for the Japanese military 'comfort women' issue and include it in textbooks.
374	2016. 3.8			- The New York City Council pushed forward a resolution on the Japanese military 'comfort women' issue. - At a press conference in front of New York City Hall, Yong-soo Lee said that the 'comfort women' agreement between Korea and Japan was not acceptable.
375	2016. 3.9			The Wednesday Demonstration was held in Washington, D.C., in front of the Japanese Embassy.
376	2016. 3.10		- Japanese civic group, "Japan Nationwide Action for the Resolution of the Japanese Military 'Comfort Women' Issue," criticized Sugiyama's remarks at the UN Committee on the Elimination of Discrimination against Women which denied forced mobilization. - Zaid Ra'ad Al Hussein, UN High Commissioner for Human Rights said "The judgment of victims of the Japanese military 'comfort women' is the most important."	
377	2016. 3.11			UN Secretary-General Ki-moon Ban met with Japanese 'comfort women' victim, Won-ok Gil at the UN Headquarters in New York, and explained that he did not welcome the agreement.

No.	Date	Korea	Japan	International Community
378	2016. 3.16	33 universities in Korea held Wednesday Demonstrationt Rallies on campus.		
379	2016. 3.17			Yong-soo Lee, a victim the Japanese military 'comfort women,' was given Merit Award by the U.S. California Senate.
380	2016. 3.22		Japan decided to remove the word "military" from the description of 'comfort women' in high school textbooks.	
381	2016. 3.27	Victims of the Japanese military 'comfort women' filed a constitutiona complaint to the Constitutional Court saying that their basic rights were violated by the agreement between Korean and Japanese foreign ministers. (Association of lawyers for democratic society)	Korea-Japan Foreign Minister-level consultation meeting was held to discuss the issue of victims of the Japanese military 'comfort women' in Tokyo. Both agreed to cooperate to early establishment of 'Japanese military 'comfort women' Support Foundation."	Yong-soo Lee. the victim of the Japanese military 'comfort women,' was given a Merit of Award by Los Angeles City, CA, USA.
382	2016. 3.31	Korea-Japan summit was held in Washington, D.C., U.S., and the leaders of the two countries agreed to make efforts for the full implementation of the "Korea-Japan Agreement on Japanese Military 'Comfort Women' issue" (2015.12.28).		
383	2016. 4.7	Korea's Foreign Ministry said, "The issue of establishing the Japanese military 'Comfort Women' Victims Foundation and the removal of the "Statue of Peace" are separate issues."	Chief Cabinet Hagiuda said "The establishment of the Japanese Military 'comfort women Victims Foundation and the removal of the "Statue of Peace" should be done in one package."	
384	2016. 4.9			The victims of the Japanese military 'comfort women' system, Ok-sun Lee and Il-chul Kang testified at the Nassau County Holocaust Center on Long Island, New York.
385	2016. 4.10	Upon request from victims living in China, support for transportation and treatment was provided.		

No.	Date	Korea	Japan	International Community
386	2016. 4.15	- Goyang Mayor Sung Choi and victims of Japanese Military 'comfort women,' Ok-sun Lee and Il-chul Kang, demonstrated in front of the UN Headquarters in New York calling for the resolution of the Japanese military 'comfort women' issue.		
387	2016. 4.26			- San Francisco Board of Education unanimously passed a resolution to include the Japanese military 'comfort women' in the textbook contents.
388	2016. 5.14		- The Japanese government claimed that the removal of the "Statue of Peace" was virtually included in the December 28th Agreement.	
389	2016. 5.18	The "Korean Council" awarded the first 'Bok-dong Kim Butterfly Peace Prize' to Durebang, Saeumteo, and Sunshine Welfare Association.		
390	2016. 5.19			- The 14th "Asian Solidarity Conference to Solve Japanese military 'comfort women' issues" was held.
391	2016. 5.25		Former Prime Minister Murayama said, "Prime Minister Abe himself should apologize to the victims."	
392	2016. 5.31	- The Korean government launched a preparatory committee for the establishment of the "Foundation to Support the Victims of Japanese military 'comfort women.'" Emeritus Professor Tae-hyun Kim of Sungshin Women's University, was appointed as the chairperson. - 14 civic society organizations from 8 countries submitted records related to the Japanese military 'comfort women' to the British War Memorial, for joint registration as Memory of the World Heritage.		

No.	Date	Korea	Japan	International Community
393	2016. 6.9	Justice and Memory Foundation for the Resolution of the Japanese military 'comfort women' Problem (Justice and Memory Foundation) Iwas launched.		
394	2016. 6.24	National Medical Center and Korea Women's Human Rights Promotion Agency signed a business agreement to providing medical services for victims of the Japanese military 'comfort women.'		
395	2016. 6.29	Seoul City held the groundbreaking ceremony for the Site of Memory, a memorial park for victims of the Japanese military 'comfort women.'		
396	2016. 7.21	Victims of Japanese military "comfort women," Yong-soo Lee, Ok-sun Park, and Ok-sun Lee submitted a petition to the National Assembly for the enactment of the "Special Act on Support for Life Stabilization and Commemorative Projects for Victims of the Japanese military 'comfort women.'"	First screening of movie, *Homecoming*, in Japan.	
397	2016. 7.28	The Reconciliation and Healing Foundation was launched.		
398	2016. 8.9			In Sydney, Australia, the "Statue of Peace" was erected.
399	2016. 8.29	On the site of the old Tonggam residence in Namsan Park, Jung-gu, Seoul, the Site of Memory of the Japanese military 'comfort women' was constructed.		
400	2016. 10.3		Prime Minister Abe said, "I have absolutely no intention what-so-ever to send a letter of apology to the victims of Japanese military 'comfort women.'"	
401	2016. 10.22			In Shanghai Normal University, the "Statue of Peace" was unveiled.

No.	Date	Korea	Japan	International Community
402	2016.12	Twenty survivors and family members of victims of Japanese military 'comfort women' filed a lawsuit against the Japanese government for their "mental and physical suffering."		
403	2016.12.30	"Statue of Peace" was erected in front of the Japanese consulate in Busan.		
404	2017.1.6		The Japanese government has announced retaliatory measures, including temporarily recalling the Japanese Consul General in Busan and suspending currency swaps, citing the installation of the "Statue of Peace" in front of the Busan Consulate General as a violation of the 2015 Agreement.	
405	2017.3.8			In the city of Wiesent, Bavaria, Germany, the "Statue of Peace" was erected.
406	2017.4.25		Japanese Diplomatic Bluebook expressed regrets over the installation of the Busan "Statue of Peace" and called for Korea-Japan Agreement.	
407	2017.5.9	The 19th presidential election		
408	2017.5.11	President Jae-in Moon told Prime Minister Abe, "The reality is that the majority of our people cannot emotionally accept the Japanese Military 'Comfort Women' Agreement."		
409	2017.5.12			The UN Anti-Torture Commission recommended modification of the 2015 Korea-Japan Agreement on Japanese Military 'Comfort Women.'

No.	Date	Korea	Japan	International Community
410	2017. 6.27	Former US Representative Mike Honda was awarded a Medal of Distinguished Service for his efforts to resolve the issue of Japanese military 'comfort women' and consolidate Korea-U.S. alliance.	Consul General of Japan in Atlanta, Shinozuka (篠塚) said "Japanese military 'comfort women' was prostitutes."	
411	2017. 7.26			UN CCPR downgraded its assessment of the Japanese government's efforts to resolve the issue of 'comfort women.'
412	2017. 7.31	The Ministry of Foreign Affairs launched the task force for the 2015 Korea-Japan Agreement on Japanese military 'comfort women.'		
413	2017. 9.13	The 1,300th Wednesday Demonstration was held.		
414	2017. 9.14	Release of the movie *Homecoming, Unfinished Story*.		
415	2017. 9.21	Release of the movie, *I can speak*.		
416	2017. 9.22			In San Francisco, USA, the Japanese military 'comfort women' Memorial Stone was constructed.
417	2017. 9.25	In the Garden of Manghyang, construction of a memorial monument for Japanese military 'comfort women' started.		
418	2017. 10.14			Won-ok Gil, a former 'comfort woman,' visited Washington D.C. and LA in the U.S., and engaged in testimony activities of the Japanese military 'comfort women' system.
419	2017. 10.31			UNESCO's World Heritage Committee decided to withhold the inclusion of records related to the Japanese military 'comfort women' issue as Memory of the World Heritage.

No.	Date	Korea	Japan	International Community
420	2017. 11.14			The UN HRC, in its 'Universal Periodic Review' of Japan, recommended to the Japanese government 'sincere apology and compensation for the victims' regarding the Japanese military 'comfort women' issue.
421	2017. 11.23	- At the plenary session of the National Assembly, a resolution to amend the 'Act on Support for Life Stabilization and Commemorative Projects for the Victims of Japanese military Comfort under the Japanese Colonial Rule' was adopted. - A day to commemorate "Victims of the Japanese military 'comfort women'" was designated.		
422	2017. 12.8			A statue of the Japanese military 'comfort woman' was erected in Manila, the Philippines.
423	2017. 12.27	- Announcement of the results of the Ministry of Foreign Affairs' Task Force review of the 2015 Korea-Japan Agreement on the Japanese military 'comfort women' issue. - Announcement of the result of the Reconciliation and Healing Foundation inspection by the Ministry of Gender Equality and Family.		
424	2018. 3.1	- President Jae-in Moon, called for "true reflection and reconciliation on Dokdo and 'Comfort Women'" in his speech at the 99th anniversary ceremony of the March 1st Movement.		
425	2018. 3.7			The 15th 'Asia Solidarity Meeting to Solve the Japanese Military 'Comfort Women' Issue' was held.
426	2018. 3.8	Yong-soo Lee, a former 'comfort woman,' visited the French House of Representatives and testified on damage.		

Chronology of the Japanese Military's 'Comfort Women' Issue 289

No.	Date	Korea	Japan	International Community
427	2018. 4.28			The statue of Japanese military 'comfort women' was removed in Manila, the Philippines.
428	2018. 5.24			The Japanese military 'comfort women' memorial stone was unveiled in Fort Lee, New Jersey, USA.
429	2018. 6.27	Film, *Her Story*, was released.		
430	2018. 8.14	Commemoration ceremony for Memorial Day for Japanese Military 'Comfort Women.'		- 5th Anniversary of the Establishment of the Peace Girl Statue in Glendale, USA. - Establishment of a Statue for Victims of Japanese military 'comfort women' in Taiwan.
431	2018. 9.27	President Jae-in Moon, in his keynote address at the 73rd UN General Assembly, stated that he would actively participate in international discussions on women's issues based on the experience of the victims of the Japanese military 'comfort women' and contribute to efforts to eliminate sexual violence in conflict zones.		
432	2018. 10.30	The Korean Supreme Court ruled that Japanese companies must compensate Koreans who were conscripted for forced labor during Japan's colonial rule.		
433	2018. 11.21	Desolution of the Reconciliation and Healing Foundation was decied.		The UN Committee on Enforced Disappearances recommended Japanese government to clarify the truth and hold responsible parties accountable.
434	2018. 12.28		Chief Cabinet Secretary Suga stated, 'Faithful implementation of agreements is an obligation to the international community.'	A "Statue of Peace" was erected at the "House of Women' in San Pedro, south of Manila, the capital of the Philippines."
435	2018. 12.30			A "Statue of Peace" was suddenly removed from the "House of Women" in San Pedro, south of Manila, the capital of the Philippines.

No.	Date	Korea	Japan	International Community
436	2019. 1.21	Under the authority of the Minister of Gender Equality and Family, permission of the Reconciliation and Healing Foundation was revoked.		
437	2019. 1.28	Bok-dong Kim, a victim of the Japanese military 'comfort women' passed away at the age of 93.		
438	2019. 1.29	President Jae-in Moon paid respects at the wake of Bok-dong Kim.		
439	2019. 2.5			Filipino human rights activist Nelia Sancho erected a statue to honor the victims of the Japanese military 'comfort women' system at the gateway to Boracay.
440	2019. 4.18	Seoul High Court, ruled that it is justifiable for the Ministry of Foreign Affairs not to disclose documents related to the 2015 Korea-Japan Agreement on 'Comfort Women' in the national interest.		
441	2019. 7.3	Registration of the Reconciliation and Healing Foundation was cancelled.		
442	2019. 7.25			- Movie, *Shusenjo: The Main Battleground of the Comfort Women Issue,* made by a Japanese American director was released.
443	2019. 8.1		'Aichi Triennial 2019' exhibited a "Statue of Peace" produced by Eun-sung Kim and Seo-kyung Kim.	
444	2019. 8.5		The "Statue of Peace" was unilaterally removed from the 'Aichi Triennale 2019' due to a notification from Aichi Prefecture, Japan.	
445	2019. 8.8	A documentary film, "Bok-dong Kim," was released.		

No.	Date	Korea	Japan	International Community
446	2019. 8.14	- The 1,400th Wednesday Demonstration Rally was held. - The Korean government held a commemorative event for the Memorial Day for Japanese Military 'Comfort Women' at the Baekbeom Kim Koo Memorial in Yongsan-gu. - "Girls Statue of Korea, China, and the Philippines" was installed at Namsan, Seoul.		
447	2019. 8.15	Honda, a former US Congressman, visited the House of Sharing.		
448	2019. 8.19			Jan Ruff O'Herne, a Dutch victim of Japanese military "comfort women," passed away.
449	2019. 8.22			The Wednesday Demonstration was held in Washington DC to demand that the Japanese government acknowledge its war crimes and issue a genuine, formal apology.
450	2019. 9.12	The House of Sharing of Gwangju, Gyeonggi-do, in collaboration with the Ministry of Gender Equality and Family, held an exhibition on the theme of "The End of The Tunnel" at the Korean Verband in Berlin, Germany, from September 12th to 25th.		
451	2019. 9.20			Miki Dezaki, the director of the right-wing Japanese film, *Shusenjo* (主戦場): *The Main Battleground of the 'Comfort Women' Issue*, was sued for defamation.
452	2019. 9.30		The Executive Committee of the Aichi Triennale agreed to resume the display of the "Statue of Peace" at the "Non-Freedom of Expression: After" exhibition.	

No.	Date	Korea	Japan	International Community
453	2019.10.27			Groundbreaking Ceremony for the "Statue of Peace" in Washington DC took place.
454	2019.11.13	Three years after the lawsuit was filed, the first trial for damages against the Japanese government by victims of Japanese military 'comfort women' took place.		
455	2019.12.6			Artworks by 'comfort women' victims were exhibited in Berlin.
456	2019.12.27	The Constitutional Court of Korea ruled that the 2015 'Comfort Women' Agreement between South Korea and Japan is not subject to its review for unconstitutionality, and dismissed the case, stating that "the 2015 Agreement was a political agreement and the court will leave the various assessments of that agreement to the political realm."		
457	2020.2.25		In response to South Korean Foreign Minister Kyung-wha Kang's mention of the 'comfort women' issue, Asako Omi (尾身朝子), the Japanese Parliamentary Vice Minister for Foreign Affairs, said, "The Japanese government has been seriously responding to the 'comfort women' issue for a long time. Many 'comfort women' have praised the projects based on the agreement between South Korea and Japan."	
458	2020.3.3		Uemura Takashi (植村隆), a former *Asahi Shimbun* journalist, lost his lawsuit for damages against the Japanese right-wingers who had attacked Uemura's reporting as "fabrications." (The original verdict was upheld.)	

No.	Date	Korea	Japan	International Community
459	2020. 3.9			In celebration of its 50th anniversary, Rhine-Main Korean Church in Frankfurt, Germany held an unveiling ceremony for the "Statue of Peace" in front of its property. It was the second "Statue of Peace" installed in Germany.
460	2020. 3.11			The U.S. Department of State, in its "2019 Country Reports on Human Rights Practices," addressed the issue of the suspension of the display of the "Statue of Peace," which symbolizes the victims of Japanese military 'comfort women,' as a matter of freedom of expression.
461	2020. 5.7	Yong-soo Lee, a victim of Japanese military 'comfort women,' said, "The Wednesday Demonstrations are not helping at all, and I don't know where the donations are going."		
462	2020. 5.12	The South Korean Ministry of the Interior and Safety requested the "Korean Council" to submit its donation records.		
463	2020. 5.19		The Japanese Diplomatic Bluebook wrote, "Korea is an important neighbor," while stating that the expression "sex slave" did not reflect the truth and that South Korea also confirmed this in the 2015 South Korea-Japan 'comfort women' Agreement.	
464	2020. 8.14	The South Korean government held an event to commemorate the Memorial Day for Japanese Military 'Comfort Women' where President Jae-in Moon reiterated victim-centeredness in his congratulatory remarks.		

No.	Date	Korea	Japan	International Community
465	2020. 8.29	Mak-dal Lee, a victim of Japanese military 'comfort women,' passed away at the age of 97 in Busan, reducing the number of survivors to 16.		
466	2020. 10.2			Japanese Foreign Minister Motegi Toshimitsu (茂木敏充) called on the German government to remove the "Statue of Peace" in Germany.
467	2020. 10.3			The 3rd anniversary of the installation of the "Comfort Women Column of Strength" was celebrated in San Francisco, USA.
468	2020. 10.7			Authorities in Berlin, the German capital, ordered the removal of the "Statue of Peace" erected in the center of the city.
469	2020. 10.13			The district office of Mitte, Berlin, announced in a press release on October 13 that a local civic organization, the Korean Verband, filed an injunction with the court against the removal of the "Statue of Peace" in Mitte District, saying that it has decided not to take any further action and to await the court's decision.
470	2020. 10.22			The 10th anniversary of the first 'comfort women' Memorial in the US was celebrated in front of the memorial erected on the grounds of the Palisades Park Library.
471	2020. 11.2		The Japanese Ministry of Foreign Affairs translated a document outlining its position on the 'comfort women' issue into English and German, and posted it on its website.	
472	2020. 12.1			Discussions began for a permanent installation of the "Statue of Peace" in Berlin, Germany, which had been the subject of a removal order, and the order to remove the statue was rescinded.

No.	Date	Korea	Japan	International Community
473	2021. 1.8	The court ruled in favor of the plaintiffs in the lawsuit filed by the victims of Japanese military 'comfort women' against the Japanese government, ordering the accused to pay KRW 100 million to each plaintiff.	The Japanese Ministry of Foreign Affairs summoned Gwan-pyo Nam, South Korean Ambassador to Japan, to lodge a protest over the court's decision. Katsunobu Kato (加藤勝信), the Japanese Chief Cabinet Secretary, said in a regular press briefing that the South Korean court's decision to compensate the victims of Japanese military 'comfort women' cannot be accepted, saying that the decision violates international law.	
474	2021. 1.19		The Foreign Affairs Committee of the Liberal Democratic Party of Japan passed its resolution condemning the 'comfort women' decision to Japanese Foreign Minister Motegi Toshimitsu (茂木敏充).	
475	2021. 1.23	As the Japanese government announced that it would not appeal against the court's decision to compensate the 'comfort women' victims, the verdict of the first trial was finalized at 12 a.m. on January 23.		
476	2020. 2.12	Bok-soo Jeong, a victim of Japanese military 'comfort women,' passed away, reducing the number of survivors to 15.		
477	2021. 2.23	South Korea told the UN Human Rights Council that the Japanese military 'comfort women' issue is a matter of universal human rights.		
478	2021. 2.24			Japan noted that the Korean representative's speech on February 23 was unacceptable and said, "The two governments have affirmed that they will refrain from condemnation and criticism of the issue in the international community, including the UN. Japan has implemented all the measures it promised under the agreement, including the payment of JPY 1 billion."

No.	Date	Korea	Japan	International Community
479	2021. 4.1		The Cabinet decided that Japanese textbooks should be written based on the views of the Japanese government, and that it is appropriate to use the terms "conscription" and 'comfort women' instead of "forced mobilization" and "comfort women serving the army."	
480	2021. 4.21	The Civil Settlement Division 15 of the Seoul Central District Court dismissed a lawsuit for damages against Japan filed by 20 survivors and family members of Japanese military 'comfort women,' including Ye-nam Kwak, Bok-dong Kim, and Yong-soo Lee, on the grounds of "state immunity (sovereign immunity)."		Katsunobu Kato (加藤勝信), the Chief Cabinet Secretary, commented on the appropriateness of the South Korean court's decision to dismiss the case.
481	2021. 5.2	A victim of Japanese military 'comfort women' passed away, reducing the number of survivors to 14.		
482	2021. 5.6	Twelve out of the 16 victims of Japanese military 'comfort women,' who filed the lawsuit for damages against the Japanese government, appealed on May 6 against the court's decision to dismiss the case.		
483	2021. 6.4	The first "Public-Private Council" was held and attended by government ministries and experts to address the 'comfort women' issue.		
484	2021. 6.14			The Rhode Island State Senate passed a resolution (LC002984) condemning Remseyer, a Harvard Law School professor, for writing an article that distorted history by claiming that Japanese military 'comfort women' were prostitutes.
485	2021. 6.15	The Seoul Central District Court ordered the Japanese government to release a list of its properties in South Korea after the Japanese military 'comfort women' compensation case had been decided against Japan.	Katsunobu Kato (加藤勝信), the Chief Cabinet Secretary, stated that the decision of the Central District Court of South Korea to accept the claim of the 'comfort women,' who filed and won a lawsuit against the Japanese government is deeply regrettable and clear violation of international law as well as the bilateral agreement between the two governments, and therefore should never be accepted.	

No.	Date	Korea	Japan	International Community
486	2021. 7.7	The South Korean Ministry of Foreign Affairs held a Public-Private Council to resolve the 'comfort women' issue.		
487	2021. 7.16		The 'Non-Freedom of Expression, Kansai" exhibition began to display the "Statue of Peace".	
488	2021. 8.14	The South Korean government held an event to commemorate the Memorial Day for Japanese Military 'Comfort Women.'		
489	2021. 9.1	The Seoul Central District Court ordered the Japanese government to release a list of its properties in South Korea after the Japanese military 'comfort women' compensation case had been decided against Japan.		
490	2021. 9.6		The Japanese government lodged a complaint to Germany over the decision to extend the installation of the "Statue of Peace" in Berlin.	
491	2021. 9.19			The 4th anniversary of the installation of the "Comfort Women Column of Strength" was celebrated in San Francisco, USA.
492	2021. 9.24	A victim of Japanese military 'comfort women' passed away, reducing the number of registered survivors to 13.		
493	2022. 5.1	Yang-ju Kim, a victim of Japanese military 'comfort women,' passed away, reducing the number of survivors to 11.		
494	2022. 7.8			The unveiling ceremony for the "Statue of Peace" was held in a newly-built park in front of the Student Body HQ at Kassel State University in central Germany.
495	2022. 7.11			Fourteen professors and scholars from Germany, France, and Japan sent a letter to the district office of Mitte in Berlin, Germany, requesting that the "Statue of Peace" be made permanent.

No.	Date	Korea	Japan	International Community
496	2022. 7.30			ReflectSpace Gallery at the Glendale Central Library held an exhibition titled "Modes of Resistance: Legacies of Colonialism & 'Comfort Women'" until October 9.
497	2022. 8.14	The Memorial Day for Japanese Military 'Comfort Women'		
498	2022. 9.15	On September 15, 2022, the Seoul Central District Court dismissed the case regarding identification of seizable properties from the Japanese government, citing "unknown address."		
499	2022. 11.6			According to the UN Committee for the International Covenant on Civil and Political Rights (CCPR), the UN issued a second set of recommendations, expressing regret at the Japanese government's lack of progress in resolving the issue of 'comfort women' issue and called for compensation for victims, punishment of perpetrators, and a formal apology from the Japanese government.
500	2022. 12.6	Ok-seon Lee, a victim of Japanese military 'comfort women,' passed away, reducing the number of survivors to 10.		
501	2023. 1			*The International Review of Law and Economics (IRLE)*, the journal that had published the article on the 'comfort women' by Harvard Professor Mark Ramseyer in 2020, rejected the academy's request to retract the article, on the grounds that his article did not constitute a violation of the rules.
502	2023. 3.6	Foreign Minister Jin Park announced the government's plan for compensation for forced mobilization.		
503	2023. 5.2	A victim of Japanese military 'comfort women' passed away, reducing the number of survivors to 9.		

No.	Date	Korea	Japan	International Community
504	2023. 6.1	The Supreme Court of Korea ruled that "the non-disclosure of the negotiation documents for the 2015 'Comfort Women' Agreement is lawful."		
505	2023. 6.14	The 1,600th Wednesday Demonstration Rally for resolving the Japanese military 'comfort women' issue took place.		
506	2023. 7.29			The 10th anniversary of the installation of the "Statue of Peace" was celebrated in Glendale, Los Angeles.
507	2023. 8.14	The Ministry of Gender Equality and Family held an event to commemorate the Memorial Day for Japanese Military 'Comfort Women,' which was recognized as a national holiday in 2017.		
508	2023. 9.14			Fabian Salvioli, the UN Special Rapporteur on the Promotion of Truth, Justice, Reparation and Guarantees of Non-recurrence, recommended the South Korean government to revise the 'Comfort Women' Agreement signed with Japan and to repeal the National Security Act

Bibliography

Chapter One

- Ishigawa Itsuko (2014), *Girls Who Become Japanese Military Comfort Women*, Samcheonri.
- Jan Ruff Ohern/Translated by Choi Jae-in Lee (2018), *I Was a Sex Slave for the Japanese Military*, Samcheonri.
- Kang Jeong-sook (1996), *Korean women forcibly taken for the Japanese military comfort women: Book of Testimony 1*.
- Kim Jung-sung (2005), *(Japanese military comfort woman on the Burmese Battlefront) Moon Ok-ju*, Beautiful People, Gyeongsangnam-do Board of Education, 2015.
- Kim Geum-sook (2017), *Grass: A Living History, Testimony of Japanese military comfort women*, Bori.
- Korean Women's Volunteer Labor Corps Association (1993-1999), *Korean women forcibly taken for the Japanese military comfort women 1-3,"* Hanul Academy.
- Korean Women's Volunteer Labor Corps Association (2001), *Korean women forcibly taken for the Japanese military comfort women 4-5,"* Pulbit.
- Lee Ok-sun, *Honors and Human Rights to Grandmothers*, produced by Korean Women's Volunteer Labor Corps Association, DVD.
- Pramudiya Ananthatur/Translated by Youngsoo Kim, Stories of Indonesian Japanese military comfort women (2019), Dongjjok'nara.
- War and Women's Human Rights Center Research Team, *The Story of Making History*, Women and Human Rights.

Chapter Two

- Ahn Byung-jik (Translation and annotation), *Diary of the Japanese Military Comfort Station Manager*, Esoop.
- An Yeon-seon (2003), *Sexual slavery and making of soldiers*, Samcheonri.
- Itagaki Ryuta and Kim Buja (editors)/ Translated by Bae Young-mi and Ko Young-jin (2016), *(Q&A) Comfort Women Problems and Responsibility for Colonial Rule*, Samchang.
- Kang Jung-sook (2015), *Do you know Japanese Military Comfort Women?*, Independence Hall of Korea Independence Movement Research Institute.

- Kim Se-jin (2018), *Drawing a Girl Statue of Peace*, Bori.
- Kwon Sung-wook (2015), *The Dragon of the Sino-Japanese War, Defeat the Samurai 1928-1945*, Miji Books.
- Ministry of Foreign Affairs (1992, July) "Interim Report on the Status of Japanese Comfort Women".
- Northeast Asian History Foundation (2015), *(Easy to understand Q&A) Japanese military comfort women*.
- Northeast Asia History Foundation (2018), *Japanese Military Comfort Women Data List I-IV*.
- Northeast Asia History Foundation (2015), *Japanese Military Comfort Women Exhibition Panel Booklet*.
- Sejong University and Yuji Hosaka (editors, 2018), *A collection of evidence on Japan's comfort women issue1*, Hwanggeum'al.
- Song Yeon-ok and Kim Gwi-ok et al. (2017), *Colonial War, Military Comfort Women*, Samin.
- Su Zhuryang, Chen Lifei/Translated by Lee Seon-yi (2017), *The Japanese Military Invasion of China*, Volume 19 "Japanese military comfort women and sexual violence", Nulpum Plus.
- Su Zhuryang et al./ Translated by Son Yeom-hong (2019) "Military comfort stations in the Shanghai area", Northeast History Foundation.
- The Korean Ministry of Foreign Affairs' Korean Women's Volunteer Labor Corps Task Force (1992), *Interim report on investigation of the status of military comfort women under the Japanese colonial rule*.
- Yoon Mi-hyang (2016), *Wednesdays of 25 Years*, Saihaengsung.
- Yoon Myung-sook (2015), *Korean Military Comfort Women and Japanese Military Comfort System*, Yihaksa.
- Yoshimi Yoshiaki (1998) *Japanese Military Comfort Women*, Sohwa.
- Yoshimi Yoshiaki (2013) *Japanese Military Comfort Women, The Truth of Its History: What is Japanese Military Comfort Women System?*, Yoksa'konggan.
- 吉見義明(1992),『従軍慰安婦資料集』,東京：大月書店.
- 吉見義明(1995),『従軍慰安婦』,東京：岩波書店.
- 内閣官房内閣外政審議室(2013a),『朝鮮半島出身のいわゆる従軍慰安婦問題について(平成4年7月6日)』.

- 内閣官房内閣外政審議室(2013b), 『いわゆる従軍慰安婦問題の調査結果について(平成5年8月4日)』.

Chapter Three

- Asia Women's Fund Digital Memorial Hall, 『慰安婦問題のアジア女性基金ディジタル記念館』. www.awf.or.kr
- Cho Yoon-soo (2014), "Japanese military comfort women and Korea-Japan relations: Focusing on the Response of Korea and Japan in the 1990s," *The Korean Diplomatic History*, 1(36).
- Cho Yoon-soo (2018), The Abe administration's perception and policy on the issue of "Japanese military comfort women": Focusing on the Korea-Japan Agreement on Japanese military comfort women," *Japan Research*, No. 48.
- Haruki Wada (2016), *To solve the problem of the Japanese military comfort women*, Yoksa'konggan.
- Japanese Ministry of Foreign Affairs (1993), 『いわゆる従軍慰安婦問題について(内閣官房内閣外政審議室/(平成5年8月4日)』.
- Japanese Ministry of Foreign Affairs (2014), 『慰安婦問題を巡る日韓のやりとりの経緯:~河野談話作成からアジア女性基金まで, 河野談話作成過程などに関する検討チーム』.
- Jeong Jin-sung (2004), *The Japanese Military Sexual Slavery*, Seoul National University Press.
- Korean Women's Volunteer Labor Corps Association (1997), *Inquiring responsibility of Japanese military comfort women: Historical-sociological perspective*.
- Nam Sang-gu (2014), "Critical Review of Kono Statement Modifications," *Research on the History of Korea-Japan Relations*.
- Nam Sang-gu (2017), "History Perception and Policy Changes of the Japanese Government's Japanese Military Comfort Women," *Research on the History of Korea-Japan Relations*, the 58th edition.
- Northeast Asian History Foundation (2015), *Think about the problem of Japanese military comfort women (with former Prime Minister Murayama)*.

Chapter Four

- Compilation Committee of the 20th Anniversary of Korean Women's Volunteer Labor Corps Association (editor, 2014), *20 Years of History of the Korean Women's Volunteer Labor Corps Association*, Hanul Academy.
- In the case of parliamentary resolutions in each country, summaries of the excerpts from home page of the Ministry of Gender Equality and Family and the e-History Museum of Japanese military comfort women
- Korean Women's Volunteer Labor Corps Association (2015), *A collection of major documents related to the Japanese military comfort women*.

Index

abuses 196
Adachi Shigeichi (足立茂一) 82
Anti-Japan Tribalism 33, 78, 79, 217, 224
Aoji Washio (青地鷲雄) 86
apology 16, 22, 23, 26, 86, 89, 136, 138, 150, 154, 155, 157, 162, 173, 174, 176~178, 182, 205, 207, 213, 219, 230~235, 237, 244, 247, 251, 257, 259, 260, 263, 265, 271, 278, 285, 288, 291, 298
Army Dispatched to Shanghai 71, 129
Army Dispatched to Southern China 60
Asahi Shimbun (朝日新聞) 135, 148, 181, 183~185, 275, 278, 279, 292
Asian Solidarity Conference 175, 176, 235, 284
asset and liability statement 103

Basic Life Protection Fund 151
Bong-ki Bae 112, 113, 191, 232
Bosnian War 196, 217
Bunbei Hara (原文兵衛) 153

Cabinet Councilors' Office for Foreign Affairs 137, 142
CAT (Committee against Torture) 204
CESCR (Committee on Economic, Social and Cultural Rights) 204
Changzhou Garrison 92~94
chief cabinet secretary Kato 134~136, 139, 142, 150, 231, 232, 234
Chung-ok Yun 228
Claims Agreement 164
clarification of the truth 135, 155, 244, 248, 255
(three-party) coalition 152, 153, 250, 252
comfort corps 35, 36
comfort station 14, 22, 32, 40, 41, 63, 75~77, 82, 93~96, 99, 100, 103, 106~108, 110, 113, 114, 120, 126, 131, 137, 146, 147, 201, 209, 236
'Comfort Women' Memorial Day 273
Comfort Women of the Empire 78, 112
'comfort women' system 15, 31, 41, 47, 109, 111, 112, 148, 149, 157, 193, 211, 215~218, 229, 231, 235, 237~241, 243~247, 249, 250, 252, 258, 260, 261, 265, 270, 272~275, 279, 283, 287, 290
Commission on the Status of Women 196, 245
Committee on the Elimination of Racial Discrimination (CERD) 182, 204
Compliance Rules for Comfort Facilities and Inn Business 102
Constitutional Court 163~165, 167, 264, 283, 292
crime against humanity 232

Democratic People's Republic of Korea 198, 216
director at the Police Bureau at the Home Ministry 71
director of the Labor Ministry's Occupational Safety Bureau 23
Dorao Harao (早尾虎雄) 119
Dutch Indonesian Official Gazette 87

East Timor 115, 158
employment contract 106
employment fraud 64
enforced sex slaves 272
EU Parliament 207, 215
Eyes of Dawn 13, 14

fact-finding / investigation of the truth 135
field diary 92

Index 305

forced mobilization 46, 139, 148, 149, 169, 180, 181, 183~187, 196, 217, 219, 235, 238, 242, 263, 266~269, 274, 275, 277~279, 281, 282, 296, 298
Fumio Kishida (岸田文雄) 170
fundamental rights (to demand compensation) 165, 166

GAHT (Global Alliance for Historical Truth) 186, 269
Gathering for Returning Ok-joo Moon's Military Postal Savings 33
Gojo Igarashi (五十嵐廣三) 153
Guangxi-sheng 84
Guilin Trial 84

Hak-soon Kim 14, 15, 21~24, 26, 35, 115, 189, 229, 234, 254
Hankyoreh newspaper 15, 228
Haruki Wada (和田春樹) 153
head of the general military government 102
human trafficking 46, 64, 73, 79, 80, 193, 211, 263, 280

identification 52, 56, 73, 74, 78, 81, 136~138, 146, 298
ILO (International Labor Organization) Committee of Experts 204, 239, 245, 246, 249, 259, 261
international treaties on trafficking of women 72, 73
International Treaty Prohibiting the Trafficking of Women for Prostitution 66
irreversible 172, 175
Isou Abe (安部磯雄) 79
issue of the Japanese military 'comfort women' 12, 16, 46, 136, 155, 197, 198, 224, 233, 242, 248, 260, 274

Iwane Matsui (松岩岩根) 48

Jan Ruff O'Herne 24, 38, 114, 156, 262, 269, 291
Japanese army in central China 48
Japanese criminal code 64
Japanese imperialism 115
Japanese Kwantung Army 118
Joseon Army 47

Keumah Im 115
kidnapping 65, 73, 76, 84
kiosks outside the barracks 100
Kono statement 78, 146, 148, 149, 152, 167~169, 176, 84, 202, 207, 210, 214, 265, 268, 271, 272, 274
Korea-Japan agreement 160, 169, 170, 173, 178~181, 185~188, 283, 286~288, 290
Korea-Japan Agreement on the 'Comfort Women' Issue 181, 187
Korea-Japan summit 163, 164, 170, 232, 253, 280, 283
Korean Council for Justice and Remembrance for the Issues of Military Sexual Slavery by Japan 41
Korean Council for the Women Drafted for Military Sexual Slavery by Japan 20, 22, 35, 41, 228, 277
Kosovo conflict 196

legal responsibility 155, 162, 163, 173, 215, 245, 251, 254, 260, 269
licensed (legalized) prostitution system 79
Life Stabilization Act 151
Linda Chavez 198, 202, 240, 246, 247

Liuzhou (柳州) 84
Lower House of the Dutch Parliament Resolution 209
Lugou (Marco Polo) Bridge (蘆溝橋) 47

Maeilsinbo 40
Makiko Takita (田北真樹子) 184
"making history right" 143
Mamoru Inuma (飯沼守) 129
McDougall Report 203, 204, 256
memorial monument 189, 190, 280, 287
merchants hired by the military 51
Michio Watanabe (渡辺美智雄) 135
Mike Honda 30, 262, 267, 278, 287
military coupon 32
military government 102, 103, 105
military personnel 27, 120, 122, 128~130, 144
military sexual slavery 20, 22, 35, 38, 41, 93, 98, 116, 198, 220, 228, 235, 259, 261, 269, 277
military ship 54
Ministry of Treasury 153
Miyazawa Kiichi (宮澤喜一) 135
mobilization of 'comfort women' 71, 181, 219, 231, 266, 268, 275
Mukden Incident 47
Myung-bak Lee 164

Nanjing 14, 50, 51, 83, 91, 92, 121, 126, 129, 270, 280
Nanjing massacre 50, 121, 270
Naozaburo Okabe (岡部直三郎) 119, 121, 122
National Fund for Asian Peace and Women 153, 246, 247, 253, 255
National Mang-Hyang Cemetry 189
Nationalist government (Kuomintang) 121

New History Textbooks 150
North Korea 17, 115, 139, 158, 229, 237, 248, 250, 269

Okinawa Guard 112
Ok-joo Moon 32~34
Out-of-Barrack Facility Rules 100

Pacific War Victims' Families Association 134, 143, 146, 228, 243, 245
postal savings 33, 34
Prime Minister Shinzo Abe 47, 210, 280

racism 11
Radhika Coomaraswamy 38, 198, 242, 276
rape centers 41, 81, 204
recruitment of 'comfort women' 15, 26, 64, 75~77, 240
Report of the Allied Forces Command 141
Rwandan genocide 196

Sakura Club 86~88
San Francisco Peace Treaty 139, 183
Sankei Shimbun 148, 167, 168, 184~186
Seiji Yoshida (吉田清治) 181, 183, 202
Seijiro Saijo 113
Seijiro Yoshizawa (吉澤清次郎) 74
Setsuzo Kinbara (金原節三) 125
sex slavery 41
sexual violence 12, 41, 50, 89, 113, 125, 126, 177, 196, 204, 221, 270, 275, 289
sexual violence against 125, 196, 217, 218, 224
Shanghai Consulate 49, 53~56, 71, 81

Shin-do Song 111, 238, 257, 258
Shinsuke Sugiyama (杉山晋輔) 183
Shoji Motooka (本岡昭次) 23
slave raid 200
southern military headquarters 102
special comfort stations 98~101, 119
special rights to national housing 151
statement by chief cabinet secretary Koichi Kato 138
Statue of Peace in Glendale 182, 185, 267~269, 273
Statute Book Decree of 1946 87
STD test 55, 59

Tae-woo Roh 21, 136, 232
Takako Doi (土井多賀子) 134
temporary work permit 54
Tesuo Aso (麻生徹男) 126
The 1st Shanghai Incident 37
"The Facts" 207, 209, 263
The Main Battleground of the Comfort Women Issue 11, 12, 290, 291
The Washington Post 207, 210, 214, 263, 267
Thomas Schieffer 167
Tomiichi Murayama (村山富市) 152, 179, 215
transfer of 'comfort women' 49, 144
Tsudao Shimizu (清水傳雄) 23
tsugunaigin (償い金, atonement money) 154, 163

U.S. House of Representatives Resolution 30, 167, 207, 210, 211, 253, 262, 264, 266~268, 275
UN Committee on Elimination of Discrimination against Women (CEDAW) 181
UN Human Rights Committee (UNHRC) 168, 182, 204, 245, 246, 248~251, 255, 257, 260, 268, 271, 272
unconstitutional 164~166, 264, 292

victims' of the 'comfort women' system 176, 177
violation of human rights 35~37

war comfort women 35~37
war crimes 51, 84, 86, 146, 149, 162, 197, 204, 211, 253, 259
war crimes of sexual slavery by the Japanese military 197
war crimes trial 84, 146
wartime responsibility 143
Working Group on Contemporary Forms of Slavery 99, 233, 239, 248, 252
World Conference on Human Rights 196
World Conference on Women 197, 248

Yamaguchi District Court 80, 230, 237, 255
Yohei Kono 15, 143, 144, 209, 211, 215
Yomiuri Shimbun 148, 184, 186
Yong-soo Lee 27, 28, 43, 262, 282, 283, 285, 288, 293, 296
Yoshiaki Yoshimi (吉見義明) 25, 135, 192
Yoshihide Suga (菅義偉) 168, 186
Yoshiko Sakurai 150
Young-hoon Rhee 33, 78, 79
Young-sam Kim 143, 150, 151, 160, 153, 238, 240, 251
Young-sim Park 17

Japanese Military 'Comfort Women'

Sharing and Remembering the Historical Pain

Published on	November 30, 2023
Written by	Yoon-soo Cho
Publisher	Young-ho Lee
Published by	Northeast Asian History Foundation
Address	81, Tongil-ro, Seodaemun-gu, Seoul, Republic of Korea
Tel	02-2012-6065
Website	www.nahf.or.kr
Printed in	Nikebooks
ISBN	979-11-7161-013-6 03910

All rights reserved. No part of this publication may be used in any way that infringes copyright without prior written permission. To obtain copyright permission, please send a written inquiry to book@nahf.or.kr.